THE ~~~~~~ ER
and Other Scoundrels

*My life and times with Luis Basualdo,
the man who befriended royalty
and seduced heiresses*

A memoir by

MARCELO MANRIQUE DE ACUÑA

Published by MAP Productions Ltd. 2025
London, United Kingdom

© Marcelo Manrique de Acuña, 2023

The moral rights of the author have been asserted.

All rights reserved. No part of this publication may be reproduced, stored in a retrieval system, or transmitted, in any form or by any means, without the prior permission in writing of the author, or as expressly permitted by law, by licence or under terms agreed with the appropriate reprographics rights organisation.

The events and conversations in this book are accurate to the best of the author's ability.

Front cover image: Luis Basualdo at the 1986 Derby, Epsom Downs Racecourse, Surrey. Photo: Desmond O'Neill | Desmond O'Neill Features

Back cover image: Luis Basualdo with HRH Prince Charles at Cowdray Park, 1977. Photo: Mirrorpix | Trinity Mirror/Alamy Stock Photo

ISBN: 978-1-0682679-0-1 (English edition)

To my loving wife, Patricia Anne Begley

Contents

	Epilogue as Prologue	vii
1.	The Plan	1
2.	When Marcelo Met Luis	8
3.	Planning Our Escape	20
4.	Aunt Clara	24
5.	Ransacking the Family Home	28
6.	Welcome to Miami	31
7.	Social Climbing in Palm Beach	49
8.	From Florida to Minnesota to Missouri	53
9.	An Adventure in New York	57
10.	Back to Square One	60
11.	And Then There Was One	67
12.	An Elusive Thief	74
13.	A Gentleman of Leisure	79
14.	The Discreet Charm of the Art Forger	85
15.	Luis Meets the Queen	95
16.	Enter Christina Onassis	102
17.	The Waiting Room	108

18.	Enter Ursula Mahler	117
19.	Vive la Différence!	121
20.	A Roman Holiday	133
21.	The Heiresses	144
22.	An Escort in London	148
23.	The Heiress Comes of Age	162
24.	The Smart Set	170
25.	Blackballed	176
26.	A Most Unusual Ambassador	183
27.	A Walk on the Wild Side	190
28.	Sarah Comes to the Rescue	193
29.	Surrendell Farm Has a Royal Guest	196
30.	The Count of No Account	199
31.	Charles Keeps His Word	202
32.	Luis, the Family Man	210
33.	Bad Company	217
34.	Hashish and Ashes	223
35.	Back in the Saddle	228
36.	The Falklands War	233
37.	Homme d'Affaires	238
38.	The Strange Case of Christina's Missing Money	247
39.	A Game of Cat and Mouse	258
40.	Ducking and Diving	266
41.	Biting the Hand That Fed Him	273
42.	An Honest Man	276
43.	Our Last Meeting	280
	Endnotes	289
	Acknowledgements	291
	Photographic Credits	293
	About the Author	297
	Name Index	299

Epilogue as Prologue
– A Sad Farewell –

It was December in Buenos Aires, usually balmy at that time of year, but in 2020, the heat was unbearable. The midday sun bore down on a handful of mourners gathered outside the church of El Pilar, a stone's throw from the La Recoleta cemetery. There, the mortal remains of Luis Sosa Basualdo were being laid to rest above ground, not in a grave of his own, but in the mausoleum of the Etcheverrigarays, his brother-in-law's family. His sister, María Teresa – Marité – had informed her friends of her brother's passing, and they comprised most of the mourners that day. Many of Luis's friends stayed away, because of Covid they said. There were so few able-bodied men present that Marité had to rely on the goodwill of strangers to join her brothers-in-law as pallbearers. They navigated the coffin through the cool of the church out into the blazing sun where the hearse was waiting. Then it travelled the short distance to the entrance of La Recoleta, where Argentina's great and wealthy lay to rest. The funeral party followed the coffin along the neat paths of the cemetery, under the shade of occasional cypress trees, and past the marble and stone mausoleums of the country's most illustrious families of presidents, writers, actors, and generals. It is customary for Recoleta mourners to have an aperitif afterwards at La Biela, a bar opposite the cemetery, but it was still closed due to the pandemic, so those present stood around the cemetery's forecourt chatting, adding to the sense of awkwardness.

For Marité, arranging her brother's funeral and final resting place became of paramount importance. Both their parents were buried in La Chacarita, a graveyard where the less fortunate end up, but she was determined to see him laid to rest at the more prestigious cemetery. While Luis was fighting for life, Marité begged her late husband's siblings to allow her brother a place in their family mausoleum. She was a rich widow of high social standing and with no heirs; did she recompense them in exchange for the favour? It's hard to believe that such an illustrious family would want to be connected for all eternity with the notorious Luis Basualdo out of the goodness of their hearts.

By the time Luis died on 9th December 2020, everything had been arranged. A notice appeared the next day in *La Nación*, Argentina's leading daily newspaper, which had no doubt been prepared well in advance. It read:

> *Luis Sosa Basualdo. His sister, Marité S. de Etcheverrigaray, is heartbroken to announce the death of her beloved brother, hoping that Jesus and Mary are already embracing him.*[1]

Except that Sosa Basualdo wasn't his name – at least, not the family name he came into the world with. Born as plain Sosa, the siblings later added the aristocratic-sounding Basualdo in the hope of attaining some social status. The double-barrelled name was part of a new identity they concocted, along with a flexible backstory, so they could set about climbing Argentina's steep and narrow social ladder.

Marité remained faithful to Luis to the very end, when most others had tired of him, and she was the central figure at Luis's funeral. His daughter, who lived in the United Kingdom, was not in attendance, probably because in her hurry to get Luis buried in the socially appropriate place, she failed to notify her in time. She also made a point of avoiding me, Marcelo Manrique de Acuña, the author of this book. She erased me from her life as she did others who had known her from the beginning and contradicted her version of events. I was informed neither of his death nor the funeral, even though I had been in contact with him up to the very end, despite our troubled and often competitive relationship. I only learned about his passing on Facebook, where an acquaintance mentioned it in a comment.

When people die, they become somehow eternal: their younger self is as present as the person they were the day they died and they are suddenly both things all at once. The young man I had met all those years ago came back to me. I recalled his cheeky personality, the studied, stiff movements he adopted, both charming and unnerving, and the way he always smoothed his hair back in a never-ending struggle to curb its natural curls.

Like his sister, Luis sought the respect of society, yet his actions wilfully and unapologetically scandalised it. As his daughter observed, he was a self-confessed gigolo who revelled in being a rogue.[2] I was no saint myself, but Luis was something else. He dazzled me at times with his self-confidence, his spirit of adventure, and his exaggerated need to be the centre of attention. His complete lack of morals often repelled me. Yet it was Luis who gave me the confidence and the tools to pursue the life I lived. We learned tricks together, egged each other on, came unstuck, and recovered; we sometimes colluded in adventures and often competed; sometimes we were at each other's throats.

Despite the different routes Luis and I took as time went on, our destinies seemed somehow linked. The account that follows is my recollection of the life of Luis Basualdo, as well as a reflection on my own.

1
The Plan

It had always been their plan. Luis and his sister María Teresa (Marité) had long shared the belief that their circumstances were not in alignment with their social aspirations, so together they decided to change reality to accord with their dreams. It was a habit that Luis perfected over the years, altering the truth to suit his needs so that no one knew what was real and what was fabrication.

Luis Sosa was born on 5th September 1945 in Buenos Aires. His sister was already two years old when he was born. She had a big influence on her younger brother and was the driving force in their quest for higher social status. From an early age, she was a voracious reader of society magazines and columns and had set her sights on joining the ranks of those she read about. It was possibly from their mother, Amanda Teresa Bissoni, that the siblings inherited this burning desire for upward social mobility. When Luis was nine, she abandoned her husband and the two children to live with a doctor who enjoyed much better circumstances than the ones she found herself in with Héctor Sosa, an army lieutenant with little money.

Héctor Sosa was born to a modest family in Pehuajó, a city located about four hundred kilometres west of Buenos Aires. Even after a couple of centuries in the country, the Sosa family had made no headway in its tight-knit society. From an early age, he had had to support his ailing mother, and his financial situation had been so precarious that he was exempted from paying fees at the military academy he attended. Héctor's ancestry was Afro-Portuguese, and it was from him that Luis derived his exotic looks, a handicap in the snobbish and Eurocentric society of Buenos Aires, but an asset outside Argentina where Luis put them to good use.

Luis's mother's family, on the other hand, were Italian and better off than the Sosas. Vincenzo Bissoni, Amanda's father, was born in Milan and arrived in Argentina as a young man at the end of the nineteenth century. He was a simple man who never really felt at home in his adopted country and only mixed with members of the Italian community. He made his money in the insurance business and bought a house in Flores, a sleepy, lower middle-class area on the outskirts of Buenos Aires. At the age of 42, he married Manuela Fazio who, although of Italian parentage, had been born in Buenos Aires and was therefore more established than him.

Amanda's parents did not warm to Héctor and warned their daughter against marrying beneath her. However, once she had married him, they were a constant source of financial support, supplementing the young army officer's wages and ensuring that the children were brought up in relative comfort in an apartment in a middle-class area of Buenos Aires. All that came to an end when Amanda left the children for the local doctor. Luis and Marité were sent to live with their now aged and mainly bedridden grandfather Vincenzo and their eccentric Aunt Ada, Amanda's older sister, in Flores.

Luis's mother's restlessness soon got the better of her again and not long after settling down with the doctor, she left him for a wealthy landowner called Arias and moved into his sizeable *hacienda* named La Avispa (The Wasp) near Mar del Plata, a four-hour drive from Buenos Aires. It was a good move for her but not for her children.

While Luis and Marité were not invited to live at the *hacienda*, they were subjected to a draconian regime whenever they visited. Arias was an idealistic admirer of Rousseau and spent a great deal of his money funding organisations that advocated liberty. However, he had no time for freedom at home, where he exercised strict discipline, particularly over his newly acquired stepchildren. Things were always tense when they stayed at the *hacienda*. Arias was horrified by the children's lack of discipline and always made comments about the way they behaved, the way they sat, the way they spoke, and what they said. There was never any doubt which side the children's mother would take, something that both Luis and Marité were acutely aware of. Luis, a rulebreaker his whole life, chafed under this authority, and the two men clashed from the start. Things came to a head after Arias discovered that a pistol, a treasured family heirloom, had disappeared from the house. Although he could not prove it, Arias believed Luis to be the culprit and a relationship that had been barely cordial became openly hostile.

Despite the instability of those years, Luis did receive a relatively good education. His grandfather sent him to the Ward School, an American Methodist institution, not to instil Methodist doctrine in him, but for the school's focus on the English language which became Luis's first social attainment. The second attainment, ultimately just as valuable, he owed to his father.

There is a long history of horse breeding and horsemanship in Argentina. For people like me, born into 'good families', knowing your way around a horse was as much a sign of good breeding as was speaking English and French. Héctor Sosa was an accomplished horseman, and Luis inherited from his father a familiarity and confidence around horses, which later developed into an aptitude for polo.

At his father's insistence, Luis's secondary school career began as a cadet at the General San Martín Military School, located in a northern suburb of the city. Although he may have been sent there to iron out his rebellious streak, it was always going to end badly.

Young cadets were often on the receiving end of brutal discipline at the hands of the senior cadets whose role it was to 'soften' cadets into compliance. This institutionalised abuse was particularly acute from a senior cadet by the name of Jorge Blanco. Eventually, Luis had had enough, so he and his friend Jorge Santa Marina, who had also been bullied by Blanco, waited patiently in a dark alley for him to pass by. They grabbed him from behind and covered his head with a sheet, then Luis set about him, hitting his head repeatedly until he collapsed unconscious to the ground. Luckily, Blanco recovered swiftly, and if he knew who his assailants were, he kept it to himself. Luis and his friend achieved their aim and suffered no more abuse.

After a year of getting into one scrape after another, Luis was expelled from the school. He spent the following two years at the Marín Boarding School, where he was also thrown out due to endless punch-ups with his classmates. With his appalling track record, the only option left was to finish his studies at night school. By that time, his father was a retired colonel and had gone back to live in the city of Mendoza. There was no question of Luis joining him: he already felt that Buenos Aires was too much of a backwater, never mind the provincial city of Mendoza, a hop and a skip from the Andes. So he asked his mother if he could stay with her at Arias' *hacienda*. But following the incident of the missing pistol, he was no longer welcome there. His mother did not argue her son's case with her husband.

Having been abandoned by both his father and his mother, Luis and Marité had no option but to move back to Flores to live with his grandfather and aunt. For Luis, the main attraction of living with doddery old Vincenzo and Aunt Ada was that he was left to his own devices. It was around this time that his restlessness and distaste for authority developed into delinquency. Unsupervised and carefree, Luis soon gravitated towards the local bad boys.

One of the more questionable characters with whom he associated was a provincial lawyer's son by the name of Eduardo Soldano. Somehow the two of them discovered that they shared a penchant for arson. They would roam the streets of Flores at night, find quiet roads or cul-de-sacs, and set parked cars alight, then decamp nearby to watch the growing blaze and ensuing explosions for the fun of it.

They then fancied themselves as gentlemen thieves and planned a few robberies. But according to Luis, only Soldano turned to burglary. After a series of break-ins into wealthy homes in the exclusive summer resort of Punta del Este on the coast of nearby Uruguay, he was caught and served a stiff prison sentence. Luis heard later that he had changed his ways, took a job with the law courts, and was happily married.

Meanwhile, Marité started volunteering at the prestigious charitable foundation ALPI, which supports people affected by motor neuron disorders and paralysis. She served drinks and sandwiches to members of the landed gentry who attended the fundraising events at the Palermo polo grounds, the hub of the social scene in Buenos Aires, hoping to catch the eye of one of them. Marité was slim and olive-skinned like her brother, but she did not have his easy charm and probably struggled to be seen. But beneath that unremarkable exterior was a steely resolve and ambition that eventually paid off. She met Fernando Castro Cranwell, an aristocratic and relentless suitor four years her senior. Fernando was built like a boxer but had a kind face, a gentle giant who brought out in her the only feelings of affection she ever likely experienced. Early in their short-lived relationship, he gave her the gift of a teddy bear, which she cherished her entire life.

Luis had a more morbid way of breaking into high society. He started frequenting the funerals of young men his age from good families. He would peruse the death notices in *La Nación*, decide on a target, put on his only suit, and insinuate himself into the funeral party. He would play at being just another mourner, tagging along with the family and friends of the deceased, going back to the dead boy's home for whatever refreshments had been organised. There, he would mingle with the guests, claiming to have some vague unverifiable connection to the young man and parroting the platitudes expected of mourners on the day. He made such a habit of this that his Aunt Ada nicknamed him 'the undertaker'. It was unclear what he hoped to achieve – to make connections with people from good families (who were bound to find out eventually that he was an impostor), or just to be in that milieu, to participate in it, even if only temporarily and in such unhappy circumstances.

This lasted until he was found out by the grieving mother of one of the deceased. The woman thought Luis was a little too old to know her son and said as much to him. He told her that even though he had been in a class two years above her son at school, they had struck up a friendship. The more he talked, the deeper the hole he dug for himself. She made her excuses and turned her attention to another guest; as usual, Luis thought he had got away with it. However, after a while, the lady returned with her husband. The next round of questions was much more probing and as Luis started to flounder, the conversation caught the attention of other mourners. When it became clear that nobody knew him, he was asked to leave and his career as a funeral-crasher ended that day.

Marité felt that to make real progress, they had to reinvent themselves by erasing their Italian working-class immigrant roots and supplanting them with something more patrician. For a while, Marité and her brother claimed that their mother was an Italian countess, but in a country where many are of Italian descent, this attempt at a social upgrade was met with ridicule. However, they soon devised a much more successful way to disguise the truth about their family background and hint at an illustrious heritage.

On 16th May 1963, following an application to the Buenos Aires Civil Register, the siblings were granted permission to add the more aristocratic-sounding 'Basualdo' to their existing last name of Sosa. Basualdo was synonymous with status and old money. The Ortiz Basualdo family were members of Argentina's aristocracy. Emblematic of their status was the Ortiz Basualdo Palace, the lavish belle epoque residence that occupied an entire block on the Plaza San Martín in the centre of Buenos Aires before it was demolished in the 1930s. As if assuming the name Sosa Basualdo wasn't enough to satisfy their egos, Marité and Luis also claimed to be related to the Ortiz Basualdo family. It was a tale Luis peddled repeatedly and what he told me when I first met him. He would often make vague references to them as his cousins without going into any detail.

The Ortiz Basualdo Palace in Plaza San Martín, Buenos Aires, c. 1910, which Luis claimed to be the home of his ancestors

To further pursue their ambitious quest, the siblings tried to convince the editors of the social directory *Libro Azul*, the *Debrett's Peerage of Argentina*, to include their family in the latest edition. To qualify for inclusion, you must be endorsed by three people who had appeared in a previous edition. Marité could not come up with even one. Despite that, the 1966 edition featured Luis and María Teresa Sosa Basualdo, owners of their stepfather's *hacienda* La Avispa. Luis later told me that it was a $1,500 'contribution' that had made all the difference. Luis and Marité had bought themselves social status and a history. Now it was time to go out into the world and put it to good use.

That was where I came in.

2
When Marcelo Met Luis

Bar El Socorro sits at the intersection of Calle Juncal and Calle Suipacha in the wealthy Recoleta district of Buenos Aires. The bar hasn't changed much since the day I first met Luis Sosa Basualdo there in May 1965. The tables are still marble-topped, the walls are still covered in wood panelling, suggesting the place is older than it is, and the waiters are still formally attired in a nod to a past that never was. Frequented by locals for breakfast and lunch during the week, on Sundays it hosted family gatherings after Mass at the El Socorro church on the opposite side of the street. But as the day wore, the respectable church-going families were replaced by a younger, thirstier, and far less devout clientele: the spoilt kids of the well-to-do. I was in this latter crowd.

It seemed little more than a sleepy café, but it was where everything happened back then – where people congregated before a night out, where friendships were made and lost. I can't remember why I had gone there that particular evening, though I certainly didn't need a reason to be out. I was an immature and pleasure-seeking young man, and there were few nights that I ever stayed in. I had to have a drink in one hand, a cigarette in the other, and I had to stay out late – the later the better. It was an itch that I didn't stop scratching for most of my life.

In many ways, I was exactly the type of person Luis was claiming to be. I was from a good family and raised in my grandparents's four-storey house, now the Czech embassy, in the district of Barrio Parque. Later, when the house was sold, I moved with my parents to neighbouring La Recoleta. If I had died at that time, Luis would no doubt have found a way to attend my funeral, claiming a friendship with me, networking with mourners, and offering his condolences.

Like Luis, I was a restless soul, and as much as I enjoyed the trappings of my privileged life, I found the expectations that accompanied it suffocating. I am the eldest of five children and was born a few months before Luis, in June 1945. If there was any claim at all in our family to social prestige, it was through my father who was a well-respected judge and a professor at Buenos Aires University; his father had also been a judge and, at one point, the Minister of Justice. But it was my maternal grandfather who counted. He was a rich banker and landowner who provided for everybody, and it was with him and my grandmother that I lived in my early years. My grandparents treated me more like a son than a grandson, and I was spoilt rotten. My parents lived on the ground floor of the house, and I shared an en-suite room on the third floor with my Irish nanny, Miss Anne Dowd; I occasionally went downstairs to see my parents.

My grandmother found Anne in a local hostel run by nuns which offered lodgings to young women who had recently arrived in the country and were looking for work in domestic service. The nuns told my grandmother that by taking Anne, she would be employing a saint, and for me, that's what she turned out to be. She was slim with pale skin, bright blue eyes, and auburn hair that she always wore tied back. Apart from teaching me to speak English, she gave me the warmth and affection that my own family could not and was more of a mother to me than my real mother. She was a devout Catholic, and the fact that I am a practising Catholic now is in no small part due to her influence. Everyone understood that I was her favourite and she was mine. I was so close to her that when she was hit by a car in Buenos Aires and died years later, in 1971, my family kept the news from me out of concern for how I might react.

Alas, my paradise ended when I was twelve. My grandparents sold their house and my parents bought their own property where I was taken to live against my wishes. My father was a heavy-handed disciplinarian and beat us children regularly while my mother did nothing about it, sometimes watching his attacks and even encouraging them. Even though my parents had a place of their own, my grandfather continued to pay for everything – the school fees, the clubs, our clothes, and all the luxuries we enjoyed. I grew up both spoilt and resentful. I wanted the best things in life without having to work for them. I resented my entire family, my parents for the way they were with me, and my grandparents for allowing what I considered this terrible calamity to take place.

As soon as we moved into my parents' new property in Calle Libertad, a few blocks from El Socorro, I wanted to run away, but like all children, I was trapped. With law being my father's trade, the path into the judiciary was open to me, but it just wasn't me. I couldn't study as I lacked concentration and my school grades were a constant source of disappointment. The more pressure that was put on me, the worse it got. My grades were so bad I repeated one of my years at school twice. Many nights I overheard my parents discuss my uncertain future in hushed tones behind closed doors.

When I turned fifteen, I was sent to a boarding school run by Irish Pallottine priests and came home only at weekends. I hated everything about it. It was a 'last resort' school, full of other kids like me who had failed their grades. After that, I was sent to another school where I could cram two years into one. My grandfather offered me a trip to Europe on the condition that I pass my exams. But even with that incentive it was no use. By that time, it was clear I had very little academic ability and that's when my life of crime began. I found someone who could forge the examination certificates and

I presented them to my grandfather who rewarded me with a short trip to Europe.

It was also around this time that I began to steal from my parents and grandparents, sometimes out of spite, sometimes for no reason at all. I took anything I could get my hands on from my grandfather – a cane-sword, an ivory carving, a platinum Patek Philippe watch, which I dismantled piece by piece and eventually destroyed just for the hell of it. As an adult, I spent as much time as I could in the bars and clubs of Buenos Aires, unhappily nursing a drink and returning home as late as I could.

That was the background to my presence at El Socorro the evening I met Luis. As soon as I walked into the bar, I heard someone call my name. I looked around, scanned the sea of faces, and spotted one I hadn't seen for a while. In the rogue's gallery that is the *dramatis personae* of my life, Beto Saavedra deserves a special place. Beto is sadly remembered for having played polo in Europe at the request of one of the Fiat heirs, Emanuele Filiberto 'Lele' Nasi Agnelli, who invited him to join his team at the Rome Polo Club. Not long after he arrived at the club, Beto got a telegram informing him that his father had died. Not having funds for the fare home, he struck a deal with Lele who provided the money for the trip in exchange for Beto's horses, saddles and equipment. The deal was struck and the horses were duly delivered as arranged, but when the boxes of saddles and equipment were opened, they contained only stones. By that time Beto was long gone, but instead of returning to Argentina for his father's funeral, he remained in Europe, partying. Interpol later took an interest in him because

Me with Leticia Arrighi at a society ball, Buenos Aires, 1963

he had declared that his horses were in transit and had not paid duty on them; he also left a hotel without paying the bill. Formal complaints were made to the Italian Polo Association and he was barred from ever playing polo in Italy. It was a story he told many times with relish.

On this particular night, it was odd that Beto should be calling my name and waving me over; he usually ignored me. I often used to see him at the Hurlingham and Jockey clubs where he played polo, but we only knew each other superficially, in the way that everyone knows everyone else in those circles. I made my way cautiously towards him. Beto was a good ten years older than me, and short but broad across the shoulders; he could make his presence felt. He sported a thin pencil moustache that accentuated a peculiar dismissive grin that looked more like a sneer.

'It's so funny that you walked in at this very moment,' he said, addressing me as if we were great friends.

'I'm always here,' I responded dryly.

'Meet Luis Sosa,' he said.

Luis stood up and stiffly shook my hand. 'Luis Sosa *Basualdo*,' Luis corrected him loudly, emphasising his newly minted surname.

If he was related to the Ortiz Basualdo family, his branch must have fallen on hard times, I thought to myself. Luis looked about my age and had an overly formal way about him. He was dressed in a suit that, although not shabby, was not particularly impressive. What stood out was his black hair, slicked back in the style of Rudolph Valentino. It was so heavy with brilliantine that it reflected the lights in the ceiling.

'I was just telling Luis that he ought to meet someone like you,' Beto said. 'I even mentioned your name and then you walked in. What do you think about that?'

What I soon realised was that Beto was trying to dump this man on me. It turned out that Luis had asked Beto for help with the necessary introductions to climb the next rung up the social ladder. Who better to enlist than someone Luis's own age?

Beto only agreed to help because he felt he owed Luis's father a favour. He had come across Héctor Sosa when serving as a conscript in his regiment, where he was assigned the care of his horses. In 1940, Héctor had been Argentina's first showjumping champion with his horse *Dragón*. A relationship of mutual respect developed between the two men, and Beto repaid Héctor's kindness by inviting his son to the family *hacienda* on the outskirts of the city. This was where Luis was introduced to polo and given a taste of 'stick-and-ball' – hitting the ball with the mallet while riding at a gallop.

That night in the bar, I made myself comfortable on the chair that Beto offered me, having nothing better to do. It was Beto who did all the talking. Many of his stories were anecdotes about Héctor – what a great honour to serve under Luis's father; how amazing it was that he had won that showjumping tournament. At that time, the Luis I came to know was still a work in progress: he said very little and seemed unsure of how he should behave. I could sense that he wasn't comfortable in his skin. He sat stiffly upright to affect confidence and good manners, occasionally checking that his hair was still smooth, and listened attentively to what we said and how we said it, watching our movements closely so he could replicate them. But he gave away just enough of himself for me to understand that we were kindred spirits, that he, like me, was looking for another kind of life. At the end of the night, I offered to share a taxi with him, but he suddenly became coy and the bonhomie that had developed between us quickly evaporated. He mentioned something vague about staying with his cousins, who I mistakenly assumed were the Ortiz Basualdos, and said goodbye while loitering mysteriously. What I discovered much later was that he was waiting for the bus to take him back to Flores, something he was ashamed of and which would have blown his story about his smart relations.

I flattered myself then, and perhaps still flatter myself, that Luis enjoyed my company, that his initial friendliness was not merely in exchange for the contacts I could provide and the doors I could open; for my part, I believed there was a genuine understanding between us and a sense of shared mission, however transgressive it became.

From that moment, our lives and our fortunes were to be inextricably linked. Even when there was distance between us, whether geographical or emotional, Luis always kept in contact. He wrote letters and phoned, volunteering information about his life and adventures. Sometimes he bragged and sometimes he lied, but that connection between us was always there. I should have seen in his disarming, mischievous grin and his unwillingness to take anything seriously that deceit lay behind all his relationships and transactions. But I too was after mischief, and we joined forces in search of it. Even this first meeting with Luis was predicated on the deceit of a coincidence, and in many ways, Beto established the template for what Luis was to become.

One of the pieces of information that Beto shared with Luis about me was that I was engaged, which I was. The unlucky lady in question was Desirée de la Grangére. She was the daughter of Gustave de la Grangére, a bald, plump, medium-built man with black opal eyes and a thick moustache. Despite his grand name, which he inherited from a family of minor French nobility, he made a living by shuffling papers in a government department. It was his older brother, Baron Armand de Vandières, who was head of the family. Desirée's mother came from good Spanish stock who had been among Argentina's earliest settlers. Short and olive-skinned, she was the breadwinner of the family, running a dressmaking business from home that produced fashionable clothes for the not-so-well-off locals who couldn't afford exorbitant *haute couture* prices.

Desirée was small and innocent-looking, although towards the end of our relationship (and certainly since then), I noticed that she had a rebellious streak, and perhaps flirted with the idea of another kind of life. Like me, she was straight-jacketed by family expectations. It was one of those engagements destined never to end in marriage (or never *should* end in marriage). From her perspective, marrying into my family was an upward move, even though I had no job and no ambition to find one. They naively thought that marrying a Manrique de Acuña would be to their financial advantage. From my family's perspective, my mother, although keen to see me settled, wanted our family to be allied with the French nobility. They were the nobles and we supposedly had the money. But it was my grandparents who were wealthy, and they were still relatively young and in no hurry to pass any of their wealth onto their children, never mind their grandchildren.

Another not insignificant factor in the shaky foundations of our engagement was that, pretty as Desirée was, I was not attracted to her. I was not attracted to women my age. It was women in their forties and fifties and even older who turned me on. I discovered this when I was quite young. When I was at school, it wasn't the girls I fantasised about but their mothers. At the parties that parents arranged for their teenage daughters so they could socialise with young men from other good families, I found myself looking not at the girls with whom I was supposed to mix but at the mothers who dropped them off and picked them up at the end of the evening. As I got older, they often caught me looking at them and knew exactly what I was looking at and why. They knew it even before I did. I would feel that little bolt of electricity running through me that indicated sexual awakening, especially the excitement of forbidden desire. Now that I look back on it, I wonder if it had something to do with my mother and her lack of interest in me. Perhaps it was her attention I sought and these other older women, of which there have been many in my life, were surrogates. Yet as a horny young man about town, all I knew was that it was older women I wanted to sleep with.

As my courtship of Desirée began to fizzle out, my friendship with Luis thrived. Shortly after our first meeting, I invited him to the Hurlingham Club for a polo session. The invitation had barely left my lips before Luis accepted; even on the phone, I could sense his enthusiasm. A little more complicated were the logistics of *how* we would meet. I suggested I'd come to his house and pick him up. At first, he made a show of politeness: he could not possibly impose on me that way. When I insisted, his evasions became more absurd and his alternatives so impractical that in the end, I told him I'd pick him up at his address. It was a sticky situation for Luis – reality was clashing with his fantasy – so when he gave me the address, he claimed it was his family's *Quinta* (a weekend house surrounded by land), and was at pains to stress that he usually stayed with his cousins, the elusive Ortiz Basualdos, when was in Buenos Aires.

I had never been to Flores. It's a long drive westwards out of the city. Knowing what I know now, I can imagine that that bus ride home after hobnobbing with the spoilt uptown kids must have been almost unbearable, Luis's resentment growing with every rattle of the bus and bump on that road. When I arrived at the address he had given me, I was taken aback. While the quiet residential streets were flanked by graceful old oak trees, the property itself was most certainly not a *Quinta*. It was just an unremarkable house, neither grand nor ramshackle, with a backyard. Luis was outside in full regalia – boots, a long whip, and a white helmet in his hand, looking more like a circus lion tamer than a polo player – standing guard by the door so that I couldn't set foot on the porch or meet any members of his real family.

'I thought you said it was a *Quinta*,' I said, more out of naivety than anything else. Although I sensed that his stories were not quite adding up, I still took him at his word in this early stage of our friendship.

'It was a *Quinta* when my grandfather originally bought the place,' he told me. 'He sold the land surrounding the house, but there is still a large garden at the back.'

Anybody could see that his house was one of several detached houses on a street in the suburbs. It wasn't a very good lie; his cover had been blown. But I decided to overlook it.

Neither Luis nor I were genuinely interested in polo. I pretended I was for my grandfather's sake; in Luis's case, it was a means to an end, a means to move up the rungs of the social ladder. The snag was that Luis was left-handed, and in polo, you have to hit the ball with your right hand. So it meant he had a handicap right from the start, although he compensated by having greater control of his horse with his stronger left arm, while at full gallop. Most players restrain their horses with both their hands. Over time, Luis worked hard on his deficiency, making him a competitive player. It was something that he put a great deal of effort into.

At that first practice session at the Hurlingham Club, Fernando Merlos, the stable owner, confided in Luis that he thought little of my prowess at the game, telling him that I often turned up drunk to practice, which was true. But despite my lack of ability, Luis was far more tired at the end of that practice than I was. Although he professed great enthusiasm for the game, he had played very little in the past and wasn't as fit as I had imagined.

To thank me for bringing him to the Hurlingham, I was invited to his house in Flores for tea with his Aunt Ada and Marité, his sister. As I entered the sitting room, Aunt Ada was sprawled on the sofa, dressed in some kind of evening gown, as though she had been sitting for Manet. From a distance, her skin looked as white as porcelain, but when I drew near to shake her hand, I saw that it was caked in white powder. Nonetheless, it was evenly caked and created the illusion of agelessness it was designed to do. I not only liked her immediately, but I also found her attractive. There was something of the Blanche Dubois about her. According to Luis, she had been jilted by a suitor and had never looked at another man, so she lived with her ailing father who spent most of the time shut in his room. Marité, on the other hand, was dressed casually in a white blouse, blue jeans, and a pair of brown moccasins. She looked very much like Luis but lacked his charm. She had the same wiry hair that he had and put on airs and graces to emphasise her 'aristocratic' background.

From Aunt Ada's and Marité's studied poses to the tea table on which the best china was displayed and piled high with an abundance of cakes, scones, and biscuits, I got a strong sense that it had all been staged. Everyone seemed to be overly keen to impress, as though I was an honoured guest.

But they couldn't keep it up. First of all, Marité's conversation about the charity work she did at the polo club, peppered by her incessant name-dropping, was punctuated by a series of foul-mouthed tirades from somewhere outside, a complete contrast to the air of refinement the ladies were trying to create.

'*¡La puta madre que te parió, vieja de mierda. Te vas a podrir en el infierno!*'

As expletives rolled out, Ada froze, her teacup held in mid-air, her little finger stiffened in forced elegance, waiting for the verbal offensive to end.

'Take no notice. That is Chacho next door shouting at his wife,' explained Luis.

Chacho Bigger, their next-door neighbour, was a notorious wife-beater, among other things. If Ada was Blanche Dubois, Chacho was Stanley Kowalski, albeit an older, unattractive pot-bellied version. The plump sixty-year-old, wearing a sleeveless vest and straw hat, was sitting on a canvas chair in his backyard adjacent to theirs. Jobless and hard-up, he regularly picked fights with his wife. Next, just as Marité was about to resume her boring story, a high-speed train passed by the house, making the china rattle and floor shake – the inconvenience of living opposite a busy railway track. Then, the unexpected arrival of Vincenzo, Luis's grandfather, finally dispelled any remaining illusions of gentility. He was mostly bedridden and under the care of a nurse on the top floor of the house. Drawn by the talk and loud laughter, he decided to join the tea party in his pyjamas. His grandchildren seemed mortified by his arrival, embarrassed by his thick Italian accent, which to me was rather charming, as much as by his lack of decorum. None of it was what I was used to, to say the least. Soon after, Vincenzo's health took a turn for the worse and he was unable to come downstairs at all any more.

While I was floating along aimlessly, drinking too much, attending every event I was invited to and seeing far less of my fiancée than one might expect from a prospective husband-to-be. In the meantime, Luis was putting together a plan, and we found ourselves spending an increasing amount of time on bringing it to fruition.

Both Fernando Merlos and Beto Saavedra had told Luis about how one could live the good life abroad as a polo player. It was simply a question of arousing the interest of a millionaire patron who would sponsor you and pay for the shipment of your horses, travel and living expenses included. So not only was polo the best way for Luis to access the social circles he aspired to enter, but it also promised the kind of easy lifestyle that he and I were attracted to, and Beto was the very man who could provide us with the means to attain it. So we visited him at his *hacienda* in Mercedes, sixty kilometres west of Buenos Aires. The property, a cattle ranch, belonged to his mother and Beto was the manager. With a well-maintained polo field, he often hosted matches between his neighbours. It was there that Luis learned the rudiments of polo.

While eating empanadas after a two-against-two game, Luis brought up the subject.

'I can't stop thinking of what you said last time we met.'

'What did I say?' Beto asked.

'All the stuff about travelling and living off polo.'

'What part of it can't you stop thinking about?'

'All of it.'

Beto did not need any encouragement to talk about his exploits and give advice on how to have a good time without doing much other than playing polo and finding wealthy benefactors. What excited him were the connections to women that polo provided. 'Especially if you're Argentinian and have other attributes,' he added.

He told stories of women who wined and dined him around Europe, all at their expense, and all he had to do was pretend to be their boyfriend for a little while. What he was describing was how to be a gigolo. Of course, Luis and I lapped all this up. It was easy, according to him. To get started, all it required were some initial funds; then we could go abroad and play polo and get noticed by a sponsor. But neither Luis nor I had any money to get started.

That was where Luis's persistence and irrepressible optimism came into play.

3
Planning Our Escape

El proyecto (the project), as I referred to it, was the plan that Luis and I concocted on the way back from Beto's *hacienda*. It involved horses, polo, rich sponsors, and wealthy women. I felt as if I had just woken from a long sleep; now I had a plan to escape the dull mediocrity that otherwise stretched ahead of me.

We swapped the confined space of El Socorro for Café La Biela as the venue for plotting our domination of the world. It was all we talked about. We each brought something to the table: Luis depended on me for resources and contacts, while he gave me the ambition and daring I needed. Our meetings in La Biela created a bond between us, further cemented by some early escapades.

For example, we took to eating out in restaurants and leaving without paying the bill, a 'dine-and-dash' as it was known. We would arrive at a place as if we owned it, choose a table near the entrance, eat whatever we fancied, and then, while the waiter was away fetching our coffees, we calmly got up, quietly left without arousing suspicion and, as soon as we were out in the street, made a run for it. For a while, it worked, but then we made the mistake of going to the same restaurant twice in one week, which, of course, was utterly idiotic. We sat down near the door as we always did and ate our meal, including dessert, after which we were stuffed. As usual, we asked for two espressos and when the waiter reached the kitchen with the order, we upped from our seats and made for the door. But it turned out that the other waiters had been on the alert and when we left, they started chasing after us. Usually, all we had to do was run around a corner and that was it, but on this occasion, we had to run like hell for several blocks. At one point, I was almost caught. How we kept down all the food we'd eaten, I will never know. The experience was enough to dissuade us from any similar escapades.

However, we continued to test each other's boundaries and push each other. The more restless we became, the more extreme our antics. One night, after hours of heavy drinking, we were stumbling through the streets on our way home and arrived at a police station. We began taunting the policeman guarding it, goose-stepping in front of him, giving exaggerated salutes, and making whatever other offensive taunts and gestures we could think of. In Argentina in 1965, the police were omnipresent and powerful; their authority was not something to play around with. But in our arrogance and inebriation, we continued until the policeman sent for backup and we were arrested.

I was surprised, partly because I was so drunk and partly because of my family's connections. At the station, I tried the 'Do you know who I am?' line.

'No, please tell me who are you?' the duty sergeant replied sarcastically.

'I'm the son of Judge Manrique de Acuña,' I pronounced haughtily.

At first, he didn't believe me, but I was insistent and he eventually decided to err on the side of caution.

Police stations dealt regularly with criminal judges and kept a list with their contact details. It was three o'clock in the morning and the duty sergeant dialled nervously. For him, it was a lose-lose situation: if the judge really was my father, he might get in trouble for arresting me; if he wasn't my father, he'd be in trouble for being an idiot and waking a judge in the middle of the night. Eventually, my father answered the phone and the officer explained the situation. After a moment's silence, he passed the phone to me. The conversation with my father was brief, just long enough for him to confirm it was me and that I was indeed as drunk and disorderly as the sergeant said I was. I passed the phone back to the sergeant rather smugly. But the smug expression was soon wiped off my face. The sergeant listened to my father's instructions, ended the conversation, escorted us to a cell, and locked us up. We were released the next morning when we had sobered up.

Once the dust settled from that escapade, I thought it would be a good idea to introduce Luis to my grandparents, just as he had introduced me to his family.

'So this is the famous Luis Sosa Basualdo!' my grandfather said when he met him.

'Yes,' Luis responded somewhat coyly, his growing social confidence suddenly dissolving when faced with my grandfather and his reputation. My grandmother saw right through him the moment he walked in the door. As though testing a potential suitor, she homed in immediately on his name.

'We must be related,' she said to him.

'Really, how can that be?' he asked.

'My grandmother's last name was Ortiz Basualdo,' she said.

'The truth is I don't pay much attention to family genealogy,' he replied, hoping the matter would end there. But she pursued the subject, asking him further questions about his connections, none of which he was able to answer to her satisfaction. In the end, she offered him what appeared to be a lifeline, naming a member of the family to whom he might be connected. He took it. It was only after he left that she told me she had only mentioned that relation to catch him out.

Luis was furious about the way he had been treated, and so was I, not because they had seen through him, but because of the way they had humiliated him in front of me. My grandmother was well aware of what she had done; they had already decided he was a bad influence on me and she wanted me to see what he was really up to. I told her that when I had gone to his house, his family had shown me nothing but kindness.

'Where does he live?' she asked.

'In Flores,' I said.

'Flores?'

'He lives in a *Quinta*. It's been the family home for hundreds of years if you must know – before it was annexed to the city.'

She looked at me suspiciously.

'It's huge,' I added, compounding the lie further.

It was the beginning of a serious deterioration in the relationship with my parents and grandparents. The options were to stay with my family and the security they provided or follow Luis and the adventures he promised, and even at that stage I was choosing the latter. If anything, the whole episode with my grandparents made me even more eager to move forward with our plans.

Over many lively discussions with many cigarettes, cups of coffee, and whatever alcohol we could get our hands on (though in those days I was the big drinker), we formulated our plans.

4
Aunt Clara

The first step in *el proyecto* was to leave Argentina as soon as possible. We concluded that the United States was a better starting point than Europe – it would be easier to find work there, and the airfare to the US was far cheaper than to Europe. Luis, always savvy, insisted that it would all be in vain if we did not have the right connections there, and he was right.

Connections were my department and I scratched my head wondering who I could turn to. I thought Aunt Clara might be able to help. I called Clara Leloir Unzué 'Aunt Clara' not because she was my real aunt, but because, in addition to being my mother's cousin, she was my godmother. When I lived at my grandparents' house, she came for lunch every Sunday and I got to know her well from an early age. After I moved away with my parents I stopped seeing her.

Clara was rich and well-connected both in Argentina and abroad, and I thought of her because her ex-husband was none other than Charlie Menditéguy, a man who excelled in different sports. He was an ace driver in both road rallying and Formula One, and a scratch golfer. But it was as a polo player that he most interested me. He had been rated as a ten-goal handicap, and with his team 'El Trébol' he was seven times winner of the Argentine Open. He had also courted many stunning women, including the legendary actress Brigitte Bardot. However, his true value to us lay in his close friendship with the polo player Stewart Iglehart, a man who could open doors for us in the most select polo circles in the US. So how could I convey my aspirations to Aunt Clara diplomatically?

On the day we agreed to have lunch, I brought her the gift of a book about pedigree dogs, forgetting that she was only interested in street dogs, which she protected through a charity organisation. Luckily, the book remained unwrapped on the coffee table until one of her servants took it away.

Lunch itself was very civilised. We ate in the large dining room of her apartment, overlooking Plaza Alemania and attended by a white-gloved butler. She couldn't understand why I wanted to meet up with her; however, from the way she looked at me, it was clear she sensed my visit was not without some sort of agenda. I didn't know how to start and went around in circles while Clara let the conversation drift without trying to direct it. I kept looking at her cleavage and she noticed, but it didn't seem to bother her. Maybe it had been a while since anyone had courted her. Between one thing and another, time seemed to disappear without me getting to the point of my visit. Finally, partly motivated by several glasses of wine and partly driven by anxiety, I ended up blurting it out.

'The truth is, Aunt Clara, I came to ask for a favour.'

'Yes dear, what is it?' she asked, smiling.

'I'd like you to help me with a trip I have planned to the United States.'

Just then, I became a bit breathless and dizzy. My aunt noticed and asked if I was feeling okay. Downplaying my discomfort, I blamed the oppressive weather and the unaccustomed alcohol.

'The thing is, I've decided to take a course in business administration at Florida International University in Miami,' I continued. 'And, well, I need a cover letter to show at the Palm Beach Polo Club.'

She looked at me in surprise and, applying impeccable reasoning, said, 'But if you're going to study in America, wouldn't you need a letter sponsoring you to enter university?'

My response – that I wanted to take a gap year before starting my studies – only raised Clara's suspicions further. However, she didn't outright reject the possibility of helping me; she just told me she was going to think about it.

When I got up to say goodbye, I staggered, but Clara held me steady, putting an arm around me. (The feel and smell of her soft, warm skin made my head spin again for a different reason!) But she elegantly and compassionately downplayed my wobble: 'Anyone can stumble in life, dear.' Outside, her driver was waiting to take me home.

It must have been almost three weeks before she got in touch again, asking me to call in to see her. It was a brief meeting, and this time very productive. She handed me two letters: a copy of the one her ex-husband, Charlie Menditéguy, had sent to Stewart Iglehart, and another from Iglehart addressed to the US Embassy in which he stated he would sponsor me on my visit to America. In a separate note to Charlie, Iglehart said he would also make arrangements for me to play polo in the US. Menditéguy had taken a chance on me!

When I got home I put the letters in a safe place so my father wouldn't discover them and immediately called Luis. I told him about the two letters, explaining the connection between me and Menditéguy and between him and Iglehart.

Luis was ecstatic. 'Your aunt did that for you! Is she hot?' He laughed. 'Did you have to pay her?'

Luis was envious of my relationships and contacts, and my situation as a potential heir to a fortune. Once he even calculated how much my grandparents would leave me in land, property, cars, and so on. From the beginning of our friendship, it was tinged with competitiveness and it went both ways. I envied Luis's audacity and thirst for conquest, while Luis craved my family lineage, wealth, and contacts. We each had what the other lacked and for that reason, we made the perfect team in pursuit of one goal – to leave Argentina.

So now that we had secured the right connections in the US, we needed money to buy the tickets to get us there. We couldn't borrow the money – we exhausted that route – and we quickly discovered that it was impossible to get free or highly discounted tickets on a cargo ship, which we'd been fantasising about. So it was decided, with little debate or moral qualms, that we would steal items from my parents and sell them.

5
Ransacking the Family Home

I met with Luis at a restaurant in La Recoleta and after a few drinks to give us courage, we went to my house around four in the afternoon. Even though my parents were on holiday at the time, we tiptoed in and whispered to each other. Luis, ever impulsive, wanted to take the first things he saw in the large entrance hall – the collection of antique Chinese ceramic figurines and the paintings on the walls. He was right to think they were valuable. Any one of them would fetch us the sum we needed, with plenty left over, but I insisted that whatever we took, it should be something that would not be noticed immediately.

We entered my father's study where a plum-wood cabinet with glass doors stood at the far end. Inside was a collection of silverware – a tureen and a complete cutlery set – along with a set of Murano glass goblets with goldwork. For some reason, I thought these items would not be missed straight away. I tried to force open the glass door and eventually broke the lock. I took out the most valuable objects, telling myself that it wasn't really stealing; it was just a loan. They were things of no use to my parents, sitting there gathering dust on a shelf, but for me they were priceless. When we'd taken what we wanted, we called a locksmith to repair the broken lock. The man was a true professional and did his job without asking questions, even though the situation was highly suspicious.

Luis suggested that we take the loot to Tommy Guerra, a Uruguayan known for his shady business dealings and his connection to Buenos Aires's gay underworld. Guerra treated us like the inexperienced thieves he knew we were, despite my story that my family had fallen on difficult times and I had been sent to pawn the heirlooms. When he saw the contents of the suitcase, he was far from enthusiastic.

'Didn't you realise that these objects you described as gold are nothing but silver dipped in a thin layer of gold?' he asked disdainfully. He called them 'trinkets'; the silver cutlery was merely 'Sheffield rubbish'. The only item he took any interest in was the silver tureen. He inspected the hallmark on the underside and immediately recognised a classic design by Paul de Lamerie, the 18th-century London-based French silversmith known as the King's silversmith. 'This will pay for a trip around the world, my commission included,' Guerra said. After the disdain he had shown the other objects, which I perversely took as an insult to my family, I was pleased that he was pleased.

Guerra took us and the items to an associate by the name of Ali, better known as 'The Turk', who operated out of Ali's Antiques, a cat pee-scented hovel not far from Luis's home. Inside, a variety of second-hand objects were piled high.

There was no pretence as to how we had come by the items. 'As this is stolen,' Ali casually remarked, on inspecting the tureen, 'I can only give you fifty per cent of the normal purchase price.' He gave me his best price and I accepted. Then he opened an old biscuit tin, took out a wad of bills, gave Guerra his commission, and counted out my share.

Needless to say, my parents immediately noticed the missing items and assumed it was a burglary committed by some expert lock pickers. The police went straight to Ali's cave of treasure, where they knew many stolen items ended up. The Turk was well used to this kind of situation and even though they roughed him up and threatened to throw him in prison for an indefinite period if he didn't produce the missing items, he didn't give in and the police left empty-handed.

Despite these setbacks, the tureen earned Ali a handsome profit, Guerra got his commission and Luis and I bought two airfare tickets to Miami. Not bad for a day's work!

6
Welcome to Miami

I neither announced nor explained my departure to my family. I simply packed my bags and waited for the crack of dawn, when Luis and his sister Marité arrived in a taxi to pick me up, and together we went to Ezeiza Airport. Once we had checked in, Marité reached inside her handbag and pulled out an image of Our Lady of Luján, the patron saint of Argentina, and gave it to Luis. 'She'll take care of you,' she said rather dramatically.

As we said our goodbyes, I had a twinge of conscience. I was expected for lunch at my grandfather's that afternoon, so I asked Marité to call him and explain why I couldn't make it. She told me much later that he was appalled; he took it as a complete betrayal.

For Luis, this was a new beginning, a chance to reinvent himself in a new country where his social status would not be such an issue and where he could fool people with his bogus family background and mix in the circles he despised. For me, the adventure was much more problematic. I was leaving behind some fractured family relationships and the certainty that my sudden departure would be connected with the disappearance of the heirloom from my father's cabinet. Sooner or later, that would have to be reckoned with, but for now, as the plane took off and I saw the city of my birth disappear from view, so too did all those worries.

The trip to the US was punctuated by an overnight stopover in Lima, Peru. After landing at the international airport there, we were driven in a mini-bus to the three-star Hotel Riviera, situated in the centre of the city. While we were checking in, we couldn't help but notice the persistent stare of two young women sitting in the adjacent lounge. Luis's reaction was typically uncouth.

'We'll pick them up and fuck them later. Let's unpack first,' he said.

I was no more refined. 'Yeah, I'm dying for a screw too!'

But when we came down from our rooms, there was no sign of the girls, so we sat and enjoyed the buffet lunch included in the airfare. After a two-hour nap in our hotel room, we showered, put on our blue suits ready for the evening, and sat in the hotel lounge. Not long after we arrived, the concierge approached us and said our presence was requested. He nodded toward the entrance where the two young girls who had stared at us earlier were standing.

I strolled over and one of them asked, 'Are you Ramón and Manuel?'

'No, no, I'm afraid not,' I said and went back to sit in the lounge.

'What was that all about?' Luis inquired.

'Nothing. The girls weren't interested in us. They wanted to know if we were Ramón and Manuel. A case of mistaken identity.'

'You stupid ass! You should have said we were them. Don't you know who Ramón and Manuel are? They're the pop duo who appear playing guitar on television. Maybe they're expected at this hotel. If that's who they thought we were, we must look like them. We could be screwing by now!'

Luis was right, and I kicked myself. There was nothing for it but to kill time until the evening meal at the hotel, so we went to have a look around the city. By seven thirty we were back, only to find a noisy crowd of girls out on the street, shouting and screaming. At the doorway stood Ramón and Manuel themselves, surrounded by photographers feverishly taking snaps. With his dark skin and slicked-back hair, Luis was indeed the spitting image of Ramón.

'See! What did I tell you,' Luis said indignantly as we went into the hotel. 'They'll be screwing tonight, and thanks to you, we'll go to bed with hard cocks.'

We finally arrived in the United States of America on 22nd of January 1966. As soon as we landed in Miami reality hit us, as did the humidity. America was expensive and the basics – where we were going to live and what we were going to live on – brought us back to earth with a painful thud.

It also turned out that Miami was a haven for every Cuban who had escaped or been expelled from the island. It was a measure of how naive we had been about the whole adventure. The cab driver who took us to the hotel spoke Spanish, the staff at the hotel spoke Spanish and the waiters spoke Spanish. At first, the familiarity was welcome – we didn't have to struggle to make ourselves understood; it was like we had never left. But in reality, we were just another couple of Latino hustlers chasing the American dream, despite our letters of introduction to the most select circles. The conversations that Luis and I were having about getting a well-paid job and how to circumnavigate the immigration laws were the conversations that every other Hispanic immigrant was having.

One of the many Cubans we came across was Pepe, a barman at the hotel where we first stayed. He was a mine of information. He recommended a nearby employment agency where we could apply for a social security number, an essential requirement to work in the US, and get a job. These were the practical things that neither Luis nor I had even remotely considered. But Pepe, who was at first so friendly and helpful, suddenly turned cold and distant, and we soon learned the first lesson about life in America: nothing is for free; everything is transactional, one way or another, even friendly advice from a fellow Latino, who we eventually tipped.

We put on our best suits, our most sober ties, and our well-polished shoes and made our way to the Rainbow Employment Agency, as Pepe recommended. We were greeted by a man dressed like one of those gangsters you see in films; he also talked like one. Bernie Blackstone was his name, though judging from his thick Russian accent, it was almost certainly not his real name. In our most formal English, we introduced ourselves and told him that we were educated young men from good families and were looking for jobs, perhaps in a bank or an office.

'Don't got no banks. What I got is a vacancy for two beach boys,' he said gruffly with a take-it-or-leave-it attitude.

'Beach boy? What's that?' I asked.

'You work at the pool. You lay towels, you pick up towels, you serve drinks, you serve snacks. And if you see anyone drowning, you go in after them. I need thirty bucks to register you.'

'Thirty dollars? You mean we give you thirty dollars?' Luis, like me, didn't understand the logic of paying to get a job. We assumed that we'd be the ones to get paid.

'Yeah, that's right. You give me thirty bucks each, or you show me a work permit. Have you got one of those?'

We spewed out some unlikely story that Bernie saw straight through. He'd heard it all before. But when he softened his attitude, we got a glimpse of his more human side.

'Look, the job's easy, and the tips are good for a couple of good-looking guys like you. It's a nice place. An apart-hotel, good class of customer. Elegant.' The word 'elegant' sounded slightly sordid coming from him.

Luis turned to me and muttered in Spanish, 'This guy's a scoundrel, but what choice do we have?' Taking a slim wad of bills out of his pocket, he handed Bernie sixty dollars.

As he counted the notes, Bernie said, 'By the way, I'm not a scoundrel.' Not only did Cuban exiles speak Spanish in Miami, but Russian gangsters did too.

We had gone in dressed in suits looking for jobs as bank tellers or office workers and came out as pool boys who'd be working with hardly any clothes on.

Marty Lewis was the pool manager at Harbour House in Collins Avenue, the apartment hotel where we'd be working. Despite his dyed dark hair, he looked like the actor Jeff Chandler. Marty had been an army officer and he bossed his beach boys around as if he were still in command of his regiment. When he saw us, dressed in our suits and ties, ready for our 'respectable' jobs, he burst out laughing. Once he had composed himself, we received our instructions and he drove us to what would be our accommodation.

The impressive Harbour House condo complex, Miami, Florida

Harbour House swimming pool area

Our new home was the Glades Motel on Biscayne Boulevard, a seven-minute bus ride from Collins Avenue, where we worked. It was a typical 1950s complex comprising ground-floor units mounted on stilts to avoid rats, summer crabs, and flooding. It was an affordable place, convenient for beach boys and hotel staff, but also for pimps, prostitutes, and many colourful characters living on government benefits. The motel was run by a man called J. P. Edwards and his wife, Beth. I never found out what the J. P. stood for – that's just what we all called him. He was a slim guy in his forties with a greying blond crew cut and muscular, tattooed arms with pumped-up veins that looked like they were going to burst. He would often make racist remarks about black and Jewish people, and reserved a special disdain for Sammy Davis Junior who, he said, had 'two strikes against him – he's black and Jewish.' This was the world we found ourselves in.

At 8 a.m. the next day, we reported for work. First, we had breakfast at the Harbour House coffee shop where we met Ruco and his wife, Juanita, Cubans who worked behind the bar. It was Ruco who filled us in about the job and the place, the tipping culture, and, crucially, how to supplement our income. Naturally, we were all ears.

'This is a springboard for other things, if you know what I mean.' He immediately noticed that we didn't know what he meant, and continued: 'Getting acquainted with customers often leads to much better tips if you play your cards right. Guys like you – young and handsome – can make some nice money by just standing around looking pretty. If an old lady wants to play with you in bed, you say yes. The men are sometimes better than the women.'

Not only did he say that in full hearing of his wife, but he winked at her as he said it. I wondered what that meant: did he play with men? Did she play with men? Or did both of them? Sex seemed so free and easy compared to Argentina; as much of a scoundrel as I was, the Catholic in me was immediately uncomfortable. We had come to the US to bag heiresses, not turn tricks with men and women for tips.

'You mean we should sleep with men?' I asked, unable to hide my outrage.

'What difference does it make – men, women? It's the tips that count.'

'I would never go to bed with a man,' pronounced an indignant Luis.

'Well, it's your choice, Chico. If that's the way you think, then maybe this isn't the job for you. You don't get prizes for morality here.'

We soon learned that this was Ruco's favourite subject. He talked about it all the time, and his wife loved it, particularly the stories of dirty old men taking advantage of unsuspecting beach boys. They never failed to make her howl with laughter, though we never quite knew whether she was laughing at us or if she was turned on.

'The pool boys here swing every which way.' With Ruco's words ringing in our ears, we started work. Marty added some of his own advice: 'People here tip for good service. Your answers should be "Yes Sir" or "Yes Ma'am", and you must come and go in a hurry. You must look busy at all times. This is not South America, where people spend their time sleeping under a coconut tree.'

That first day we spent all our time putting mats on the white plastic reclining chairs and giving out towels to customers. It was a rude awakening for both of us. We returned to the motel exhausted and slept until seven the next morning. It took a couple of weeks for us to adjust to this routine, let alone think of venturing into the city for a night out.

It wasn't long before I came upon one of those opportunities to make extra money, and I did not hesitate. A lady lying on one of the lounge chairs by the pool called me over. She was an American woman in her fifties with dyed blonde hair and wearing a large hat, the brim of which she had tipped up so I could see her face.

'You're new here, aren't you?' she asked in a husky voice.

'Yes, I am.'

'What's your name?'

'Marcelo.'

'Marr-se-lo,' she repeated, rolling my name around her mouth in an attempt to mimic my accent.

Me (right) with fellow beach boy, Harbour House, 1966

Me (left, seated) with fellow beach boys, Harbour House, 1966

She handed me the tanning lotion, turned onto her front, and muttered something, which I guessed was an instruction to rub the lotion into her back. I proceeded to do so, careful to avoid the straps.

'Aren't you going to unfasten my top?' she said.

For a twenty-year-old who was attracted to older women, it was all too exciting. I fumbled with the fastener, letting each strap fall to the side, and rubbed in the lotion. From that first interaction, it was clear she was the boss. She gave the instructions – higher, lower, 'now my legs', 'now my ankles', all the time very much in control.

Then she turned over and lay on her back.

I hesitated for a moment. 'You want me to do your front?'

'Well, I don't want to get burnt, do I? The skin around there is very delicate. Don't you have a mother and sisters?'

'Yes Ma'am, but I don't rub their breasts!'

She laughed for a second before becoming business-like again. More instructions: softly, gently, please don't rush. Then she sat up, ordered a drink, which I got for her, and introduced herself as Ruth Goldberg. She proceeded to ask me a series of questions: where was I from? Was I a student? Was it hot in Argentina? Were all the men in Argentina as attractive as me? Despite her dark glasses, I could feel her studying me, noting my nervousness, my fumbled answers, and my cock, which by this time was protruding through the skimpy tight shorts we had to wear, despite my best efforts to hide it.

'Why don't you come to my apartment this evening?' she said. 'It's number thirty-six on the third floor.'

After work, I raced back to the motel to change and got to Mrs Goldberg's flat for seven o'clock. This time, she was wearing a revealing white blouse, tight black satin pants, and open-toed stilettos. Her blonde hair partially covered her face, like Veronica Lake, and she had on false eyelashes. She poured me a whisky and handed me the glass, her bright red manicured nails flashing seductively.

'What are your plans here?' she asked. 'Don't tell me you're an actor.'

'Why do you say that?' I replied.

'I can spot them a mile off. My husband is a theatre producer. He's producing a show on Broadway, where he'll be for months. Just in case you're wondering, I'm not interested in young men, or mature men for that matter. My husband is gay and we have an arrangement that suits us both. The reason I asked you back is because I was feeling lonely. By the way, you should meet my husband when he returns.'

'I don't think that would be necessary,' I said.

'But I thought you wanted to be an actor.'

'Well, yes, but …'

She then produced a yellow capsule, crushed it, and stuffed it under my nose, ordering me to inhale, which I did. Almost immediately, I felt a wave of what I can only describe as complete and utter abandon. It was as if I was on another planet. I felt like I was going to explode.

'What was that?' I asked eventually.

'Poppers.'

'What are poppers?'

She looked at me incredulously, checking that I wasn't joking, and then said, 'You, my dear Marcelo, have a lot to learn. But it's getting late and I have a long day tomorrow.' She scribbled something on a sheet of paper and handed it to me. 'This is Ruth Foreman's office number. She's a drama teacher. Don't mention my name or she'll put two and two together and won't be able to keep her mouth shut.'

There was no goodbye kiss, no embrace, just that number scribbled on a piece of paper. I half expected to be tipped; I guess Ruth Foreman's number was my tip.

Ruth Goldberg and I saw each other regularly over the next few weeks, but just as friends, given the fact that she was not interested in men. She never paid me any money, but she did buy me expensive presents. If I needed something, she would pay for it, but she never took me out; she was careful not to be seen with me, even at the pool, despite the obvious nature of our initial encounter. From then on, we met almost exclusively at her apartment. It was my first foray into the world of the gigolo and I felt disappointed as there was no sex involved, no money either. It wasn't as glamorous as I thought it would be.

Meanwhile, the relationship between Luis and I was beginning to show its cracks. We were very competitive about everything, and Luis was often envious of the smallest of my successes. Even a generous tip from a guest would bother him. He would denigrate or trivialise any acquaintance I made and was always comparing everything, including the size of our dicks which we measured in front of a mirror (I always won, which made things worse). His mood would darken for days if he felt I had somehow achieved more than him. Jealousy seemed to eat him up, so I learned to be vague about where I had been and who I had been with. But I didn't go out of my way to boost his confidence either; joking about his lack of success with women probably wasn't the best way to go. Instead of meeting heiresses, as he hoped, he often ended up with maids or prostitutes whose drinks he had to pay for and I mocked him pitilessly for it. His other failings were his lack of social graces, his inability to make small talk, and his poor general knowledge. The wider the gap between us, the more pleasure I took in humiliating him. I didn't tell Luis about my appointment with the acting coach Ruth Foreman; I was no actor and had never had any ambition to be one until Ruth Goldberg put the idea in my head. But I was vain enough to go along with it, and why not? Wasn't I in the Land of Opportunity?

Ruth Foreman had the look of a glamourous school teacher. When I arrived at her office, she asked me to read a part she thought I might be good for. I looked at the script and read it like I was reading the newspaper, with no emotion or energy and none of the qualities an actor should have.

'Aren't you going to stand up?' she asked.

I stood up, but my delivery was no better. She gave me a little direction, which I barely knew how to interpret. I was hopeless and I knew it; she most certainly knew it. But she took me on all the same, on her beginner's course, and I was elated. It meant she had seen promise in me; it was a first step in a great career. But I soon realised that Ruth Foreman accepted anyone on her course as long they paid the fees.

The lessons themselves were pointless. She did most of the talking, not just about acting, but also about how to break into the industry. Occasionally she would call two people to the front of the class to perform a sketch, which was almost always awful. Most of my fellow wannabe thespians were Cuban and spoke English with a worse accent than I did. Indeed, some of them could barely speak English at all; I doubt they understood when Ruth asked us to dig deep into our own life experiences and channel them into the roles we were assigned in class. It was farcical, she with her doggedly serious approach to method acting, and the Cubans who talked amongst themselves about what job paid good tips and where to find cheap accommodation.

One day, just as my interest was waning, Ruth approached me after class.

'I've been watching you, Mario,' she said.

'It's Marcelo.'

'... and I think you have something special. It's what we in the business call raw talent.'

I felt flattered and allowed myself to get a little excited.

'For four hundred dollars a week, I can give you private coaching,' she went on.

I barely made four hundred dollars a week, tips included. I told her I'd think it over, but by that time I'd learned that when someone pays you a compliment it's because they want one of two things: money or sex. I decided that what I needed was not more acting lessons but a car.

I had been putting a little money aside each week and was eventually able to buy a grey 1957 Pontiac for one hundred dollars. Somehow it improved the combative relationship between me and Luis. Up to that point, we had been taking the bus to work, or spending a small fortune on taxis when we stayed late drinking at a bar. Now, here I was at the wheel of a big American car like the ones we'd seen driven by Cornel Wilde or Rock Hudson. We felt like we had gone up a notch in the world and got that bit closer to living the American dream.

Ruco, the Cuban barman, hadn't been lying when he mentioned the close relationship between pool boys and clients. Our evenings began to be organised around the people we met at work. He was also right about the attention we'd get from men as well as from women. We were always fending off advances from men. 'It's just the beginning, boys, you'll see,' Marty said, laughing at our uptight attitude. 'We're not from Havana!' I'd protest whenever he teased us.

By that time, I'd learned that I didn't have any talent as an actor; I also knew I didn't want to be a pool boy for the rest of my life. However, what I did seem to have a talent for was chatting up women, especially older women.

As Ruth's husband now spent more time in Miami and I was seeing less of her, I became more available to offers from other generous ladies. It was around that time that I met Betty Meyer. She sat right next to me at a bar and, without so much as an introduction, offered to buy me a drink, which I of course accepted. She told me she was a missionary, and that her main interest was helping young people. I listened with some scepticism, thinking she was after something, just like everyone else I had met. But Betty was different. She not only asked questions, but she listened to the answers. I'd already had a few drinks by then, so my tongue was loose enough; then Betty paid for a few more. Among the things she got out of me was my background in swimming. I had always been a good swimmer, and as uncommitted and unenthusiastic as I was about polo, I loved going to the pool. Back home I joined a local club and won a few cups. Mind you, there were only four of us competing with each other at any given time.

'Is that what you're doing here?' she asked.

'I've come here to pursue a career as an actor. I'm taking drama classes,' I said without thinking. This flimsy excuse had now become the alibi I shared with strangers in bars after a few drinks.

To my surprise, it turned out that Betty knew Ricou Browning, the director of the successful *Flipper* TV series that ran from 1964 to 1967. She was a friend of Ricou's mother and had known him since he was a baby. She said she'd reach out to him and see if he had a part in the series for a very handsome young man. A couple of days later, a note from Betty was left for me at the motel with precise instructions to contact Ricou Browning at the Ivan Tors Studios. Betty had made good on her end of the bargain. I soon found out what *my* end of the bargain would be and she often swung by the motel in the evenings when she knew I would be in. She might have been a missionary, but she was also a randy middle-aged woman with an insatiable appetite for sex. She had everyone fooled, even J. P. and Beth, who met her one evening when I was out. She told them she wanted to help me spiritually, and they actively encouraged me to listen to her advice as she was a woman of God.

The TV series, named after Flipper, a dolphin that aided the marine park rangers in often dramatic endeavours to keep people safe, was harmless all-American family fun and people loved it. Following Betty's introduction, I arranged to meet Ricou at the studios where a young woman led me to his office. All the time I had Ruco's words ringing in my head, that I would need to service men as well as women, and I was apprehensive about our meeting.

Browning was an imposing six-foot-something ex-stuntman who knew his business inside out. He had a brisk, no-nonsense way about him, which was a little intimidating.

'Betty told me you're interested in acting,' he said.

'Yes, I'm a student of Ruth Foreman's acting school.'

He looked perplexed. 'What school?'

'Ruth Foreman's. She's one of the most well-known and prestigious acting coaches in the United States,' I said, repeating what she had told me.

He politely said nothing, opened a drawer, and took out a script from which he asked me to read. It was only then it became clear that I'd have to prove my acting skills; none of my other 'skills' would be required. All my many weeks of acting lessons came down to this moment. Clearing my throat I gave it everything I had, but I was as awful as I had been on that first day with Ruth Foreman. He interrupted me before I got through the first sentence: 'I think I might have something for you.'

Essentially, I became an extra on the show. My role was to hang around in the outdoor scenes, naked from the waist up; occasionally he let me mutter a word or two, which may or may not have made it into the episode that aired. So I still couldn't get a job without having to be half-naked.

My first day on set was for an episode titled 'Deep Waters', shot at the Miami Seaquarium and in Biscayne Bay. It was easy work as all I had to do was stand around in a skimpy bathing suit looking pretty and wait for the director to call 'Action' and 'Cut.' There was always lots of hanging around, waiting for shots to be set up and the dolphin to do what it was supposed to do, and that was it. I appeared daily at the studios at 8 a.m., whether we filmed or not (there was no filming on cloudy days), and I received my wages once a week regardless. It wasn't a fortune, but it was more than I made as a pool boy and I had more fun. I met lots of people, women particularly, who were also half-naked, a definite perk of the job. Lowly extra or not, half-naked or not, all of this went to my head, despite my obvious lack of talent.

I felt like things were taking off, that this was the beginning of what would be a new and exciting career in TV, the next step – the movies.

No sooner had my acting career taken off than it sank to the bottom of the sea, too deep even for a dolphin. Once filming for the season ended, I spent time searching unsuccessfully for another job in film or TV while my savings rapidly dried up. Eventually, I had no choice but to go back to Harbour House and ask for my old job back. 'Hey chico, what happened to the film career then? Did you fall off the casting couch?' asked a gleeful Ruco. I hated every moment of being back where I had started, hustling for tips.

Luis, of course, had been incapable of taking pleasure in my good fortune and loved to make jokes about me appearing shirtless next to a dolphin. By that point, we were barely talking, and once I left Harbour House to work on *Flipper*, I hardly saw him as he tended to disappear on his days off without saying where he was going. Something had changed between us, and not for the better. Things that had previously amused us now ceased to even cheer us up. The jokes I told at his expense did not help, jokes that in Buenos Aires he might have laughed along with. In Miami, they took on another meaning and seemed snippy and critical. For example, I'd tease him about being the only pool boy I knew who swam like a dog, splashing anyone within ten metres of the pool, or that more often than not, the women he tried to pick up were hookers. And I never failed to mock his table manners and domestic habits. All I did was remind Luis of all the things he had been trying to get away from in Argentina. Yet I also suspect the real reason our friendship deteriorated was because I was less useful to him in the US where my only contacts, via Aunt Clara, were in Palm Beach.

Luis valued people in terms of what he could get out of them and he was constantly in search of the next prize. When I came down with a fever and joint pain that prevented me from even getting out of bed, he deliberately ignored me. He could see I was in pain and becoming increasingly delirious, suffering uncontrollable feverish sweats that drenched the bed and left me dangerously dehydrated, but he never even asked me what was wrong, let alone offer to help. It was my first glimpse of the cold-hearted inhuman side of Luis that

I came to know so well. In the end, it was Shirley, the motel cleaner, who, seeing the state I was in, bundled me into her old car and took me to a local doctor's surgery where she paid cash for a strong shot of antibiotics. Shirley, a twenty-seven-year-old black gospel singer at the local Baptist church who sang as she cleaned the rooms, saved my life and I learned the hard way the perils of not having health insurance cover.

If Luis felt he had no more use for me, he still found my Pontiac indispensable. He took it to Palm Beach in the hope of joining the exclusive Gulf Stream Club. Happy to borrow the car but ashamed of how it looked, he used to park it a hundred metres from the entrance so no one would know it was his.

Once inside the club, he made the acquaintance of Benny Gutiérrez, a dark-skinned Mexican professional polo player with whom he immediately identified. With an impressive seven-goal handicap, Benny liked to hang around the clubhouse offering his services to potential sponsors. He told Luis that he was employed by the millionaire Adolphus (Dolph) Orthwein, a beer magnate from St. Louis who was a regular competitor in Gulf Stream's winter season. Luis soaked up everything his new friend told him. One of the things he discovered was that the person in charge of the Gulf Stream Club was none other than Philip Iglehart, brother of Stewart Iglehart, the man who had sponsored my visa application to enter the US.

He asked Benny to introduce him, claiming that he was related to the Ortiz Basualdos. The introduction worked well, and Philip kindly let Luis stay at his spare bungalow and borrow his ponies. But over time Philip got suspicious; too many things didn't ring true about Luis. For example, he was told by several people that Luis handled the horses in an alarmingly rough and brutal way. What also struck him as odd was that an Argentinian from a good family would come to work as a groom in Palm Beach while he waited to start a course at Florida International University. Most men from good families played polo in the US or Europe at the invitation of a sponsor. They most certainly didn't suggest bringing horses from Argentina to sell at the club, as Luis started to do. Philip, who had known the Ortiz Basualdo family for many years, made discreet enquiries and his suspicions were confirmed. Luis was exposed as a fraud and told he was no longer welcome. 'He conned me,' Philip told his groom, Ike Walton.

However, what was amazing about Luis was his ability to brush off these setbacks. Even when he was caught red-handed and ejected ignominiously from the club, he dusted himself off, returning to the scene of his crime as though nothing had happened and deploying the same tactics over and over again, until eventually they bore fruit.

Not long after Luis was exposed as an impostor, he met Bob Wickser, a middle-aged, roguish New Yorker who knew everybody in the Palm Beach social scene. A confirmed bachelor, Bob stayed with his mother in her apartment on Seaspray Avenue when he was in Palm Beach, and drove a classic Studebaker as old as my Pontiac. When he met Luis, they hit it off immediately because they both needed a friend. Wickser introduced his new friend to some influential people and Luis made himself useful by cruising the bars of Palm Beach picking up willing young ladies for Bob who, not being blessed with good looks, wouldn't have had a chance on his own.

It was a fair exchange for introductions, however it didn't pay the bills. With only a few dollars in his pocket, Luis desperately needed to find a job. The Palm Beach polo season was almost over and the sponsors were getting ready to go home. Luckily for Luis, Benny Gutiérrez told him about two potential jobs. The first was for Dolph Orthwein who was looking to hire a groom to take back to Missouri. 'He's a cheapskate. He'll pay you a pittance. He often saddles himself to save paying for grooms,' Benny warned him. The second was for Jim Binger who was also looking for a groom at his Minnesota farm. 'Jim's your best bet,' Benny advised. 'Go see Virgil Christian and tell him I sent you. He's Binger's right-hand man.'

The interview was brief and Luis got the job. That same night, Luis called me.

'I finally got a job. I'll be leaving Palm Beach in a few days,' he told me. 'Can you lend me three hundred dollars till I get my paycheck?'

The devil on my shoulder was outraged: 'The nerve! How dare he ask for money after the way he's behaved towards you!' But the angel on the other side won out: 'You're his only friend here. How can you not help him?' I not only advanced him the three hundred dollars, but I also let him keep the Pontiac that he'd already taken.

7
Social Climbing in Palm Beach

While waiting to go Minnesota, the trip there delayed because of Jim Binger's prior arrangements to conclude in Palm Beach, Luis began courting the adolescent María Beatriz de Holguín, the daughter of Alfredo de Holguín Pombo, a prominent Colombian landowner, and Beatrice Murray Fairbanks, an American socialite, journalist, and author of *Tales of Palm Beach* (under the name Beatrice de Holguin), among other books. Luis thought that meeting the young lady seemed promising … until her mother intervened. A savvy but understanding lady, Beatrice had met Luis at the bar at the Gulf Stream Club and instinct told her he wasn't right for her daughter.

'Keep away from María. She's still very young,' she said. 'But if you're looking for a good match, I'll be able to help you.'

'Why did she assume I was a social climber?' Luis asked Wickser indignantly. Beatrice promised she would put him in touch with the right people and promote his interests on condition that he kept away from her daughter. It was a subtle way of threatening him. So in the end, he accepted her friendship.

Luis's strange relationship with Beatrice Fairbanks began with a lecture on image and style advice.

'You look like a spic straight out of West Side Story!' she told him.

'What's a spic?' he asked.

'What New Yorkers call Latinos. Don't worry, that's what they call my Colombian husband too. But at least you could disguise your appearance by refraining from using that greasy brilliantine on your hair.'

Beatrice's 'lessons' extended to guiding him through Worth Avenue, the upscale shopping centre where the fashion houses and artists' ateliers were located. But she was nonplussed by his reaction when she suggested a visit to the Flagler Museum and art galleries: 'I avoid gay-controlled environments,' he said. The only person Luis wanted to meet in the art world was David Stein, the successful art forger who had recently made headlines in the press. He had successfully penetrated the social circles of Palm Beach 'to spread modern art' by offering Picassos at reduced prices. The philanthropic Mr Stein ended up in jail after admitting the paintings he sold were forgeries. Unfortunately, the law had caught up with Stein before Luis had a chance to meet him.

In the end, Luis was frank with Beatrice about what he was looking for: 'I came here to succeed in polo and achieve my goal of bagging an heiress. To do that, I need to mingle with established members of Palm Beach families who belong to the rich list.' Beatrice got the message, but she wasn't one to give up easily. She was convinced she needed to be a sort of Pygmalion to Luis, training him in the airs and graces necessary to succeed with the best of the best in the Palm Beach circuit.

To fulfil that mission, she offered to introduce him to a Chilean by the name of Guy Burgos. Regarded as a glamorous figure, he was the owner of a mythical art gallery in Miami who in a short period had become intimate in the most exclusive circles in Florida.

'I already told you I don't want to hang out in faggot circles. Can't you tell he's one of them?' Luis complained.

'You're so prejudiced, Luis. No gay would hook up with Lady Sarah Spencer-Churchill, the daughter of the Duke of Marlborough, and granddaughter of Consuelo Vanderbilt, heiress to the American railroad fortune.'

Luis quickly changed his mind and asked to be introduced to Burgos. Predictably it happened at a cocktail party, and right from the start, Luis knew that Guy liked him very much. So he took advantage of Burgos's friendliness to learn strategic approaches to try out on unsuspecting heiresses. But Burgos, a man of the world, smelled a rat and replied tactfully to Luis's questions, not wanting to offend him, and left the party without giving much away.

The next day, Luis called me. I had already agreed to lend him money, but now he decided he needed an accomplice and he told me the story of Burgos and the rich duke's daughter to wet my appetite.

'Are you listening to me? Are you listening to me?' Luis kept repeating. I could tell he was on a high. 'This guy is so effeminate and he doesn't look half as good as you or me. Yet he hooked up with the Duke of Marlborough's daughter. Do you get what I'm saying? She's a powerful, influential woman, and loaded to boot. Come on, come on! The two of us could make a killing here if we work together.'

But Luis's pleas could not convince me. It was one thing to give him money, but it was quite another to trust his fantasies.

Guy Burgos and Sarah Churchill were by far the most glamorous couple on the Palm Beach scene in 1966. However, their relationship was doomed from the start, and Luis wasn't wrong in pointing out the Chilean's sexual disposition. His hunch was confirmed when not long after Luis met him, Sarah unexpectedly filed for divorce. She had caught Burgos passionately kissing a burly black man fresh from the Bronx.

When he heard the news, Luis savoured his small triumph over Beatrice: 'So I was prejudiced, was I? What did I tell you? I knew he leaned the other way from the start. All that smarmy talk of how much he loved his wife! I can smell them a mile away.'

Following Burgos's scandalous divorce, and on Beatrice's recommendation, Luis turned his affections to Count and Countess de Lugar Nuevo, an ambitious couple trying hard to mix in Palm Beach's high society but not quite making it. Their Spanish-style house, Villa Ave María, was the ideal home for a nobleman and much enhanced by authentic Spanish antiques, bought by the devout Count at a cut-rate price from impoverished nuns who desperately needed to raise funds. Furthermore, the Count's title dated back to 1895, and his sister had been a lady-in-waiting for the Spanish queen, Victoria Eugenia de Battenberg. But all their authentic grandeur cut no ice with the members of Palm Beach high society who were only impressed by wealthy WASPS of consequence, not middle-of-the-road Catholics like the Count and his wife. It turned out there was no chemistry between Luis and the Count and they never hit it off; ironically, they thought of each other as phoney social climbers.

Despite these small hiccups, Luis followed most of Beatrice's advice. He no longer used brilliantine, but he was still unhappy with his hair. It was either flat as a pancake or wiry, a sore point for Luis, as failing to find the right balance became the tragedy of his life.

8
From Florida to Minnesota to Missouri

Virgil Christian finally got the order from his boss, the philanthropist Jim Binger, to make a move to his Minnesota Rainbow farm. Luis was given the task of accommodating the eight thoroughbreds on the heavy gooseneck trailer, while Virgil took care of filling the petrol tank and checking the truck's engine. It was early morning when Luis gave Beatrice a heartfelt goodbye hug. 'I may seem tough, but I do get emotional at times,' he told her. He didn't have to pretend with her as she had become his closest friend.

The journey to the northern state of Minnesota took a couple of days; they made a few stops along the way. It took a huge effort for Luis to endure those 3,000 kilometres with a baleful stranger – Luis nicknamed Virgil 'the servant.' They passed through lost landscapes and dusty valleys that looked like scenes from the Westerns he used to watch as a boy back home in the local cinema. At one point he began to nod off, and the image of John Wayne riding into the sunset crept into his dream – until a sharp poke in the ribs brought him back to reality. 'Your job isn't to sleep, but to talk to me to keep me awake,' he was told. *I'll make you pay for this, you bastard!* Luis thought to himself.

He didn't have to wait long to take his revenge. During the first overnight stopover, the two men shared a motel room. The next morning, Virgil discovered that his telecommunications card and twenty dollars were missing from his wallet. Nothing was said at the time and everything carried on as normal.

Virgil's trailer was at the head of the convoy. Behind them was a van transporting black boys who had been hired to do the heavy lifting at Binger's farm. *Surely they won't be working as grooms*, Luis thought. At one point, they stopped at a diner attached to a roadside motel in the middle of nowhere, a large neon sign with an arrow indicating the parking spot. They all went in, but as soon as the black boys crossed the threshold, the owner told them they had to sit elsewhere as the place was segregated. The boys did as they were told as if the Civil Rights Act of 1964 hadn't been passed. Two years had gone by since its proclamation, but in some states, it hadn't yet been implemented. It was a close call for Luis; with his wiry hair and Latino look he might have been segregated too. He called me after this harrowing experience: 'Can you imagine what it would have been like for me if I hadn't straightened out my afro hairstyle?'

When they finally arrived at the farm, Luis discovered that the job wasn't what he had expected at all. Instead of playing polo, he found himself having to work shoulder to shoulder with the young blacks in the van doing fencing work, unloading trucks, and other heavy jobs. It made him feel more like a farmhand than a prospective polo player. However, the experience was to be short-lived. Virgil intercepted him as he finished cleaning a stable and aggressively barked at him, 'You're fired. You must leave immediately!' When Luis asked why, Virgil reminded him about the stolen telecommunications charge card and the money. Luis was glad not to be seeing Virgil again, but he didn't relish the prospect of being back on the road without Beatrice or me nearby.

It was probably the stolen charge card that paid for his call to Benny Gutiérrez in Palm Beach to see if he knew of any other opportunities. Benny told him that Dolph Orthwein was still looking for a groom at his farm in St. Louis, Missouri. Luis immediately rang Orthwein, who told him the job entailed turning difficult foals into docile ones, a tough test for any novice and the best way to learn the trade. Luis packed his bags and immediately headed for St. Louis.

It was the beginning of June and the polo season had begun. Dolph was at his base ready to participate in the local tournaments with his St. Louis team, strictly a family affair – Dolph, his twin sons Stephen and Peter. Benny Gutiérrez was a fourth player only when they played in high-goal tournaments. Luis was a substitute for lesser tournaments.

In the beginning, it was going well for Luis until one day Dolph arrived unexpectedly at the stables and found one of his sons bandaging a pony.

'What are you doing, Steve,' Dolph asked.

'I'm helping Luis. He doesn't know how to bandage, Dad.'

A staunch enemy of work, Luis always did his best to offload his obligations onto others, and already he was putting this new job in jeopardy. It wasn't the only incident that exasperated Dolph, who was stingy by nature. One day he suddenly burst into Luis's room.

'Enough. This has to stop!' Dolph yelled at him. 'Over the last three weeks, you've consumed forty-two bottles of Coke and seven boxes of ice cream.' Luis was speechless. 'And Martha tells me yesterday you ate three slices of apple pie with cream. Don't you think you're abusing our agreement, quite apart from the fact that you're getting fat as a pig! I've told Martha to lock up the pantry.'

Luis continued to listen without flinching.

'And while I'm here, there's something else – my wife doesn't like the way you look at the young girl she hired. Did you fuck her?'

Luis was astonished and indignant in equal measure. 'Of course not! I wouldn't do a thing like that!'

But later that night, while Dolph slept, Luis shared his bed with the young girl.

On other occasions, Luis took his boss's convertible to pick up good-time girls and bring them back to the house. He was incorrigible, and though his days in St. Louis seemed numbered from the start, he managed to keep the job for the whole season.

The task of turning surly foals into docile ones and regularly playing practice games was the best way for a novice to learn the trade, and Luis did improve. The US Polo Association acknowledged this and raised his handicap to two goals at the end of the season.

Later on, Luis reinvented his life in the US and the time he spent in the Midwest. He told people he had been sent to New York by his father, who had connections in the polo world, and was taken on by a prestigious polo team in Minneapolis, where he caught the eye of a prominent sponsor. The truth was rather different.

9
An Adventure in New York

The fact that Luis took off was a double annoyance for me. Even if we were drifting apart, sharing a motel room with him had given me an anchor, a point of familiarity, amid the uncertainty of the adventure we were on. But I was most annoyed that he had gone off in my Pontiac. Not only did I have to resort to using public transport but it meant that I had no means of escape.

I desperately needed to take a break and get away from my job. My prayers were answered when I overheard one of the resort's patrons tell a friend that he needed someone to drive his car back to New York.

'Don't look any further. I am your man!' I exclaimed.

We agreed on a fee, I said goodbye to Marty again and picked up any wages I was owed. The next day, I was happily driving a De Soto convertible – one of the last models Chrysler produced – up Interstate 95 to New York. On the way, I stopped several times at gas stations and thoroughly enjoyed the freedom of driving a beautiful car through foreign landscapes.

After delivering the car to its owner, who had travelled by plane from Miami, I discovered that what I thought was a great opportunity was simply a nightmare. The money was not enough to cover the price of my return ticket to Miami. So, with nothing else to do, I wandered around New York City.

I had a hamburger and decided to gamble the few dollars I had left on a night out, in the hope of picking up a woman who could rescue me from my miseries. That evening, while having a drink at the bar in the Taft Hotel, I felt the lingering gaze of a blonde in her forties sitting nearby. I confidently walked over to her table and introduced myself. We were soon involved in a promising tête-à-tête, and an hour and a half later she called the waitress and charged both our bills to her room. Then she looked lovingly at me and said, 'Come, I'll take you to dinner.'

Her name was Doris Pullen and she was an American who worked as a real estate agent in Puerto Rico but was currently home on vacation. She discovered that she loved having adventures with young men when on her travels. By way of confessing to a stranger, she told me her friends and colleagues thought she and her husband were the ideal couple when in fact she was having an affair with the husband of her best friend.

While walking through Greenwich Village, we passed a restaurant that displayed a black bowler hat and cane in the window.

'You see that?' she said, pointing her finger. 'It means it's a lesbian joint.'

'How do you know that?'

'I like to try everything once.'

Then taking me by the hand, she led me inside the restaurant. We enjoyed the meal, and she took the opportunity to flirt with the waitress, which was a bit of a blow to my pride. But my fears vanished when after coffee she said, 'It's getting late. Let's go back to the hotel.'

In terms of lewdness, Doris was on par with Ruth Goldberg. At eight o'clock the next morning, breakfast was delivered to our room.

'I'd better rush,' she said. 'I have a plane to catch.'

As Doris got into the shower, I leaned back on the bed and wondered how I was going to pay for my ticket back to Miami. I looked around the ornate room and saw her purse sitting on a table. Without any hesitation, I dived into it and helped myself to a hundred-dollar bill. Then I got dressed at the speed of lightning and with my shoes in one hand, I rushed down the three flights of stairs and exited the hotel. Hailing a cab in the street, I went straight to the Greyhound station to catch the next bus to Miami.

10
Back to Square One

By this time, *Flipper* had swum off into the sunset, taking my career with him. I had no chance of getting any other acting jobs and I came back to earth with a thud, realising what everybody new to America soon discovers, what every Latino busboy, waiter, and taxi driver will tell you: America is great but only if you have money.

I was behind with my rent at the Glades Motel, and to make things worse, there was no one to share the bills with now that Luis had left. I needed a job, but I refused to go back to Harbour House. Then I remembered Stewart Iglehart and the introduction I had been given but hadn't used. When I contacted Stewart he invited me to stay at La Centinela, his Delray Beach residence, for the weekend.

Stewart was born in Valparaíso, Chile, to an American father, a president of the Grace Line shipping company, and Aida Birrell, who was from a prominent Anglo-Chilean family. Stewart was always willing to help South Americans in need and had a special interest in Miami University's polo team. Since I had been introduced as a prospective student, he was eager to hear my story. As we chatted about his life in the US, he told me about a 'slick Argentinian bandit' he had recently come across. It soon became clear that he was talking about Luis, who had behaved shamelessly throughout the polo season. Of course, I couldn't resist asking for more details. He said that Luis had bragged that his family owned two *haciendas* in Argentina and then proceeded to wreck his brother's horses by mistreating them. He was later given a groom's job but was fired for stealing soon after. I sat there listening to these stories, being careful not to give away the fact that I was friends with this reprobate, while making the appropriate expressions of horror and surprise. Then the conversation turned to my predicament.

'So you want to play polo,' Stewart said.

'Yes, I do. Very much.' The more enthusiastic I tried to sound, the less convincing it was, even to me. So I decided to come clean. 'The truth is that I do play polo, but I can't say it's my passion. What I want to do … is become an actor.'

Stewart scratched his head as I told him about the acting school, the promising feedback I'd received, and my role in *Flipper*.

'That all sounds wonderful,' he eventually said after a long silence. 'But there's not a lot I can do to help you there. If you like, you could come and work for me as a salesman.'

Stewart was a partner in a real estate company that was putting up buildings in the Palm Beach area. His offer was a huge load off my mind as I would at least have a stable job, which was just what I needed. So I decided to buy myself some new shirts and a tie in preparation for the next phase of my American dream. But all did not go according to plan.

The next day, while I was having a shower at the motel, I was interrupted by a series of urgent knocks on my door.

'It's the police! Open the door!'

I turned the water off and, with a towel wrapped around my waist, I opened the door to a uniformed policeman. 'Have you been working illegally in the country?' he asked.

I denied doing any such thing, but he'd had a tip-off of some sort. 'We've had a complaint from the Deauville Hotel that says different.'

'Complaint! What complaint?' I asked angrily.

'I need to take a look around,' he said, pushing past me into the room.

I thought about closing the door, locking him in, and running, but my towel wouldn't have stayed on for long and I wouldn't get very far running naked through the streets of Miami.

The policeman went through my possessions and took a special interest in the entry visa stamp on my passport.

'You're under arrest!' he announced.

'What for?' I shouted.

'Working illegally on a tourist visa. That's what for.'

He let me dry off and put on a t-shirt and shorts before escorting me to his car. Then he took me directly to the immigration department, *La Migra* as Latinos called it at 79th Street and Biscayne Boulevard. A guard the size of a bear led me to a room where three officials were seated, a file lying in front of them on a round table. This was the jury that would try me for working illegally in the United States while on a tourist visa. I was just another Latino who had broken the terms of his visa. They wasted no time.

'You stated in the application form submitted to the embassy in Buenos Aires that the purpose of your trip was to play polo while on vacation,' one of the officials said. 'The application form contained a clause stating that visiting tourists were prohibited from carrying out paid or unpaid work.'

'That's true,' I said, all too conscious that the shorts and t-shirt I was wearing were the uniform I wore for work as a pool boy. 'And I signed the statement, but if anyone had asked me, I would have admitted that I intended to make it a working vacation.'

The next official along perused my file and looked up. 'I see in the original application that Mr Stewart Iglehart invited you to play polo in this country,' he said. 'Is he the gentleman who represented the United States against the British at the Westchester Cup?'

'Yes sir, he is. The same one,' I replied, my voice brightening in the hope that my situation was about to improve.

Sadly, it didn't. After answering a few more questions, I was taken to a cell and told shortly after that they had arranged for me to be deported to Buenos Aires on a Braniff flight, courtesy of the US Government. My fingerprints were taken and then I was offered a cup of coffee and a sandwich. I remember how my fingers left inky marks on the white polystyrene coffee cup and on the bread of the sandwich, which I ate all the same.

Two immigration officers took me back to the motel to pack my things. At the time, I had been seeing a woman called Dorothy Elsmore, a divorced mother of two on state benefits; she lived next door at the motel. She had heard of my arrest and was waiting for my return. As soon as she saw me escorted back by the officers, she burst into tears. That somehow made me feel that my stay in America had not been for nothing. I packed up most of my belongings, put on my blue double-breasted suit, and asked Dorothy to give Luis the clothes I was leaving behind. These included a dinner jacket I had optimistically brought from Buenos Aires, thinking my American life would be a whirlwind of high-class social engagements. Weeping uncontrollably and hugging me, Dorothy suddenly pulled away. 'What if I'm pregnant?' she exclaimed. 'What am I going to do?' (The same question was on my mind when I returned to Argentina. Months later, when Luis eventually came back to Florida and visited the motel, he was able to put my mind at ease. Dorothy was 'still thin as a rake', he said.)

From the motel, I was taken to the county jail and thrown into a large communal cell where I immediately felt at home. It was full of people just like me, Latinos all of us, telling our stories, bonding over the injustices that had been dished out at the hands of the authorities. It was strangely reassuring to be there and to feel part of something, if even briefly. When they came to take me away, we said our goodbyes as though we had known each other forever.

The two immigration guards who had escorted me a couple of hours earlier were waiting for me at the entrance gate.

'You're a very lucky man,' one of them said.

Again, I got my hopes up for a reprieve.

'The jury saw you were a clean-cut sort and ordered us not to handcuff you,' he went on. 'And they put us on overtime so you could catch the next available flight and avoid spending another night in jail.'

That was the extent of my 'luck'.

We set off for the airport and after a few miles, we stopped at a gas station where one of them bought cigarettes. But when he came back, the car wouldn't start, even after a few tries. So they jumped out and began pushing it. Instinctively I joined them, and when they saw me pushing the car alongside them, they couldn't believe it.

Once we got the car started again and were back on the road, we laughed pretty much all the way to the airport. Rod and Fred – we were on first-name terms by this stage – worked it into a neat little story that I'm sure they continued to retell for many years. The friendly atmosphere persisted at the departure gate. As I moved through passport control, I turned to give them one last wave, to which they responded with exaggerated military salutes. The other passengers must have wondered who the VIP was who was being given an official send-off, accompanied by the airline representatives.

My adventure in the United States had only lasted seven months.

It was the afternoon when I arrived home in Buenos Aires. I still had the key to my parents' house and I entered with some trepidation. My father was there alone. He had come back to rest before going to a friend's wedding anniversary party. My mother was at the hairdresser's having her hair done for the event. So when he heard the front door open, he assumed she was back early.

'Is that you, dear?'

I said nothing but made my way to the living room where he was sitting in his usual chair. He'd been napping and was confused to see me standing there.

'What the hell are you doing here?'

'I got fed up with Miami,' I said. 'The American way of life isn't for me.'

I didn't know how he would react. He remained very serious and, after a while, stood up and approached me. At first, I thought he was going to slap me, but instead, he hugged me. When my mother arrived, she acted as if I had been away for the weekend. She offered me her cheek, which I kissed, and that was my homecoming.

The fact is I was crestfallen to be back in Argentina, especially as I was returning with even less than I had when I left. I made some calls, hoping to catch up with friends, but no one was interested in seeing me. It was as if I had betrayed them by going away. Old girlfriends had new boyfriends, and my associates were all busy – or not answering. Life seemed to have moved on in the seven months I had been away.

I headed for El Socorro, where the astonished regulars greeted me with many jokes about my unexpected return, my deep tan, and the colour of my hair, which had been lightened by the chlorine in the Harbour House pool. The next morning, I avoided breakfast with my parents and walked reluctantly to my grandparents' house. I was relieved that my grandmother was not going to be at home. If I had to endure my grandfather's wrath, it was better not to have her as a witness.

'I'm not particularly interested in the reasons for your exodus,' he said sternly when I arrived. 'But I would be interested to know what happened to my platinum Patek Philippe watch, my binoculars, my father's cane-sword, and my Chinese ivory carving.'

I tried to remember what I had learned in Ruth Foreman's drama classes and attempted an excuse about how difficult things had been for me in Argentina, but he saw right through me. 'I recommend you don't play the victim because it doesn't suit you,' he said.

The meeting did not go well. However, a few days later I received a call from his office, not from him but from his secretary. She told me that a job interview had been arranged for me. I would be working as a metals salesman at a subsidiary of the multinational Hochschild Mining Group, of which my grandfather was president. At the interview, all I heard was what a great man my grandfather was; they had no interest in my ability or interest in the job. There were no CVs in those days; only connections mattered. No matter what impression I made, the job was always going to be mine if I wanted it. It was my grandfather's way of keeping me on the straight and narrow.

In this case, the straight and narrow took me to the Chacarita area of the city where the famous cemetery was situated, the largest cemetery in Argentina and the one that Marité and Luis had such a horror of ending up in. My job was to visit clients, mainly small foundries that produced plaques and metal letters to be fitted to headstones. I had felt alive in Miami; now back in Buenos Aires, I felt desolate as I spent my days talking about headstones, monuments, bereavement, and the deceased and my nights washing it all away in the city's bars with as much alcohol as I could afford. Perhaps I looked back on my time in Miami through rose-tinted glasses, idealising Ruth Goldberg, Dorothy, and all the other women I had met and exaggerating my part in *Flipper* and my prospects of an acting career. But I had got a taste for what life could be like, full of adventure and fun; it was the complete opposite of this dull, monotonous existence in Buenos Aries. I knew that one way or another I would be leaving again, and soon.

Meanwhile, back in St. Louis, on the day after my deportation, Dolph Orthwein's housemaid rushed into the barn where Luis was grooming a thoroughbred and told him he had an urgent call from Miami. When he picked up the receiver in the office, Dorothy told him that I had been deported. Luis was shocked and had to sit down, but it wasn't out of sympathy for me; it was because he thought he could be next on the list. However, his fear didn't last long for he soon discovered he wasn't on the immigration authority's radar.

Over the years, Luis took great delight in reminding me of my deportation. He saw it as an amusing failure on my part and never let it go.

11
And Then There Was One

With the St. Louis polo season over, Luis decided to go back to Palm Beach where the first thing he did was to track down his old pal Bob Wickser. As usual, Bob was depressed about his love life, or rather the lack of it. Knowing what his friend craved, Luis lifted his spirits by inviting young women to his place. In return, he was once again allowed to stay at Bob's mother's place as a guest, which gave him that essential base from where he could continue his Palm Beach social climbing.

One night, when he and Bob were having a drink at the bar in the Colony Hotel, a place made fashionable by regulars like Porfirio Rubirosa, the Dominican playboy and gigolo, they noticed a woman on the other side of the bar staring at them. She wasn't just looking casually around the room; her gaze was fixed on Luis in a way that left no doubt about what interested her. Knowing who was who in Palm Beach, Bob recognised her immediately. She was Mary Sanford, the Queen of Palm Beach (as she was better known) and founder of the Polo Ball. She was married to Laddie Sanford, heir to the Connecticut Bigelow-Sanford Carpet Company, who was a former top polo player and sponsor of The Hurricanes, the team that won the American Open five times. Sadly, Laddie's polo glory days were behind him as by then he was in a wheelchair following a stroke.

As Bob was filling Luis in on Mary's life story and net worth, a waiter approached them with a message from the lady herself, inviting them to join her at her table.

They went over and Luis's direct manner captivated her immediately.

'I am Luis Basualdo from Argentina,' he said, failing to introduce Bob who waited unnoticed as the other two flirted.

'Well, what a small world this is,' she purred.

'How is it a small world?' Luis's cheeky grin hid his vulnerability: having acquaintances in common could be either good or bad for a professional liar like him.

'My husband and I were close friends with Luis Ortiz Basualdo. Are you connected to him?'

'He's my uncle. You're right, it is a small world!'

It was only then that Luis introduced Bob, mainly to put Mary off asking any more about his family connections. The flirting, however, continued as though Bob wasn't there and by the end of the evening, she had invited them to a dinner party at her mansion the next day.

Luis called me when he got back from her house that night, waking me and the rest of my family at 2 a.m. It was the first time we had spoken since I had been deported, but he barely acknowledged that. Indeed, my deportation seemed to have renewed our friendship, probably because I was no longer a threat or competition. I should have been annoyed, but it was at moments like these that I realised what a strange friendship we had. Despite our estrangement, he knew I was the only person with whom he could share his experiences and gloat.

'It was like something out of a movie,' he said. 'What a house! ... Actually, it wasn't a house, it was a castle.'

Luis skipped most of the details about dinner and the guests and jumped straight to the part where he made love all night.

'All night at her place? Where was her husband?' I inquired, trying to catch him out on inconsistencies in his story.

'They sleep in separate rooms at opposite ends of the place. It has forty rooms! You could get lost in there. Anyway, he's in a wheelchair. It would take him all week to find her.'

It turned out that not only did they sleep in separate rooms, but they had an arrangement. He had a mistress he met through his wife after his stroke.

'That's the way these people live. They do what they want,' Luis went on. 'They don't care what people think or how they're going to get to heaven. She fucks who she wants and spends his money, and he doesn't care because he's fucking someone else on the other side of the house.'

He then proceeded to tell me all the things that Mary liked about him, especially what she thought of his cock and how it made her feel.

At that point, I ended the call; I'd heard enough. And I had to get up the next day to sell bronze ingots to embellish the gravestones of the city's recently departed.

The bottom line was that Mary Sanford invited Luis to accompany her to the April in Paris Ball at the Waldorf Astoria in New York, at which, he informed me gleefully, he would be wearing my dinner jacket. It seemed my dinner jacket was having a much more exciting life than I was!

Luis and Mary arrived a week before the Ball to enjoy the city. I got a letter from him, dated October 1966 and written on Waldorf headed paper:

> *I am having a great time ensconced in the Waldorf Astoria, in my double bedroom facing Park Avenue, all paid for by Mrs Sanford who brought me to New York on her husband's private jet. I'm thinking of having a card printed saying: 'Luis Sosa Basualdo, official lover of Mrs Mary Sanford.' From my window, I can see the formidable MetLife building. It is all skyscrapers, just like in movies.*[3]

The Ball, which was attended by artists, journalists, and the very rich, along with a generous sprinkling of Kennedys, was the event of the season. When Luis and Mary entered arm in arm, he could see that everyone was looking at them, openly gossiping about the young man on the arm of Laddie Sanford's wife. But it wasn't just the women who looked; some of the men did too. A few of them approached him and asked for his number, which he happily supplied. 'You have no idea how much fun it was to say they could find me at the Waldorf,' he added in his letter.

As a parting gift before her return to Palm Beach, Mary Sanford paid for Luis to stay another two weeks at the Waldorf with a reserve for his daily expenses. However, the reserve proved to be insufficient for his lavish consumption, and once he'd outspent it, management brought the bill to his attention. Staggered by the amount of money he owed, he made all the right noises about paying, quickly packed his case, and tried to make a discreet exit. But the hotel staff was onto him in a flash, having encountered many people who enjoyed the good life without the funds to pay for it, and two security men asked him to accompany them to an office. They also informed Mrs Sanford of the situation and confiscated everything, my dinner jacket included, more as a punishment than anything else as it had no value.

One of the men with whom Luis had exchanged details at the April in Paris Ball was Martin Fabri, an architect, and designer, and when he found himself with nowhere to go and no money, he called on Martin, who eagerly put him up at his house on East 56th Street. Martin also lent him clothes, gifted him some others, and others I am sure Luis helped himself to. What the besotted Martin received in return Luis never said. It could be that he was merely content to have a handsome young man in the house, but Luis told another acquaintance years later that he was present at the men-only orgies that took place in the house, though more as a spectator than a participant. In all his letters and calls, Luis insisted that he was using Martin, that there was nothing sexual between them, and that the thought of being with a man repulsed him. I thought Luis insisted a little too much; he was certainly very comfortable in Martin's company. And so Luis replaced the protection of Mary Sanford with the hospitality of New York's gay community, who welcomed him with open arms.

Luis understood that to operate comfortably in the social circles he aspired to join, he needed some education and culture. Martin, who had impeccable taste, schooled him in art and accompanied him to art gallery openings and theatres. To further his knowledge Luis regularly read *Time* magazine's art supplement and grew more confident when attending these events. He began to speak with an increasing if somewhat affected authority on these matters. Previously, he had always steered clear of such conversations, fearing that saying the wrong thing might reveal his suburban background. He read and reread Vance Packard's *The Status Seekers*, underlining the parts he felt were relevant. What he was interested in was understanding the hidden barriers faced by people like himself – the signs of rank and evaluations based on the right addresses, clubs, friends, values, membership of communities, and even church affiliation. It was his mission to be accepted, and he put together a strategy to overcome the barriers he had experienced all his life.

However, his benefactors soon became tired of him as familiarity dulled the attraction of his good looks. Luis stretched their patience to the limit with his insatiable curiosity and constant questions. One day, when Luis asked Luis Palacio, owner of an exclusive boutique on Lexington Avenue and one of his other gay mentors, what the word 'baroque' meant, Palacio brusquely replied, 'I'm sorry, Luis, I can't start teaching you things you should have learned at school.' Relationships began to sour as they realised that most of the stories that he told them didn't add up. He soon found their generosity drying up too.

As Luis ran out of credit in New York's gay community, he found someone happy to answer all his questions. This was the Sicilian nobleman Fulco di Santostefano, Duke of Verdura. At sixty-eight years of age, Fulco was old enough to be his grandfather, but despite the age difference, they became very close. A leading figure in the international jet set, Fulco was a prominent jewellery designer; his clients included the Duchess of Windsor (Wallis Simpson), Princess Grace of Monaco (Grace Kelly), and Jackie Kennedy, among others. Perhaps because he had been around so long, seen it all, and heard it all – or because he was Sicilian – he did not hold back in telling Luis exactly what he thought and letting him know when he knew he was lying. One of the first things Fulco dismissed as complete garbage was Packard's *The Status Seekers*, which Luis constantly dropped into conversation, assuming it made him seem clever.

'It gives you away when you say you've read it and how enlightening you found it, recommending it to everyone as if it were a great work of literature. It's nothing more than a manual on how to be a social climber,' Fulco told him. Instead, he recommended *The Leopard*, Giuseppe Tomasi di Lampedusa's story of the displacement of the Sicilian nobility, which was close to his heart, not just because he was Sicilian himself but also because Lampedusa was his cousin.[4] 'Whatever you were looking for in *The Status Seekers* you'll find in *The Leopard*, although the two should not be mentioned in the same breath.'

It was Fulco who stressed to Luis that everything in life was about alliances, and that supply and demand was the name of the game. His theory was that to succeed in this world, you needed at least one of three things: an outstanding physical appearance, a great fortune, or a noble title.

'You lack the last two,' he said. 'Your only assets are your appearance and the fact that you play polo.'

Luis protested, repeating the old story that his family had money and that they owned ranches in Argentina.

'Don't you know that everyone sees through your lies?' Fulco said. 'They're all thinking it and they talk about it behind your back. People with money and titles don't want to be fucked by other people with money and titles. They want to be fucked by good-looking young men, ideally with big cocks. Are you one of those?'

Luis wasn't sure how to reply and was worried to what this line of questioning might be leading. However, a diplomatic Fulco didn't pursue it.

'There's nothing worse than someone who pretends to be something he's not. Everyone sees it, they can smell it. Eventually they'll run a mile. Act natural and you'll be fine. You have something people want. Use it. Enjoy it.'

Luis had been a pupil of Beatrice Fairbanks, Mary Sanford, and Martin Fabri, but it was Fulco di Santostefano more than anyone else who instructed him in the ways of the world. He promptly replaced quotations from *The Status Seekers* with Fulco's pearls of wisdom and didn't waste his time reading *The Leopard*.

12

An Elusive Thief

On Thanksgiving Eve in 1966, Luis escorted the beautiful Wendy Sherman to the debutante cotillion in the ballroom at the Plaza Hotel in New York City. She was the daughter of one of the heads of the United States Polo Association. There, Luis met Russell Corey, the son of legendary nine-goal player Alan Corey, a five-time winner of the American Open, who at the time was with his wife in Argentina to watch the American Polo Team play against Argentina for the Cup of the Americas. Luis's Argentine connection prompted Russell to invite him to spend the Thanksgiving weekend at his house in Old Westbury, Long Island. It was under these auspicious circumstances that Luis mentioned his desire to play polo in England. Russell had played in England the previous year for John Coleman's Radiation team where they proudly won the Benson Cup. Unable to play in the forthcoming season, Russell recommended Luis as a substitute and luckily he got the job. It was a tailor-made replacement as both men had the same handicap; it was also a time of transition for the hapless Luis.

Coleman was an atypical sponsor as he didn't subsidise his players. His invitation was merely to join his team; his guests had to pay for their board and lodging, the freight of their horses to the UK, and for their grooms. It was Luis's biggest challenge so far – having no money, he felt thrown in at the deep end. But he didn't lose heart. 'God will provide,' he told himself.

Things changed when in March of the following year, Luis bumped into his mentor Fulco di Santostefano at a cocktail party held by octogenarian Mary Vanderveer Hall at the Ritz Tower, the luxurious residential building at 465 Park Avenue in Manhattan. Fulco was not surprised to run into his social-climbing disciple there who, after greeting him affectionately, walked away as if he had an urgent appointment elsewhere.

Fulco tried to find out who had invited Luis to the party but he had no success. Later he learned that Mrs Hall's daughter's lawyers were looking for a Mr Basualdo to recover money her mother had loaned him to evict tenants for some of his ranches in Argentina. Fulco was greatly amused – so Luis was still insisting that he owned ranches – and was even more delighted when he found out the loan had been a gesture of affection from the octogenarian to her fiery Argentine lover.

But the most disturbing thing about that evening at Mrs Hall's residence was what happened there to Berlin-born ex-hostess Rita Lachman, wife of Charles Lachman, the brilliant chemist who, along with the Revson brothers, founded Revlon in the 1930s. The Lachmans lived in Paris and Rita had returned to New York especially for Mrs Hall's lavish reception. At one point in the evening, Rita had gone to the bathroom and taken off her valuable engagement sapphire ring set in platinum to wash her hands. She forgot to put it on again, but when she returned to the bathroom, it was gone. 'What am I going to tell my husband!' she shouted at the top of her voice. 'What am I going to tell my husband!'

Private investigators were quietly called in by Mrs Hall's aides and they discreetly questioned the staff and some of the guests, but they could only gather vague leads and useless rumours. Then the Lachmans' insurers started an independent investigation. The general impression was the ring had been taken by a young black-haired man who, according to a couple of witnesses, walked into the bathroom soon after Rita Lachman had left it. Fulco, realising his friend had the finger of suspicion pointing firmly at him, chose to keep his thoughts to himself.

Two weeks after the party and more than five thousand miles away, a well-dressed young man with a slicked-back hairstyle entered a renowned jewellery store on Avenida Alvear in Buenos Aires and asked to see the owner.

'My name is Luis Sosa Basualdo and I have a family jewel I'd like to sell.'

The receptionist conveyed the message on the internal phone and a few seconds later, a tall, mature, elegant gentleman emerged from the back room clutching his glasses as if he had been interrupted in the middle of something.

'They tell me you have a jewel for sale,' he said. 'Please follow me.'

The jeweller spent a few seconds carefully scrutinising the visitor sitting across from him. Then he asked Luis to show him what he had brought. Hands shaking, Luis took from his jacket pocket a sapphire ring that matched the exact description of the one Rita Lachman had reported stolen and clumsily placed it on the desk.

'It belonged to my grandmother and I would like to sell it,' he explained, 'although it depends on the price. I wouldn't part with a memento like this for a trifle.'

The jeweller, an Auschwitz survivor and master at his trade, was not about to be duped by a brilliantined upstart. Without uttering a word, he picked up the ring and took his time inspecting the gem with his loupe as if Luis were not present.

'It is beautiful, but perfect gems are usually not genuine,' he said eventually, placing the ring back on the desk. 'If it looks too good to be real, that's probably because it isn't. Only a Mohs test will determine whether it is genuine or not. You must go to Banco Municipal where they perform such tests. They will issue a certificate in the unlikely event that it turns out to be genuine.'

What the jeweller omitted to tell Luis was that his name would have to be entered on the certificate for insurance purposes, so if the ring was stolen, the culprit's name would be known. Luis took a taxi straight to the bank where a technician held the gem up to the light coming through the window and handed the ring back to Luis.

'You'll be wasting time and money paying for a test. It's too perfect to be genuine. I can tell just by looking at it.'

All that drama for a phoney gem, Luis thought to himself. So he went back to the jeweller hoping that he might at least be offered something for his trouble; after all, it had to have some value. But the jeweller maintained that the Mohs test needed to be done and sent him back to the bank. Luis returned to the bank and insisted on paying for a test, though the technician was still adamant that the gem was synthetic. After filling in the paperwork, the technician disappeared with the gem. Twenty minutes later, he returned with an official in tow. A wave of panic swept over Luis: had they deduced the ring's provenance and called the police? He looked around for the nearest exit in case he had to make a quick getaway, but the official was there to offer the bank's most sincere apologies. It turned out that the sapphire was real and worth a small fortune. With the certificate in his pocket, Luis rushed back to the jeweller's shop.

'Do you have any idea how much this is worth?' asked the jeweller.

Luis spun a line about its value being mainly sentimental, which the jeweller dismissed.

'I have a deal for you,' he said. 'I can offer you $70,000 in cash, right now. Take it or leave it.'

Minutes later, a black leather case appeared on the desk and was opened in front of Luis. It contained the equivalent of $70,000 in a variety of currencies, a common practice in such transactions.

It was not long after this that Luis made contact with me. Up until then, I had not known he was in the country. He invited me, along with some other friends, to a small gathering at his house in Flores. We were taken to his bedroom where, as if was performing a magic trick, he switched the light off while we all waited in the dark. When the light was turned on again, an open briefcase full of cash was sitting on the bed. We all asked where he had got the money from and he told an unlikely story about it being a gift from a lover. After most of his friends had left, however, he revealed to the select few who remained how he had come to acquire the ring (though he later regretted having so many witnesses to his ill-gotten stash).

Twenty-three years later, gossip columnist Nigel Dempster wrote in Christina Onassis's biography that Luis had inherited $70,000 from his parents. The story became 'official' and was reported in other accounts of Christina's life. Until now, only a few close friends knew the truth.

It was with this money he bought the ticket and the horses to play polo in England. It also set him off on his journey to scale the heights of the British aristocracy.

13

A Gentleman of Leisure

Now that Luis had come up with the money to finance his trip, his next challenge was getting arranged in time for the start of the polo season. He had agreed with Coleman to be in London at the beginning of May, just before the season began. At the beginning of April, Luis was still in Buenos Aires with the money in his coffers but without the horses. He decided to visit the Anchorena family's *hacienda* near Chascomús, just south of Buenos Aires. There he acquired three ponies, Picasso, Pascualito, and Milagro, but being new to the game and feeling flush after coming into all that money, he paid $4,000 for the three when a reasonable price would have been between $800 and $1,000 per animal. He wasn't especially concerned since he could sell each one for at least $2,000 in England. With hardly a dent in his $70,000 fortune, the operation ended up being profitable, even allowing the cost of the shipping, and he and his horses arrived in the UK on the liner France in time for his meeting with Coleman.

By early May 1967, Luis was playing at Cowdray Park Polo Club where it is said the best polo in Europe is played. The club was the creation of John Churchill Pearson, 3rd Viscount Cowdray and owner of the 16,500-acre West Sussex estate where it is situated. Lord Cowdray was a leading figure in the revival of polo in England after the Second War, having been involved in the sport since he was young, despite losing an arm at Dunkirk. He also took care of his business empire, S. Pearson & Son, which was the controlling company of influential publications like the *Financial Times*, *The Economist*, and *Penguin Books*.

Luis was now swimming in a much bigger pool than he was used to. He mistakenly believed that he would be a guest at John Coleman's residence, but instead he had to book himself into nearby Park House, the less glamorous boarding house where most of the players lived. The other members of Coleman's Radiation team included the English sugar millionaire Robert de Pass, and Bob Wickser, Luis's old Palm Beach associate. It was at this time that Luis started calling himself 'Captain' Basualdo. His mentor Fulco had told him there was nothing like a title to help one become more socially accepted and Luis mistakenly thought a military rank would do.

Coleman's team competed in low-handicap tournaments, which meant the rota was constantly changing, depending on the availability and suitability of the players. Not short of money but always anxious to profit in any given situation, Luis got involved as a middleman between burly Héctor Barrantes, a member of Lord Vestey's team, who had some horses to sell, and Coleman, who was an interested party. Barrantes asked Luis to mediate the sale for a commission and provided him with some horses on consignment for his boss to test. It was then that Luis's cruelty towards animals was first noticed in the UK, and it was something he would become notorious for over the years. It was an indicator of the utter lack of compassion he also had for people, particularly the women in his life. On this particular occasion, when 'trying out' the horses, a vet had to be called. He gave the horses painkillers and advised that they should be left to rest, but Luis completely ignored the advice and rode them all the same. Not long after, one of the horses was in such a bad way that the vet had to put it down. A couple of days later, when most of the players were present to play practice chukkas, Barrantes confronted Luis, grabbing him by the throat in full view of the other players.

'You treat horses with no respect, you *hijo de puta!*' he yelled.

Luis managed to free himself, and instead of reacting to his aggressor, he turned to the other players. 'Do you think I'm an *hijo de puta?*' he asked them.

They had all witnessed Luis's mistreatment of horses and instead of taking his side, as Luis had hoped, they agreed he was a son of a bitch. With no support from his team members, he made a quick exit. Either Coleman never knew of this incident or he turned a blind eye to it because of his team's Benson Cup victory. Whatever the case, Luis was invited to play the following season. This time he suggested that Coleman keep Bob Wickser but include Sandy Carden and Peter Orthwein, the son of his previous US employer. Even with his poor treatment of the horses and an altercation with Barrantes that almost came to blows, Luis was slowly making a name for himself.

At the beginning of the 1968 season Luis and Peter Orthwein joined forces with high-goal professional Howard Hipwood to play for Lord Brecknock's team, Pimms, in the final of the Argentine Ambassador's Cup. They lost on that occasion, but in September the Park House team were winners of the Farewell Cup, the last tournament of the season. On their return to the US, Peter Orthwein went straight back to college to make up for lost time, while Luis went back to New York's social scene.

He wasn't long back in the country before he started claiming that Yale University was his *alma mater*. It came about when one of the Yale polo team's players was injured and Peter Orthwein, the captain, had the bright idea of replacing him with Luis; the scheme was backed by Sandy Carden. Orthwein took the decision fully aware his father's ex-groom had barely attended school, let alone Yale, and he warned Luis never to admit, under any circumstances, that he wasn't a Yale student. Orthwein could have saved his breath as Luis did nothing but brag about it. It was another of his many lies; he simply repeated it so often that it became fact.

At one point, Luis flew back to Argentina to buy horses, an activity that allowed him to stretch his original capital from the sale of the sapphire ring. While he was in Buenos Aires, he called into his old haunt, El Socorro, but the shy apprentice I had met there not so many years earlier had disappeared. His loud voice carried over the general murmur of the bar and he had put on weight, which only added to his presence. He boasted to everyone within earshot about the success of the Yale team, bragged about his bogus law degree, and, of course, his conquest of women. I was fascinated by his capacity for misbehaviour, his affectations, his total lack of guilt, and his ability to make others feel special, that effusive way he had of greeting people and looking them in the eye as if they were the centre of the universe. This was the Luis who would go on to scale ever higher rungs of the social ladder, overwhelming and defrauding those he met on his up.

The Yale team was the current title holder of the intercollegiate polo championship, and at the beginning of 1969, they set out to defend it with a tour of Central America, which took them to El Salvador, Nicaragua, and Costa Rica. The Nicaraguan stopover was undoubtedly the most exciting. When they arrived in Managua, the team was surprised by the reception they received. A large crowd had gathered and a marching band heralded their arrival. The polo players responded enthusiastically to this rapturous welcome, waving to the crowds as they advanced toward the awaiting shiny black Cadillac. But when Luis tried to open one of the doors of the car, a soldier elbowed him in the ribs, twisted his arm, and restrained him. The cheers of the public soon turned to laughter as it transpired that neither the pomp, the crowds nor the Cadillac were there for the polo players. They were all there to welcome Mrs Hope Portocarrero Somoza, wife of the Nicaraguan dictator Anastasio Somoza, who was returning from an official visit to the White House and happened to be on the same plane. An embarrassed Donald Gordillo, director of the Nicaraguan Polo Association who had come to the airport to meet the players, had to plead with the captain in charge of security to get Luis released. He then ushered the team into a battered old van and drove away like a bat out of hell.

As time was short, that same afternoon they played a friendly match against Nicaragua's local team and won, despite Luis's bruised ribs and sore shoulder. The match was followed by a tea dance in the Hotel Nacional with attractive *señoritas*, and later they attended a cocktail reception and dinner given by the president of the Nicaraguan Polo Association. It was a late night for everybody as this special occasion also brought in the New Year.

The 1969 Yale team tour to Costa Rica. Left to right: Russell Corey, Peter Orthwein, Luis Basualdo and Charlie Armstrong.

After two days in Nicaragua, they travelled on to Costa Rica where they were to defend the US Inter-University Trophy. As before, a shortage of time meant they had to start playing on the day they arrived. The games took place at the colourful Santa Teresa Polo Club, with its beautifully kept grounds surrounded by palm trees and set against an idyllic background of mountains. They played every day against a different university and in the final they came face to face with Cornell. They won and remained the title holders for another year.

With the championship over, more fun began when players formed independent teams as if they were at home. Luis was invited to join King's Ranch heir Charlie Armstrong's Texas Rangers team as captain, along with Russell Corey and Peter Orthwein. After they defeated a couple of teams, the Texas Rangers managed to beat the local team Los Halcones by 6–5 in supplementary time.

Stories that Orthwein, Carden, and Luis repeated often about the good time they'd had playing polo at Cowdray Park in England made such an impression on Charlie Armstrong and Russell Corey that they asked Luis if he could arrange for them to play in the UK later on that year. Luis couldn't believe his luck.

Back in New York, the Yale gang celebrated their victory at a cocktail party given for them at the Waldorf Astoria by the Polo Association. Luis hadn't set foot there since the day his belongings had been confiscated when he tried to abscond without paying the bill. Luckily enough, no one at the hotel recognised him.

It was during this time that Luis met the woman who he would later claim was the love of his life. Her name was Justine Cushing, but it was her sister who Luis first met on a date. He had escorted her back home after their date and was asked inside. Justine was there, visiting her parents. The two of them clicked straight away and they started dating. After a few weeks, Luis moved into her apartment on the Upper East Side. Slim and languorous, Justine was a foot taller than him. Her father, Alexander Cushing, owned Squaw Valley, a ski resort and sometime home to the Winter Olympics. A true Bostonian blue blood, he was related to both James Roosevelt, son of the former president, and Vincent Astor, the richest man in the country following the death of his father on the *Titanic*. By the time Luis met Justine, Luis's unsavoury reputation was already preceding him. Mr Cushing had heard negative reports and was naturally concerned that his daughter was dating such a man. He told close friends that if she didn't break up with him, he would disinherit her. But Justine was undeterred and their relationship continued ... until Luis found bigger fish to catch.

14
The Discreet Charm of the Art Forger

Hearing about Luis's adventures, even if they were exaggerated or downright lies, gave me a sense of panic that I would be stuck in Buenos Aires forever, working in that awful place selling bronze ingots for headstones. It symbolised the death I felt inside. It was 1970. Four years had passed since my deportation from the US, and I would have given anything to go back to my old job as a pool boy in Miami. I no longer visited the clients who ordered bronze from our company; I just spoke to them on the telephone and took their orders. I didn't even have to try very hard to sell them anything. People carried on dying and I kept selling the bronze for their headstones.

I typically slept until noon and stayed at home doing very little for most of the day. At night, I inevitably made a tour of the usual bars. One morning, I returned home from one of my rounds of bar-hopping, drunkenly crashing along the corridor to my room, when my father appeared. He took one look at me and grimaced.

As inebriated as I was, I will never forget the look of total disgust on his face.

'This has to end,' he declared.

'What has to end?' I retorted defiantly.

'You know very well what I'm talking about.'

'I don't know what has to end that isn't already finished.'

I'm not sure what it was about what I said that triggered him, but out of nowhere, my father produced a cane and struck me with it, the metal tip catching my head with such force that I fell to the floor. It immediately sobered me up. By the time I got to my feet, my shirt bloodied down the front, he was no longer there. I left the apartment and took myself to the police station to report the incident. When I told the officer on duty that the perpetrator was my father, Judge Manrique de Acuña, his whole demeanour changed. He stopped writing, sat back in his chair, and folded his arms. It was clear the case would not be processed.

'These things always require witnesses,' he said as a way of getting out of it. He listed a few other reasons why the case would most likely not progress and eventually suggested that I try and resolve it at home. He then ordered an assistant to take me to the Rivadavia hospital to have the wound sutured.

I was relieved to arrive home and see that none of the lights were on. I was sober and silent this time as I walked along the corridor to my room. When I woke up hours later, I found a note that had been slipped under my bedroom door. I immediately recognised my father's handwriting. The note read: 'Take your clothes to the dry cleaners. I will take care of the bill.' That was it. No apology, no enquiry as to how I was. All he wanted was to erase the bloodstains on my clothes and with them, all trace of the brutality that he, a respected judge, was capable of. I decided that I had to leave not just my home, but my country. If I stayed, it would end in tragedy; I saw no other way out.

That strike from my father's cane left a permanent sting; it was the wake-up call I needed to get me to leave. The situation in Argentina was becoming more complicated by the day. Life on the surface was the same, people went about their business, and the restaurants and bars were open as usual, but it all felt tense. Violence was never far away.

One night, walking home from El Socorro to sober up before getting home, a pale blue Peugeot turned the corner near the Brazilian embassy at full speed, its wheels screeching. I just assumed the driver was drunk. But the car came to a standstill in front of the embassy, two young men got out and ran towards the lone policeman guarding the building. He put his hands in the air, and it was only then I realised that the two men were armed. One of them pointed a gun at the policeman while the other frisked him for weapons. I hid behind a truck parked nearby, and from there I heard a volley of shots ring out as the guards inside the embassy exchanged fire with the two men. The policeman was hit, as was one of the two assailants. When his accomplice tried to drag him away, a bullet hit him in the chest and injured him badly, possibly fatally. Within seconds, sirens began to wail in the distance. I decided to make my escape before more police appeared. It felt like another sign that I should leave Argentina.

According to the law, after deportation, a new passport could not be issued until five years had passed. I still had one year to go, which seemed like an eternity to me. I decided that the only way to speed up the process was to get a fake passport. I got in touch with Tommy Guerra, who had been the middleman when I tried to sell the family silver. First I had to listen to his complaints about how the police had hounded him for months on suspicion of being involved in the theft of property from a prominent judge. Once he'd got that off his chest, he gave me the name of a contact who could help with a forged passport.

Rodolfo Ruiz Pizarro lived in a perfectly ordinary-looking apartment in the prosperous Recoleta district of the city. The door opened as much as the security chain would allow and I got a first glimpse of the man, who eyed me with suspicion.

'Tommy Guerra sent me,' I said.

'And who might you be?' came a surprisingly smooth voice from the other side of the door. As soon as I introduced myself, his attitude changed. 'Manrique de Acuña, as in the judge?'

It turned out it was my name, not Tommy's, that got me through the door. Why that was would soon become clear.

Rodolfo was in his forties, tall, with an aquiline nose. He was inquisitive and suspicious by nature, but even more so as he had just been released from prison after serving a stiff sentence for art forgery. He had broken the golden rule of art forgers, which is to never forge the work of a living artist. He admired the work of Raúl Soldi and he had painted a portrait of a young woman in the artist's style. When the painting was being sold, it was shown to Raúl Soldi to be authenticated, but he denounced it as a forgery.

'Passport forgery is not my thing,' Rodolfo said when I told him what I needed. 'But I can reproduce a US visa. No one will ever realise it's counterfeit,' he assured me.

I explained that I needed to have a passport in the first place to put a visa into. So he agreed to ask a 'colleague'.

I returned to his apartment a few days later with high expectations, already imagining myself on the first flight out of the country, but as soon as he opened the door and I saw his face, I realised it wasn't to be. It turned out that the man he had in mind was currently behind bars. However, he suggested other ways he might be able to help ... and ways that I could help him. When he began to explain his situation, I realised why he had been so keen to open the door as soon as he heard my name.

He had just received the offer of work as an art restorer at Old Masters, a leading New York gallery, but as an ex-convict, he was unable to get a passport. So he asked if I could use my family connections to help him get one.

'The truth is, I not only need a passport but a clean record,' he said. 'Otherwise, I'll have to change my identity, which entails much more work than forging a document.'

Given the disastrous relationship with my father, I said I couldn't make any promises but I'd try. We said our goodbyes and I'd got halfway down the stairs when I heard him call out my name.

'There's something else you could help me with ... or that we could help each other with.'

I was curious. The whole time we'd been together, it felt like he had been testing me, getting to know me. I returned to his apartment and he closed the door.

'You know what I do, don't you?' he began.

'Yes,' I said.

'So tell me, what exactly is it that I do?'

Again he was testing me, letting me do the talking so that he wouldn't have to commit himself to anything.

'You're an art forger,' I said.

He encouraged me to continue.

'You make copies of paintings – very good copies from what Tommy said – and then you sell them.'

That was enough to allow him to open up about his work. 'What I do takes more skill than the original artist has. I must be precise about what I do while the original artist can let his hand roam freely.'

That would never have occurred to me.

'Everyone knows me,' he went on. 'They know what I do, so I can't sell my work directly, but someone like you, a Manrique de Acuña, is another matter.'

What Rodolfo was proposing was that I go out into the world and sell his forgeries, claiming they were heirlooms from our family's collection.

'You're a presentable young man from a good family. One of the best families,' he added with a smile.

It was a measure of my desperation that I didn't even hesitate. Selling his forgeries would be far more interesting, and more profitable, than selling bronze ingots at the Chacarita cemetery. He took me to his studio where three paintings in various stages of completion were arranged on easels. One was a large painting of

William the Conqueror; the other two were family portraits in an eighteenth-century style, commissioned by a client who wanted to invent a family history for himself. They were not therefore actual forgeries. He then pointed out three sketches that were pegged and hanging from a line like freshly washed clothes.

'You know of Jean León Pallière?' he asked.

Although I had grown up around art and the subject had always interested me, I admitted that my knowledge of the artist was not great. I soon got a crash course in Pallière, a Frenchman who settled in Argentina in the early nineteenth century and who specialised in gauchos and country landscapes.

Art forgery, I discovered, was as much about creating a work in the style of the artist as it was about copying an existing work. Rodolfo was not only an expert forger but also a good storyteller; he had created a whole new provenance for these artworks, which was just as important as the art itself. He proposed that I start by offering these three works by Pallière to a gallery or collector, and if I was able to sell them, I could keep fifty per cent of the profit. I was given instructions to take them to a picture framer called Veltri in Calle Vicente López, who was also a dealer and who would offer to buy them.

'What if he doesn't?' I asked.

'He will,' he replied nonchalantly. 'But if he doesn't, just ask what he thinks they're worth.'

Jacobo Veltri was plump, with slicked-back, jet-black hair conspicuously dyed and a long thin moustache to match, like a poor man's Salvador Dalí. As I entered his cluttered establishment, he was standing behind the counter as if he had been waiting for me. I opened up the folder that Rodolfo had given me and asked how much he would charge for framing the sketches.

He examined them as though he was evaluating them, and didn't even bother to ask about the kind of frame I had in mind. Holding them up to the light to check the watermarks, he produced a magnifying glass from a drawer for closer scrutiny. His response was as Rodolfo predicted.

'Would you be interested in selling them?' he asked.

And so my performance began.

'Uh, well, they're not mine. I'd have to check with my parents.'

I then recounted the provenance story that Rodolfo had concocted, elaborating on it with some details of my own. 'How much do you think they're worth?' I asked.

'I can offer you $150 each.'

The figure excited me so much that I immediately accepted, forgetting the script I had prepared.

'Didn't you just tell me you'd have to consult your parents?' Veltri said.

'I'm sure they'll be delighted when I bring them the money. My family isn't in the best financial situation right now.'

Back at Rodolfo's flat, I was ushered past his wife into the kitchen. I took the notes out of my pocket and put the $450 on the kitchen table. Rodolfo couldn't contain his emotion and hugged me. It was his first sale after leaving prison. He kept his end of the bargain and we split it fifty-fifty. I too was elated; it was the most exciting thing that had happened to me since I'd been hauled back to Argentina. I felt neither guilt nor remorse. As far as I was concerned, I had done a good job, irrespective of the ethics. The way I justified it was that I was creating new value in the market. It was the justification I used throughout my career as a peddler of forged art.

My part in the bargain was to see if my family could help Rodolfo get his passport so he could travel to New York to take up the job he'd been offered. With that in mind, I invited my parents to a fish restaurant my father was especially fond of to discuss the matter. During dinner, I casually brought up Rodolfo's situation. My father listened to the whole story with interest. 'I'll make some inquiries,' he said afterwards.

In Argentina in those days – and perhaps still now – who you knew mattered, and I was lucky that, despite the difficulties in our relationship, my father pulled some strings and spoke to the judge in charge of Rodolfo's case.

'How do you know this person?' my father asked a few days later.

'Oh, he's just someone I met. A friend of a friend. He's very talented and knows so much about art.'

'Your friend's a master of deception. He's an art forger, and a very good one at that.'

'He no longer does that. He needs the restorer's job to turn his life around,' I explained.

It wasn't clear which way it would go, but a few weeks later my father informed me that Rodolfo's passport request had been granted. This good news cemented my association with my restorer friend and we decided to embark on a few more transactions.

The next painting to be offered was by the renowned artist Bernaldo de Quirós. This time I had to work a little harder to deceive potential buyers. I had to play the part of a young landowner who had come in from the country to sell a family heirloom. I put on a pair of boots my grandfather had bought me and a tweed jacket and made the rounds of the galleries in Recoleta. My acting talent was put to use once again, but my performances were more convincing than they had been in Miami.

Finding a buyer would not be easy, not because of the work's quality but because of the price. It occurred to me that George Feldman, who ran Pacific Galleries in Calle Libertad, might be the ideal candidate. A convert to Catholicism, he never missed Sunday Mass at the Socorro church, nor the social gathering that followed at the bar opposite. I had often seen him there, and sometimes we had chatted over an aperitif. Sure enough, that was where I found him. I tried to persuade him to buy the Quirós painting, but Feldman was a tough nut to crack.

I threw myself into these endeavours with great passion and inventiveness and began studying the art on the walls of my grandparents' home with renewed interest. My eyes were drawn to a valuable painting my grandmother Elvira had in her reception room. The painting was of a woman dressed in black lying on a red sofa. It was by the nineteenth-century French artist Henry Fantin-Latour and it had special significance because her Uncle Antuco had given it to her as a wedding present. I made a point of visiting her and worked the painting into the conversation, showing great appreciation for it and suggesting that it would benefit from a restoration. I mentioned that I was in contact with one of the best restorers in Buenos Aires and asked if I could invite him for tea to advise her on the painting. Luckily, she didn't tell my father about our conversation as he might have told her about the restorer's other trade.

When Rodolfo called to advise her, he confirmed that it was indeed a valuable painting but added that it needed a good clean to 'bring out the original colours' and reveal certain details that had been covered in grime for decades. 'I could do it at no cost,' he told her. 'Marcelo has brought me a lot of business and I'm indebted to him.'

She was fascinated by Rodolfo's knowledge of art and his appraisal of the painting she now saw with fresh eyes and she accepted his proposal immediately. We wrapped up the painting in a towel and rushed out of the house before she could change her mind. Back in his studio, Rodolfo got to work, and within a couple of weeks, he had made a convincing copy of the Fantin-Latour and had restored the original. He then summoned me to his studio, where I saw the two paintings side by side. They looked identical; in both of them, the colours were as vivid and attractive as if the artist had painted them yesterday. He asked me which I thought was the original and which was the copy. After inspecting each painting closely, I pointed at one. 'Wrong. It's the other one!' he announced gleefully.

I took the forged painting to my grandmother, who was thrilled with the result. 'Now it glows,' she said, admiring it anew, and together we rehung it. The sheer joy it gave her diminished any guilt I felt. To this day, I don't know why we didn't return the original to my grandmother and keep the copy – the two paintings were identical.

With the original still in Rodolfo's studio, I had the task of finding a buyer for it. Mr Feldman declined the offer, but he suggested someone else. That person turned out to be Baron Armand de Vandières, a renowned collector and connoisseur of French artists who also happened to be the uncle of my ex-fianceé, Desirée. Although the end of our engagement had not gone down well with Desirée's parents, Armand was not especially close to his brother Gustave, and I felt confident that my personal history with the family would not jeopardise the potential sale.

The baron was a tall, thin gentleman; his jet-black hair contrasted strongly with the grey at his temples. On the little finger of his left hand, he wore a platinum ring bearing his family's coat of arms engraved in a blue agate stone. He looked like an aristocrat from an extras casting agency. He was also a man in a hurry. He dispensed immediately with any niceties and got straight to the point: what was I doing there? I told him that my grandmother had tasked me with selling a Fantin-Latour and I wanted to show it to him before anyone else saw it. I peeled back the brown paper in which the canvas was clumsily wrapped.

'Too bad it's not flowers,' was his first comment before explaining that Fantin-Latour's speciality was flowers and that any other subject matter by the artist tended to reduce interest.

'For that reason, my best offer is $3,000,' he said.

I accepted the offer with no haggling and told him that the only condition of the sale was that no one was to know or mention its provenance as my grandmother was embarrassed by the circumstances that motivated her to sell it. We shook hands on it, and within a few hours, I had $3,000 in my pocket, more than enough for my escape from Argentina.

15
Luis Meets the Queen

With Luis's help, King Ranch owner John Armstrong arrived in London at the start of the 1969 polo season with his family (a wife and four children, all boys) in his private jet, behind which a plane full of his horses landed. It was a piece of cake for him: one of his businesses was livestock transportation. After that initial display of magnificence, Armstrong rushed to register his team, Plainsmen, for the Gold Cup, the most emblematic and coveted trophy on the British circuit and contested by ten top teams.

John Armstrong, his son Charlie, and brothers Steve and Peter Orthwein took to the field with well-trained horses and managed to reach the semi-final, where they were defeated by the Windsor team consisting of Lord Patrick Beresford, his elder brother John (the 8th Marquess of Waterford) and the Duke of Edinburgh. They also reached the final of the Royal Windsor Cup, thanks to the inclusion of Luis Basualdo who gave an outstanding performance; they unfortunately lost at nail-biting extra time. The Queen presented the runners-up, including Luis, with a souvenir. The ex-groom had come a long way from the suburb of Flores to shake hands with Her Majesty, and to stress the point, he sent us all photos of her handing him the trophy.

Royal Windsor Cup, 1969. HM Queen Elizabeth presents Stephen Orthwein (centre), Luis Basualdo (left) and John Armstrong with the runners-up trophy.

When the polo season came to an end, Luis spent Christmas at the Corviglia Club in St Moritz, which was – and still is – the winter stomping ground for the very rich. Considered the most exclusive of all clubs, its policy was not to welcome people like Luis, whose reputation had by that time preceded him. The essential requirement was to be recommended by a member. For Luis, this was an irresistible challenge. He had achieved so much in such a short time – after all, he had just met the Queen of Great Britain – and he was determined to be accepted in the most select of circles.

Knowing that one of the founding members of the Corviglia was the Argentinian millionaire Luis Ortiz Basualdo, whose name he had appropriated and who he claimed was an uncle, he put this to good use. The mere mention of his fictitious uncle's name had already opened many doors for him in the past, so he confidently walked into the reception of the club and asked to see the manager. He introduced himself as the nephew of Luis Ortiz Basualdo and waved about an apocryphal letter of introduction, purportedly signed by his uncle. If the manager suspected any deceit, he did not let on. Accustomed to the delicate egos of the rich and powerful, he didn't want to take chances, and so Luis was admitted.

While in St Moritz, he struck up an acquaintance with the legendary Peppo Vanini, who ran a club in the basement of the Palace Hotel with his English girlfriend, the actress Victoria Tennant. It was through them that he was offered a discount rate at the hotel of a mere fifteen dollars a day, all meals included. These rooms were set aside for good-looking young men like Luis who could not afford St Moritz prices but whose presence added sex appeal to the club's mix. Peppo loved to have attractive young people in his establishment as it was good for business. For Luis, it meant he could save his resources for the expense of socialising at the Corviglia. From then on, the Palace Hotel was his home when he was in St Moritz.

Soon after Christmas, Luis returned to New York where he ran into Martín Iribarren who he had originally met in Buenos Aires through me. It was Martín's second trip to the Big Apple. During his first trip, he worked as a restaurant bus boy, and at the time, Luis had introduced him to some of his friends from the gay scene, one of whom was real estate agent and property consultant Larry Kaiser. On this second visit, Martín told Luis he had been living beyond his means, particularly because of his expensive courtship with the heiress Susan Engelhard, who he was trying to impress. Luis suggested that they visit their old friend Larry, hoping to borrow some money. Larry listened to their stories, and although he made sympathetic noises, he did not put his hand in his pocket.

A few days later, Larry's office received an urgent call from Bloomingdales. Two well-dressed men described as Puerto Ricans had bought goods on his credit card to the tune of $4,500. The signature did not match the original on the card, and when asked for identification, the two men quickly left the store, taking their purchases with them. When the store's security video was reviewed, it clearly showed Luis trying to complete the transaction, with Martín standing by his side. Larry's attorney wrote to both of them, threatening to press charges if the money wasn't returned. Since Martín was debt-ridden, Luis had to foot a bill that included previous transactions and legal fees – a total amount of $14,000. Facing the possibility of prison, Luis secured one last favour from his octogenarian mistress, Mrs Hall who, despite her previous experience with Luis, lent him the money. It was Martín's unenviable job to return the money in cash to Larry. Despite this, whenever Luis bumped into Larry at social events later, he greeted him as though nothing had happened.

Luis arrived at Cowdray Park a few days before the start of the 1970 polo season, and after the first practice match, his sponsor suggested they have a drink. Like many other Americans who played polo in the UK, John Coleman wanted to mingle with the aristocracy and hoped to get the chance to meet the royal family. But the costly endeavour of coming to the UK had not paid off the way he'd hoped and he decided to throw in the towel. Luis tried to talk him out of it, but he knew only too well what it felt like to be excluded. For Luis, Coleman's departure meant he would have to find a new sponsor, which would not be easy, especially as his mistreatment of horses and general unreliability had become well known. Then out of the blue appeared 'Atti' Albert Darboven, Germany's most successful coffee importer.

With his thick, wavy slicked-back hair and impressive stature, Atti looked like he was born into wealth, but he was very much a self-made man and, like all the rich polo patrons, he was eager to make the royal connections that had eluded Coleman. When Luis and Darboven met, they immediately clicked. Luis impressed him with stories of how close he was to the British aristocracy and he soon became Atti's escort and adviser, introducing him to the right people. But what Darboven needed more than social connections and success on the polo field was moral support and companionship. His marriage to a Costa Rican lady much younger than himself was coming to an end, and he was a fragile man as a result. The Mexican professional polo player he had hired, 'Chamaco' Antonio Herrera, famous for training horses by whispering in their ears, had taken to whispering in his wife's ear.

Fiercely loyal to Darboven, at least in those early months, Luis began undermining the Mexican by spreading rumours about him. It was something he would do regularly to many others, myself included. Luis put it out that Chamaco was a cheat and had been banned from playing in France for lying about his handicap. It worked. Chamaco was not only kicked out of the team but also banned for life from playing in France.

However, Darboven wasn't equipped to play in the UK because he hadn't brought enough ponies to compete, let alone mount, his team. Fortunately, Luis found a solution to his potential sponsor's problem. His name was Michael Cárcano, a wealthy Argentinian polo player who had his ponies for sale. With strong aristocratic connections in England,[5] Cárcano lived in Paris and had just arrived to compete in the Gold Cup with his team San Miguel, comprising Spanish sherry tycoon Perico Domec Jr., and other two equally wealthy gentlemen of leisure. Taking over a suite at Claridge's Hotel in Mayfair, he travelled to and from the polo fields in a chauffeured limousine. But alas, not long after his arrival, he had to endure a similar fate as Darboven. He received a telegram from his wife, Rosine, announcing that she was filing for divorce. The shock was unbearable as not only did he truly love her but the money was mostly hers. As an honourable man and no longer able to afford the kind of luxuries he had grown accustomed to, he first apologised to his wealthy teammates and moved out of Claridge's to a more modest hotel in South Kensington. Then eager to disengage himself from his financial commitments, he put his ponies up for sale. This was when he had the misfortune of running into Luis, who told him his new boss might be a potential buyer.

The prerequisite for the sale was that Luis would first 'try out' the ponies, and the deplorable 1967 Barrantes episode repeated itself. Luis overworked the animals to the point of injuring a couple of them. However, Darboven did well out of it – with the extra horses his team was able to compete throughout the season – but the hapless Cárcano had no sale. A satisfied Darboven sacked Chamaco and offered Luis a job in Germany.

Luis was contracted to procure, ship, and train Darboven's horses. He also had to play in his Idee Kaffee Hamburg team in low-handicap tournaments, all in exchange for $2,500 a month, a car, and lodging. Under those terms, he was to start work the following season at his boss's estate near Hamburg.

Determined to make a favourable impression at Cowdray Park this time, Luis had brought his glamourous girlfriend, Justine, and they both stayed at Park House. Her affable nature helped distract from Luis's sometimes disturbing attitude and also helped him in his business. She convinced New Yorker socialite Amanda Haynes to buy the last two ponies he had bought in Buenos Aires from Manolo Santa María. At the time Haynes thought she had got a good deal, but she later told friends that the horses Luis sold her were 'dogs'. As Luis would later discover, one of the people she told was her close friend Christina Onassis.

But Justine's presence also caused Luis some inconvenience due to his inability to remain faithful. He was used to doing as he pleased and now he had to be more discreet. He used to ensure that Justine sat on the uppermost tiers of the Cowdray Park stands, but hid her glasses so she couldn't see what he was up to.

Although they appeared a glamourous couple on the surface, guests in the adjacent rooms at Park House could not help but overhear their almost nightly rows. There were tales of physical abuse, of slapping and sobbing, as well as a story that he had even tried to drown her in the bathroom's wash basin. Complaints galore were made to the management but duly ignored. Luis told me that they were not rows; they simply enjoyed a sadomasochistic relationship and it was all consensual.

Luis with Justine Cushing, Cowdray Park, 1970

There may have been something in that, at least as far as the sadism was concerned, but how consensual it was is another matter. When I met Justine years later, I found her to be as poised and reserved as Luis had said she was. When I asked her about the quarrels, she merely said, 'People on this side of the Atlantic tend to exaggerate everything.'

She was a lady to her fingertips and loyal to Luis … until he let her down one time too many. Eventually, their relationship fizzled out, only to be resurrected many years later, something she would pay a very high price for.

16
Enter Christina Onassis

In September 1970, Justine returned to New York, and Luis, who was due to move to Hamburg to fulfil his contract with Darboven, was left once again to his own devices. At the end of the year, he returned to St Moritz for the Christmas season and stayed as usual in one of the discount rooms at the Palace Hotel. With no time to waste, he made his way to the Corviglia Club where he met up with the playboy Peter Bemberg, a New York resident and grandson of Otto Bemberg, one of Argentina's greatest industrialists.

As soon as Luis joined Peter, a young woman approached them. They both recognised her as Christina Onassis, heiress to the shipping empire that her father, Aristotle, had built. Christina seemed to know who Luis was, but not for a good reason.

'You're Luis Basualdo, aren't you?' she said, interrupting their conversation. 'You're the one who sold those lousy ponies to my friend Amanda Haynes.'

'Lousy ponies? No, you must be mistaken. I deal only in the best pedigrees.' Luis was delighted that she knew who he was; it didn't matter what she was saying.

'According to her, they were useless,' Christina went on.

'Maybe they were spoilt by the transportation,' Luis said.

'Or maybe you sold her some bad horses.'

Luis let her win that little battle and, making light of the incident, invited her to join them.

Christina, who had grown up in the glare of the world's press, was eighteen at the time and already showing signs of the headstrong, eccentric behaviour that she would become known for. She had recently had plastic surgery and was eager to explore her sexuality. She was a strange creature, sometimes boring and insecure, sometimes fun and animated, and often capricious and unstable, particularly later in her life when her increasing dependence on barbiturates affected her mood. She was already showing her father's dogged determination to go after whatever she wanted, which in her case was usually a man. She didn't seem to have any particular taste when it came to men and she was often attracted to anyone who gave her attention. When she fell for someone, she fell hard … until she got bored. It soon became apparent that it was Luis she had set her sights on this time.

Although her parents were on the hunt for a suitable match for her, she was less exacting. She probably wouldn't have cared if Luis had told her the truth about his life, but he told her the old story about his mother being Countess Bissoni and that he had been given an advance of $70,000 in lieu of his inheritance. To Christina, this amount would have been a pittance, but it was enough to get him in the door.

Whenever Luis was in slightly intimidating company, he became the Luis Sosa I met that first night at Bar El Socorro: he let others talk while he listened. Christina always had a lot to say and he listened. She was still a teenager and had a lot of gripes about her family, particularly her mother, Tina Livanos, who disapproved of much of her behaviour and with whom she had a very strained relationship. It was her mother with whom she was staying at the nearby Villa Bambi, and she tried to conceal her courtship with Luis because she knew her mother would disapprove.

The new couple established a routine that consisted of skiing in the morning, then lunch, sex in the afternoon, followed by dinner, and then dancing at the King's Club. The only cloud on the horizon was that Luis had arranged to meet Justine Cushing at the Austrian ski resort of St Anton. Christina didn't take kindly to the news and she pressured him to stay with her in St Moritz, already displaying the intensity for which she would become well known. Up until that point, Luis had thought of the relationship as nothing more than a fling, but the prospect of a union with Christina was becoming a real possibility. Peppo Vanini encouraged Luis to stay: 'Gaucho' (that's what Peppo called him), 'you can't leave. It's Christina Onassis we're talking about here! Do you know what that means?'

Luis, of course, knew exactly what it meant and had thoroughly considered his options. It was clear Christina was the bigger catch – her father was one of the richest men in the world – but attractive as all that wealth was to him, he knew that the chances of him getting his hands on any of it were remote. The mere possibility of an engagement between him and Christina would probably mean she'd be disinherited. Justine Cushing was a much safer bet, although her money was tied up in a trust fund. For all Luis's claims that Justine was the love of his life, she came with a price tag, just like everyone else.

The night before he left for Austria, he met Christina at the King's Club for what was supposed to be their last meeting of the season. By that time, Christina was openly desperate. After an evening of conversation that went round and round in circles, Luis told her that he needed to go; she said that if he went, it meant he didn't love her.

The young Argentinian finally extricated himself and made his way back to the hotel. No sooner had he put his case on the bed and started packing than there was a knock on the door. It was Christina who had not quite given up just yet. She lay down on the bed and tried to distract him from his packing. And Luis eventually succumbed to temptation and joined her in bed. Although Christina did not prevent him from going to Austria, she got his telephone number there so they could keep in touch.

Before he had even arrived at St Anton, the anxious Greek lady had already called several times, and she kept calling during his entire stay. She knew Justine was there and it was often Justine who answered the phone. It didn't take long for Justine to realise who it was who kept calling and what had been going on in St Moritz. Justine had had enough and gave Luis an ultimatum: her or Christina. Luis chose Christina.

So he returned to St Moritz and what followed for Christina was two blissful months of more skiing, lunches, sex, dinners, and discos with Luis. It was this period of romance between them that solidified their relationship and formed the basis of their lifelong friendship. She even grew fond of his weird sense of humour, something that not everyone liked. Christina's long-time friend Marina Dodero (neé Tsomlektsoglou), once commented to me, 'He tells stories that nobody understands and the only one who laughs at them is him.'

But it began to annoy Luis that she talked incessantly about money and the ships that her father, mother, and uncle owned. Her attitude to her family's wealth was odd. She was used to it, of course, and had known nothing else, yet she was always drawing attention to it. It was as if she didn't understand its value and had to watch other people's reactions to get a sense of it. Despite all this money talk, Christina never actually carried any cash with her and Luis always had to pay the thirty Swiss francs for the taxi home after their nights out. One day he'd had enough. 'If you have so many fucking ships, why don't you pay for your own fucking taxi fare!' he exploded. According to Luis, she never let him pay for a cab again. Christina respected strong men who gave her orders, as most people just fawned over her.

When I saw Luis in Buenos Aires shortly after, he was telling anyone who would listen about his 'conquest' of Christina Onassis. I met her myself for the first time in Buenos Aires in early 1972, just before I came to live in London, and the question of who would pay the bill became a running joke, which most of the time was on me or another unsuspecting punter. Things just magically happened around her without her needing to do a thing. Bills got paid without her even looking at them; she ignored bills when they arrived as though they were beneath her. I came to understand Luis's frustration only too well.

It was only a matter of time before Tina, Christina's mother, found out that her daughter was sleeping with Luis, and when she did, she was furious. A year earlier, Christina had become pregnant by her American boyfriend, Danny Marentette, and the episode had ended in a family storm and a miscarriage. Tina had little faith in her daughter's ability to choose appropriate partners and immediately saw Luis as yet another gold digger. In what Christina described as 'a very unpleasant showdown', Tina called Luis every name under the sun, throwing in every term for money-grabbing, greasy Latino she could think of. What was most hurtful to Christina was her mother's taunt that no one could possibly be interested in Christina for anything other than her wealth.

'This is different. He's a Catholic,' Christina insisted, as if that made Luis the ideal partner.

'Don't you dare even think of marrying that man!' her mother shouted.

Luis told me many times that the family would have disinherited her if their relationship ever became official. Of course, without the Onassis fortune, she would no longer have any appeal for him. He tried to make her understand that his income as a polo professional was barely enough for one, let alone two. Whatever the intensity of feelings between them, he was not about to get involved with someone who had been disinherited.

Eventually, the St Moritz season ended and Luis left for Buenos Aires to buy horses for his boss before reporting for work in Hamburg. During that time, he didn't stop talking about Christina, and she didn't stop calling him (in those days, long-distance calls were prohibitively expensive).

As much as he liked the idea of a relationship with Christina, he knew he wouldn't be able to get his hands on her money. Nor was Justine's money going to be available to him. However, there was a third heiress in the background whom he had his sights set on. She was the Honourable Lucy Pearson, Lord Cowdray's teenage daughter. During his last season at Cowdray Park, she had followed him everywhere. Since then, she had written him love letters full of teenage longing. Initially, he had disregarded her infatuation, but as time went on he came to take it more seriously. Apart from the fact that she was naive and malleable, she was an open door to the British aristocracy, whose acceptance he craved. Even better, there was the $800,000-a-year income from a trust fund she would be getting when she was eighteen. There was only one problem: she was still only sixteen.

17

The Waiting Room

Back in Buenos Aires, my new career as an 'art dealer' came to a sudden end when Rodolfo Pizarro received his passport and made the move to New York, the irony being that it was me who had facilitated his departure. I had freed the goose that laid the golden egg, losing both my means of support and my way out of Argentina in one fell swoop. However, during my brief association with Rodolfo, I discovered that my interest in the art world was not merely financial but genuine; the vocabulary of the art world came naturally to me. For someone who had never excelled at anything much, it was a pleasant surprise. My grandmother used to endlessly discuss artists and sculptors, and lunches and dinners with her had been a series of lessons in art history that I had absorbed without even realising.

But what I knew even more about, thanks to my time in Miami, was relationships with older women. It was my specialist subject. During this time in Buenos Aires, I moved restlessly from one relationship to the next, and many of them went by without making too much of an impression while others left an indelible mark. One of the more memorable was with an Italian divorcee by the name of Guillermina.

She was like something out of an Antonioni film. She drove a convertible Mercedes around the city with dangerous abandon. I saw her many times in the neighbourhood, ignoring traffic signals and speed limits, her striking mane of red hair billowing out dramatically behind her.

Me with Cecilia Tiscornia at Mau Mau discotheque, Buenos Aires, 1971

One day I ran into her at the Rond Point bar and decided to talk to her. I had the feeling that a woman like her, oblivious to rules and decorum, would respond to a direct approach. I went up to her and, without introducing myself, told her that I had seen her driving around many times and would love to have the experience of being a passenger in her car.

She was somewhat puzzled by my request. 'You want me to give you a lift somewhere?'

'No, no, I just want you to drive me around. I don't care where we go. You decide that.'

It worked. She finished her drink, and said, 'Let's go.'

We got in her car and she drove with a lack of regard for lights, rules, or other drivers that I found inexplicably attractive. We ended up driving around the city for most of the day and later, we had dinner at the Plaza Hotel. She was a dominant woman, which turned me on even more – she knew what she wanted from the menu, from the waiter, from life, from me. After dinner, before I could make a pretence of fumbling for my wallet, she handed over her Diners Club card to pay the bill. She was my kind of woman. I learned that Guillermina was a lady of means, thanks to a family inheritance and a generous divorce settlement from her ex-husband who was a psychiatrist to the rich and famous. Later that night, I discovered that she was also sexually insatiable, as had been my hope. That fire burned red hot for a while before burning itself out.

Then came Eva, who was roughly my mother's age, with intense eyes and dark hair. She was the mother of a boy I went to school with who used to invite me to his house for parties. I had fantasised about her when I was a boy and now that fantasy came true. Eventually, it was that childhood connection that became a little awkward to manage as her son grew increasingly suspicious about the nature of our relationship and began to openly question why it was I was spending so much time talking to his mother. We concocted some story about a mutual love of art until he caught us holding hands on the sofa. He stood there a moment, frozen to the spot and saying nothing, before leaving the room and storming out of the house. It was all too much, and we stopped seeing each other after that.

After Eva came a widowed mother of two who made a living as a dressmaker. Her name was Mara Rivera, a whip-thin widow fifteen years my senior with a body like an ironing board. I can't say exactly what attracted me to her but I fell hard. Ordinarily, these affairs didn't last very long – they were intense but ultimately superficial – but in this case, not only did my crush not wear off, it intensified. I only had to look at her for my heart to beat like a drum. I spent the proceeds from the Fantin-Latour sale on her. Maybe it was this very intensity bordering on desperation that put her off. She lost interest and eventually left me. I sank into a deep depression triggered by the break-up.

When I tried to find virtue in myself, I couldn't. My transgressions had been many in my life so far. The forgeries, the deceptions, the stealing, the deportation – I could only see sins, faults, and vices. I spent an entire week locked in my bedroom, sleeping most of the day, vowing to remain celibate for the rest of my life. When I finally emerged to face the world, I discovered it was a worse place than the one I had left a week earlier.

Me with Cecilia Tiscornia going into the Africa discotheque, Buenos Aires, 1971

One morning I woke up to the news that Rodolfo Pizarro had been arrested in New York. This time he was not accused of forgery but of drug trafficking. The whole story he'd fed me about being offered a job as an art restorer had been a lie. He was employed to conceal cocaine inside the frames of the paintings he was supposedly restoring. His activities were reported all over the press and the story kept growing, making the front pages and threatening to involve not just me but my father.

In a joint operation between the Argentinian, French, and American police, an investigation led to the Corsican mobster Françoise Chiappe, a former French soldier and leader of a vast criminal network, who was arrested in Buenos Aires. It turned out that Pizarro was part of the international drug trafficking ring that Chiappe operated. It was then discovered that Pizarro's passport, originally confiscated, had been restored at the behest of Judge Manrique de Acuña. In a further twist to my father's connection with this story, he was the judge chosen to decide on a request from the United States to extradite Chiappe, and it was he who ordered Chiappe to be jailed in the Devoto prison in Buenos Aires. Despite his link to the case through Pizarro, he was not taken off it and his impartiality was not questioned. During the trial he received various threats from the Corsican Mafia. It was partly because of that, and for his work over the years, that he was awarded an honour by the President.

As the situation developed, I tried to steer clear of my father as much as possible. I spent many evenings drinking late, or doing whatever I could to avoid going home. I knew he would somehow blame me for what had happened (not without reason). However, I couldn't avoid him forever.

'I take it you heard about your associate Rodolfo Pizarro,' he said one evening when he found me in the kitchen eating on my own.

'He wasn't my associate. He was just an acquaintance,' I said between mouthfuls.

'Whatever you want to call him. Did you know he was involved with some very serious criminals?'

'If I'd known that I'd never have had anything to do with him,' I replied.

'Well, you did get involved with him, and you dragged me into it. Did it occur to you at all that it could have been very serious for me to be associated with this criminal? Does that even matter to you?'

I finished my dinner and shut myself away in my room. He was right – I had dragged him into this sordid business. It could have been disastrous for him and all of us. Of course, I followed the case in the papers with great interest. In the end, Chiappe was not extradited to the US and so for reasons that are still unclear, though most likely involving corruption, he managed to evade American justice. He enjoyed a special status in the main Buenos Aires prison until he escaped in March 1973, purely by happy accident. Armed leftists broke into the prison to release political prisoners, and although Chiappe was not the object of the rescue, he managed to mingle with the leftist guerrillas and fled alongside them. His story was the inspiration behind the film *The French Connection*. I saw it at the cinema when it was released in 1971, but didn't make the association until many years later.

It was about this time that I met Linley Dagwood, and it was with her that I broke my rather half-hearted vow of celibacy. In some respects, we resembled and complemented each other. She enjoyed the company of young men like me as much as I enjoyed the company of older women like her, and both of us liked drinking. She represented for me the prototype of a beautiful, mature woman with whom I had great sexual chemistry and who could hold my attention without boring me. When I told her after we had sex for the first time that my recent experiences with women had led me to months of celibacy, her response was a dirty laugh.

'A good banging is the best cure for anxiety and stress!' she declared, lighting one of the menthol cigarettes that she chain-smoked. 'A good fuck releases endorphins that make you feel great – about life, the world, everything. You must have felt that. How do you feel now?'

'Good,' I answered sheepishly.

'Good?' She seemed almost offended. 'Don't you feel great?'

She was another one of those amazing women I've been lucky to meet in life. She was so sure of herself, so free of any restrictions or need to conform to social norms that she was inspiring. I wanted to live like that too. Of course, I was very attracted to her physically, but I was also attracted to her attitude, even the way she spoke so openly about sex. After so many lovers, I thought that maybe there wasn't much more I could learn, but Linley proved me deliciously wrong.

After graduating from Stanford Business School, Linley travelled to Argentina for a change of scenery and to see what fate might have in store for her in the southern hemisphere. Her goal upon setting foot on Argentinian soil was clear: to find a man who could keep up with her, and share her lifestyle and her taste for the finer things in life. That person turned out to be Raúl Sánchez de Bethancourt, a wealthy landowner and one of the most eligible bachelors of his generation. Many ladies had had their sights on him and they never forgave Linley for snapping him up. It was only because of her marriage to him that she was accepted in the patrician circles of the Río de la Plata.

Mistakenly thought to be a fortune hunter, Linley was not short of money. Orphaned in her teens and raised by a guardian, she had inherited a sizeable chunk of shares in the famous Harley-Davidson motorcycle company. So it wasn't money she was after in her newly adopted country but a position of power in which she could do as she pleased. Her marriage to Raúl was an open one, which very few in Argentina's hypocritical, hidebound society looked upon favourably. Having affairs in secret was permitted, but agreeing to them in advance was considered scandalous. I soon discovered the set-up was a little more complicated. Husband and wife lived under the same roof in their luxurious apartment in an art deco building on Avenida Alvear, where she was free to bring her male guests, but he had to find other venues for his extramarital business. It was a pact imposed by the dominant Linley, as everything was always on her terms. When her aristocratic mother-in-law commented on the number of young men visiting the house, Linley replied, 'I cultivate friendships with them so that when I'm ninety, they'll come to play cards with me.'

She was not only my lover but also my closest friend at the time, though she was as faithful to me as she was to her husband. I was just one of her many lovers invited to her apartment where she kept an open house. Around seven in the evening, people – mostly men, both gay and straight – would drop by for a drink. Then we spread out around her spacious drawing room, having helped ourselves to drinks, and engaged in passionate debates on current affairs.

Linley towered above us all like a goddess, her slender six-foot frame in heels sometimes even eliciting applause from the crowd of admirers. She was an actress who played her role to perfection. She was very well-read and could converse on any subject, although when it suited her she concealed her intelligence. To us, she seemed exotic and we listened intently to her stories, which mainly involved jet-setters and foreign aristocracy. For a while I was her favourite; it was me who was asked to stay after everyone else had left, and it was me she exchanged knowing glances with.

Being the chosen one, I came to depend on the emotional bond I had with her and poured out all my frustrations about life, my family, and myself, which she listened to with great patience until I realised that I had turned this fascinating woman into my counsellor. From then on, the relationship was doomed. She began lecturing me, telling me truths about myself that I didn't want to hear, though I was the one who had asked for her advice. Then I received the following note from her, in which she listed all my attributes before getting to the point:

> *Marcelo, there is something called reputation, which, as you can see from my lifestyle, I don't give a damn about. I am a free spirit and I do what I want. Being Mrs Sánchez de Bethancourt, everybody wants to be my guest. Your case is different from mine.*

You're a young man from a good family but with no money. Unfortunately, you like older women and that puts you in a very delicate situation since that inclination is misunderstood. You are a well-known gigolo, and there is no easy way out of that predicament. Therefore, my suggestion under the current circumstances is that you wash your dirty linen abroad. To be clear, you should go and live somewhere else, where nobody knows you and you can act without feeling the weight of the judgement of others.[6]

18
Enter Ursula Mahler

Linley's suggestion that I leave the country was her way of breaking up with me. Maybe she realised that if I was to be helped, the first step would be to cut the umbilical cord that joined me to her. The message was received loud and clear and I did not see her again, until one day, weeks later, I received an unexpected call. She wanted to see me immediately.

I arrived at her apartment in the hope that our relationship was going to be revived, but as soon as I got there, my hopes were dashed. Linley was not alone. She was accompanied by Fabián Guerrico, an interior decorator who was one of her many gay friends. It seemed unlikely that he would have been invited to the rekindling of our relationship. She had clearly invited me for some other reason. All three of us chatted about nothing for a while until she got to the point.

'Do you know who Ursula Mahler is?' she asked me.
'No. Should I?'
'She's a very glamourous divorcee about my age,' Linley explained. 'She moves between Paris and Buenos Aires and I wondered if you'd ever come across her.'

'Well, I haven't.'

'I've just decorated her apartment,' Fabián said, playing his role in this performance.

'Fabián has been telling her very complimentary things about you,' Linley went on and she handed me a piece of paper with Ursula's telephone number on it. It was clear that she was passing me on to someone else. Only Linley could have done it like that.

'Good luck!' said Linley. 'And whatever you do, don't bring that bitch to my house.'

Ursula Mahler, I was informed, was half Chilean, half German, and very stubborn. She had had an affair with a minister in the Peronist government who she fleeced. She later married an aristocrat with whom she had a daughter, but she was never accepted into Argentinian society because of her chequered past. The other piece of vitally important information for me to know was that she did not get up before noon, so I had to ensure that I called her in the afternoon.

I decided to play it cool and called her three days later with a speech of sorts prepared – something about a mutual acquaintance. The telephone was answered by a woman with a slightly masculine, confident, and sensual voice. All I had to do was to ask for Ursula and introduce myself as Marcelo; the rest, it seemed, had been done for me.

'Oh Marcelo,' Ursula said with great familiarity. 'Why did you take so long in calling?' Rather than enter into the immature games of courtship, she just cut to the chase. 'Why don't we have dinner?'

I responded by honouring her spirit of directness. 'What are you doing tomorrow?' I asked.

'Tomorrow?' She spat the word out in disgust. 'What the hell's wrong with tonight?'

And that was Ursula – why wait until tomorrow for something you could have right that instant?

Well-groomed, and generously splashed with Vetiver Carven, like all perfect 1970s Latin lovers, I arrived at Ursula's apartment at seven o'clock sharp. A woman in her mid-fifties, dressed as though she was playing a French maid in a film, opened the door and included in our exchange words such as Madame and s'il vous plait that she'd learned from her boss, perhaps to add a touch of refinement, when it was obvious she was as Argentinian as me. She showed me to a room where *Madame* was waiting, also looking as if she was playing a part in a movie. She was stretched out on a Louis XVI chaise longue and, without getting up, she extended her hand to me.

At first glance, Ursula reminded me of Ruth Goldberg. She was in her fifties, well-groomed, with dyed blonde hair but fair-skinned enough that it looked natural on her, and dark, rather dramatic eye shadow, which for some reason put me in mind of a horror film. She flirted the whole time, adopting a series of suggestive poses on the chaise longue as I nervously sipped my drink. It was clear from the outset that Ursula was another in a long line of women I came to know who liked to control things. That made her even more attractive in my eyes.

She took me to a French restaurant where she ordered for both of us, and when the bill came, she took care of that too. When we got back to her place, she invited me into the bedroom where she slowly took off her clothes and carefully placed them on a chair at the side, which inspired me to do the same. Then, in the most direct way, she said, 'I don't know if Fabián has already told you about my sexual preferences,' and she went on to explain exactly what they were.

Had she really told Fabián that, I wondered. He certainly hadn't passed that on to me.

We did end up in bed, but after a few hours I was asked to leave. I later found out that she didn't want me to see her without make-up in the morning.

Our meetings continued daily with an almost military routine: drinks, dinner, dance, back to hers and make love, just the way she liked it. In return, I received expensive gifts: a gold Dupont lighter with a matching ballpoint pen, a gold chain, and cufflinks, and a variety of French silk scarves. It wasn't long before she gave me the gift I had been waiting for since Linley told me about her – the gift of an exit from Argentina.

'Would you like to come to Paris with me?' she asked one day as we were having dinner, casually dropping it into the conversation as though it had just occurred to her.

'When do we leave?' I asked.

19
Vive la Difference!

On 4th April 1971, Ursula and I boarded the Air France flight that would take us to Paris. Five years had passed since my deportation from Miami and I had finally been granted a new passport.

Although I had known Ursula for a while and was getting to know her well, when you travel with someone, you often see a whole new side to them. Ursula, it turned out, was not just dominant with her men; she wanted to dominate everyone and everything around her, and she demanded that they do what she wanted. When the captain of the plane announced, to her fury, that we would be making a stopover in São Paulo, she called the air hostess and demanded that the plane continue directly to Paris as she had been told it would. For once, she did not get her way. Stopover or no stopover, I was delighted to be leaving Argentina.

When we arrived at Orly Airport, Ursula made a beeline for a middle-aged man with white hair who was holding a piece of cardboard with the words 'MME MAHLER' written on it. She told me he was her usual driver, but I wondered why her usual driver would need a sign for her to recognise him. It was the first time I noticed that things did not always add up with Ursula. Then instead of going to her apartment, which she informed me was being redecorated, we went to the Hôtel Brighton in the Rue de Rivoli, a cosy four-star hotel with a room that overlooked the Tuileries Gardens.

The mysterious apartment was being redecorated the whole time we were in Paris. In the end, I never saw it and I never knew where it was. I rather doubt it existed. True to form, Ursula had everything planned and didn't ask if there was anything specific I wanted to do. It so happened I had nothing in mind; I was just happy to be there. I was fascinated by every person we passed in the street, every shop window, every café.

The night of our arrival we went to dinner at La Belle Ferronnière to meet Susi Wyss, a Swiss ex-model of great notoriety who was an old friend of Ursula's. La Belle Ferronnière, as I discovered, was where the *Paris Match* boys and girls, the fashion people, writers and jet-setters went to be seen and photographed. It was one of the places that Ursula also liked to frequent.

Susi had modelled for Salvador Dalí, amongst others, and was a close friend of David Bowie. Her Paris apartment had been bought for her by Paul Getty Jr, the son of millionaire American oilman Paul Getty. It was the scene of many famous parties with guest lists that included Yves Saint Laurent, Baron Éric de Rothschild and Dennis Hopper.

During the dinner, Susi and Ursula mainly ignored me, most of their conversation being conducted in German (some of it may even have been about me). At one point, Susi suddenly switched to English to inform me, apropos of nothing, that she had recently dated Björn Andrésen, labelled 'the most beautiful boy in the world' after playing Tadzio in Luchino Visconti's *Death in Venice*. 'He is inexperienced but wonderfully enthusiastic,' she said in her German accent. After that non sequitur, they immediately went back to talking German and I was left to ponder what that had been about. Was it simply name-dropping or perhaps a statement of intent? I turned away from them to watch the *Paris Match* crowd as they preened and looked impossibly beautiful, feeling very much the gigolo in the company of two older women.

As I recall, that night was the first night since I'd met Ursula that we did not have sex. I wondered if I was seeing a new, softer Ursula there in Paris, but it turned out she was just tired after the long journey. It was business as usual from then on.

The next day, Ursula had an appointment with a car dealer to buy a car and I was left to my own devices, as I always was when she was dealing with financial matters. I had embarked on the trip without a penny to my name, so I was entirely reliant on her. Before she left, I asked her if she could leave me a little something for a coffee or lunch. Ursula nonchalantly took two one hundred franc notes from her purse and handed them to me. That was my pocket money for the week.

I put the money away and went straight to the hotel's corner kiosk to buy a copy of *Hello* magazine. While standing at the newsagent's flicking through the pages of the magazine, I was struck by the headline of an article: 'Christina Onassis in Love with Mystery Argentinian.' No name was given, but when I looked at the photograph closely, I saw that the mystery man was Luis. Shortly after, Luis phoned the hotel to tell me about their affair in detail, having tracked my whereabouts through the polo community, but the real reason he'd called was to find out what the Argentinian press might be reporting about it.

Ursula was not at all interested in museums, cultural activities or sightseeing. She thought all that sort of thing was a waste of time, so I was left to explore Paris on my own. After breakfast at Angelina's, the famous tea house next to the hotel we were staying in and where they served the best hot chocolate, I would walk to the Louvre nearby, stroll to Notre Dame or Les Invalides, or just get lost in the architecture and atmosphere of the city.

On one of those walks I discovered the Rue de la Paix, where all the fashion houses had their boutiques, and in the Rue de Castiglione I stumbled across a small jewellery and engraving shop. One bore a sign reading 'We sell and engrave signet rings' and I decided that I deserved a gift like that. So the next time I was out with Ursula, I made sure we passed the little shop and, pretending spontaneity, stopped in front of it and stared into the window like a child outside a toy shop.

'What are you looking at so entranced?' Ursula asked, falling into my trap.

'Those rings,' I said. I told her that my family descended from the first Count of Casa Tagle de Trasierra, governor of Peru at the time of the conquest. 'When I make some money, I'm going to buy one of those rings and have it engraved with my family crest,' I added.

'Say no more. If that's what you want, that's what you'll get.'

Once inside the shop, I discovered a wall-to-wall display of books with details of every registered family crest and every European title imaginable. I picked up a book and there it was: a mounted Saint George spearing a serpent. Ater carefully studying the selection of rings in various shapes and sizes, I chose the classic oval shape in gold. I was so excited to have the ring that I kissed Ursula on the lips, put my arm around her waist and led her out into the street, where she had another surprise for me.

'We never went into the Louvre. We only walked by it. I think it's time I got some culture,' she said.

That was certainly unexpected, but from then on, we started visiting museums and art galleries regularly together.

As Ursula had made her first connections in the city through fashion, every time she was in Paris, she made sure to meet up with some of her old friends and colleagues from that time, people like Yves Saint Laurent. We met him at Le Sept on Rue Sainte-Anne, the premier gay club of the time where the fashion icon was having dinner with their mutual friend Susi Wyss. Ursula proudly introduced me as her young Argentinian chevalier servant. Saint Laurent, who must have seen immediately that I was an escort, could have treated me with disdain, but instead he was very cordial. 'Any friend of Ursula's is a friend of mine,' he said.

Susi invited everyone to a party the next day at her famous apartment in the fourteenth arrondissement. When Ursula and I arrived, we were greeted by a young German man with short blond hair whom Susi described as her slave. He opened the door wearing nothing apart from a maid's short frilly apron that just about covered his front, though not his backside, which was slapped regularly by Susi and anyone who fancied it, so it was red raw by the end of the evening. His name was Eckhart, and he spent the evening circulating with a tray of drinks and another one with cocaine. He was impressively nimble in high heels.

By the time we arrived back at the hotel, the receptionist informed Ursula that there had been a few calls for her during the night and passed on the messages. When we got to our room, Ursula spent twenty minutes on the phone talking in German, and as much as I wanted to get to sleep after a hard night's partying, all I could hear was Ursula talking animatedly. Finally, she came to bed.

'We've been invited to a party,' she announced.

'Is that what that was all about? It sounded more you like were arguing.'

'That's how I always talk to Rita.'

'Who's Rita?'

'Rita Lachman.'

I had heard Luis mention Rita often over the years but I hadn't met her personally. 'What kind of a party?' I asked.

'A party, Marcelo. Just a party.'

Rita and Ursula had been friends for years and had a lot in common. Given what had happened with Luis, I did not especially want to meet her.

I needn't have worried about it. It turned out to be nothing more than a cocktail party at Rita's apartment on Avenue Foch. To my surprise I ran into some well-known Argentineans there. They were competing in local polo tournaments at the Bagatelle polo club in the outskirts of Paris. As they greeted me, Jimmy Dodero and Delfín Rueda looked at me up and down, taking an interest in the diamond brooches on the lapels of my black velvet jacket. I stuck out like a sore thumb, even in such a flamboyant company.

'Beautiful, aren't they?' Ursula said.

I was feeling more and more ridiculous. Apart from being her sex toy, I had become her mannequin whom she dressed and undressed according to whim.

With their youth and glamour, the polo players seemed to be the main attraction of the party, but I eventually moved away from them. They couldn't measure up to the stature of the international nobility, people such as Princess Ghislaine de Polignac and Baroness Marie-Hélène de Rothschild. Those were the people that really counted. Marie-Hélène de Rothschild's companion, who had been watching me throughout the evening, approached me and introduced himself. Alexis von Rosenberg, Baron de Redé, was his name.

'I heard you speaking in Spanish with the Argentinians. Are you also here to play polo?' he asked.

'I do play, but no, I'm here on vacation with my girlfriend,' I said.

Suddenly Ursula appeared out of nowhere, jealous of the attention I was receiving, and crudely interjected herself into the conversation, trying to ensure that she was in control as always. To her frustration, Redé continued talking to me as though she wasn't there. Before he moved on, he said, 'Don't worry, I'll be in touch.'

Five minutes later, I was approached by Marie-Hélène de Rothschild. She was the wife of Guy de Rothschild, head of the French branch of the famous European banking dynasty. She confidently introduced herself and made polite conversation, finding out as much as she could about me, no doubt to pass it all on to her friend, the baron.

The next morning, Rita Lachman phoned Ursula with an awkward request: Marie-Hélène de Rothschild had contacted her on behalf of Alexis de Redé, who wanted to invite me to dinner, and she wondered if she could borrow me for the evening. Ursula didn't even try to conceal her irritation. 'Of course he won't accept. He's my boyfriend and we always do things together,' she said before slamming the phone down. The truth was that Ursula wouldn't have minded me going if she thought she could get something out of it. Later that day, there was another call; this time it was Marie-Hélène de Rothschild herself. I'm not sure what was discussed or what deal was concocted between them, but that evening I was released to meet the baron on my own.

Alexis von Rosenberg was forty-nine years old at the time and lived on the ground floor of the seventeenth-century Hôtel Lambert in the Île Saint-Louis. His father, Oscar von Rosenberg, had been ennobled by Emperor Franz Joseph of Austria in 1916 and his mother was a member of the von Kaulla family, who partly owned the Bank of Württemberg. Alexis became the lover of millionaire Arturo López Willshaw, a Chilean he met in New York who was married. Arturo brought Alexis back to Paris and installed him in luxury. But Alexis was a canny investor and businessman, and he increased his lover's wealth; after Arturo died in 1962, he inherited half of his estate. The other half went to Arturo's long-suffering wife.

It was obvious what Alexis wanted from me; what was less clear was what I wanted from him. I had no objection to the company of gay men, but I had never had a sexual encounter with a man for the simple reason that I was not attracted to them. I wondered if Ursula had led Rita or Marie-Hélène to think otherwise and if she was considering pimping me out to men.

I was immediately impressed by the luxury and good taste of the baron's apartment – the priceless art collection, the sheer volume of books on the shelves, the furniture, silver, porcelain, crystals and other objects all exquisitely arranged. It was completely overwhelming. Alexis was dressed casually in navy slacks, an open white silk shirt, gold oval cufflinks engraved with his initials and monogrammed black velvet slippers. After a few drinks in that lily-scented atmosphere, I was finally able to relax.

A man of the world, Alexis knew that I was someone standing on the edge of the *beau monde* looking for a way in. He pointed to the ring on my finger and I told him that I'd had it engraved in a small shop in the Rue de Castiglione.

'The crown on the shield has to do with our eighteenth-century Spanish title, granted at the time of the Conquest by—'

'Say no more,' Alexis interrupted me. 'I don't need an explanation.'

It was a sensitive topic for him because for years he had put up with people calling him a *faux* baron and saying his title had been bought.

When Alexis decided it was time to go to dinner, I breathed a sigh of relief. I wanted to get away from his residence and be on neutral ground. As soon as we walked into Le Sept, he paused briefly to greet Yves Saint Laurent, who was sitting with a young man. Saint Laurent, who recognised me from our meeting a few days earlier, said to him, 'I'm sure this handsome Argentinian has become your nephew.'

'I wish,' was Alexis's reply. 'But unfortunately not.'

Shortly after we sat down, Alexis left the table to greet someone in a corner of the room, and I took the opportunity to look around me. It was one of those moments when I felt like I was actually in a movie.

Sitting at a table next to us was an exotic and glamorous lady dressed in black with matching gloves and hat. She wore a patch over one eye and smoked through a long, shiny ebony and ivory cigarette holder. With her was a pale, thin young man with black, slicked-back hair, wearing an outdated and eccentric fashion style; he looked like a character from a silent movie. A platinum blonde with an old-fashioned English lord sporting a monocle sat at another table, and not too far away were a couple of men, plastered with rouge and silver eyeshadow, holding hands. But what caught my attention the most was Andy Warhol sitting at a table with some of the cast of his film *L'Amour*. He was wearing a fuchsia wig and looked dazed, either from drugs or drink. The whole evening, I tried to signal my clear preference for women to the baron, while trying not to offend him or jeopardise whatever friendship was in the making. I even asked him to introduce me to Paloma Picasso, who had greeted him affectionately when he entered the club.

Suddenly, he said, 'I totally understand your situation.'

'What situation is that?'

'You and that woman. For many years I was with an older man who I didn't love but who generously supported me. In my case, that relationship held some advantage for me, because at a later point, I had financial problems and he took care of my needs.'

'What makes you think Ursula won't take care of my needs?'

'To begin with, that place where you're staying tells you all you need to know. You should be living in a suite at Le Meurice, or the Plaza Athénée, not at the third-rate Hôtel Brighton.'

'It's only temporary. She has an apartment in Paris. In fact, she has two.'

'Oh, she has two!' A smile was playing around his lips. 'Then why are you staying at that hotel?'

'One is let to tenants, and decorators are working on the other.'

'Of course they are!' he exclaimed sarcastically. 'Take a tip from an old dog – you're giving her more than she gives you back.'

He knew he had hit a nerve. I was her plaything and she paid for my services; everybody knew it and I knew they knew it. For the most part, I didn't mind; everybody here did as they pleased and I did too, but I was feeling increasingly suffocated by the way Ursula managed my every move, her insistence on having sex almost every night, and the way she jealously kept me to herself. But I was enjoying the good life that came with it, even if it was all on the cheap, not to mention being away from the claustrophobic environment of Argentina.

One day as Ursula and I were walking down the Boulevard des Capucines, she saw someone waving in our direction. Given that she knew half of Paris and that I barely knew anyone, she assumed they were waving at her, but as we got closer, she realised that she didn't recognise them. Turning to me she said, 'I think that woman is waving at you.'

'What woman?'

No sooner had I uttered the words than I saw my grandmother sitting at a table outside the Café de la Paix next to my grandfather. He was not waving, and even from a distance, I could feel his disapproval radiating towards me.

'Oh God, my grandparents,' I said and, like a child caught in the act of doing something naughty, I immediately let go of Ursula's hand.

We made our way towards them. I kissed my grandmother, shook my grandfather's hand, and introduced Ursula. They invited us to sit with them, but the conversation was tense from the outset. They commented on my clothes, which they thought garish, and the diamond brooches on my lapels, which they described as feminine. I was studied from head to toe and found wanting. My grandmother, who didn't miss a trick, also noticed my new signet ring and enquired about it as she sipped her café au lait.

'You're looking at the coat of arms of the Count of Casa Tagle de Trasierra, which I'm entitled to wear,' I said, raising my hand to display the ring.

'You mean that *I'm* entitled to wear!' snapped my grandmother. She added that her branch of the family had more of a right to the title than the present Count, but she didn't want to waste time and money proving her point.

'How do you know all this?' asked a surprised Ursula.

'I was brought up to be able to sift through the complex web of precedence and rank of my family,' my grandmother explained. 'It's the key to my identity.'

What started as a conversation about our lineage moved on to Ursula's background.

'Mahler,' mused my grandmother. 'Like the composer?'

'Exactly,' Ursula said.

It was the first time I had seen her even slightly nervous.

'That's a Jewish name,' said my grandmother. 'Are you Jewish?'

'My parents are German Jews of Russian origin, but I was born in Chile and educated in a convent as a Catholic.'

'You can change your religion, but not your race,' my grandmother observed. 'Are you in Europe visiting relatives?'

'My relatives were made into soap,' Ursula said almost glibly as if to warn my grandmother not to go too far.

As we talked, my grandfather sat there saying nothing, which only added to the unbearable tension. He still bore me a grudge for leaving Argentina twice and failing to inform him on both occasions.

When we were leaving, my grandmother said to me, 'Maybe I'll see you at La Madeleine for Mass on Sunday,' and then she whispered in my ear: 'Don't bring your friend.'

When I met her for Mass, she did not immediately mention Ursula, although I knew that sooner or later the subject would come up. But as soon as Mass was over and we stepped out into the street, she began.

'So how old is this Ursula?'

'You of all people know not to ask a lady her age.'

'I'm not asking her, I'm asking you.'

'She's a few years older than me,' I said vaguely.

'Well, whatever age she's told you she is, you can add on another ten. A lady will always make a little subtraction herself.'

'What does it matter what age she is?'

'Oh Marcelo, don't be ridiculous,' my grandmother said. 'Of course it matters. What about when you want to have children? Don't tell me age doesn't matter.'

'We don't want to have children.'

'I think the problem is that she can't have children, not that you don't want any.'

We walked on for a while in silence and then she said, 'How do you pay for all this? Do you have a job?'

'I have my savings from when I was working in Buenos Aires.'

'What savings? You spent more than you made. You always have.'

There was nothing I could say to that. I'd never had any money or saved any. Mercifully, she changed the subject entirely.

'You know who invited me to lunch? Florinda! You remember Florinda, don't you? Why don't you come? She'd love to see you. She still remembers you from her trip to Argentina when you were a child. You made quite an impression.'

She didn't need to tell me not to bring Ursula; it was clear she wasn't invited. Neither did she have to say that all this was a ploy to get me back into the fold, to see the error of my ways, and to stop mixing with undesirable people like Ursula.

In the company of my grandmother, I arrived at 72 Rue de Varenne, the home of Florinda 'Flor' Fernández de Anchorena, Marquise de Castellane. She came from a prominent Argentinian family who moved to Paris when she was a girl. She had married Georges de Castellane, war hero and son of the legendary Boni, Marquis de Castellane, and Anna Gould, the daughter of Jay Gould, the American financier and railroad king.

Flor greeted my grandmother effusively before introducing us to the other guests, among them Diane and Wanda de Guébriant, the latter a leading expert on the works of Henri Matisse. They were the daughters of the French Ambassador to Argentina, and I had met them at several parties in Argentina when we were all in our teens.

Please to see me, Diane asked me to accompany her to a dinner party the next day. Later that evening, when I told Ursula that I would be dining with some old friends, she was not at all pleased, but I finally wore her down and she released me for the evening. At dinner, I struck up a conversation with Dora Efthymios, a very attractive and elegant young lady whom I later took to the Chez Castel nightclub for one last drink. When I arrived back at Hôtel Brighton, late and drunk, Ursula was waiting up for me, demanding to know where I had been. I told her I had gone to a club on my own, but she didn't believe me. For a while, I thought that a relationship with Dora might become serious – she even wrote me love letters after our time in Paris – but it ended up being nothing more than a very short fling conducted behind Ursula's back. A decade later, Dora was in London staying at the Berkeley Hotel and I was reintroduced to her. I greeted her enthusiastically, but she had no recollection of me – or at least she pretended not to have. So much for love.

As for Ursula, I felt an increasing sense of relief whenever I was away from her and it was becoming clear to me that our days together were numbered.

20

A Roman Holiday

After just a few months in Paris, Ursula announced that we would be moving to Rome. This sudden and unforeseen decision may have had to do with the fact that I had made new friends in Paris and was feeling increasingly comfortable there, something she did not like to see. Alexis's warning and my grandmother's assessment of the situation had got through to me; I no longer believed in Ursula's financial solvency or her apartments. Nevertheless, I decided I was not going to miss out on a visit to Rome. We loaded our bags into her old second-hand Peugeot and made the 1,400-kilometre trip to the Park Hotel in the Roman suburb of Parioli.

On first impression, it was a cheap three-star hotel in a residential area, away from the sights – typical of Ursula, I thought. However, I soon realised that it was very well located.

'In Rome, the most glamorous and cultured people are called Pariolini, after this area,' she explained as though she had sensed my initial disappointment. She was right about that. Parioli was – is – one of the most elegant suburbs of Rome, mercifully distant from the city's hordes of tourists. Its tree-lined streets are dotted with elegant palaces and luxuriant gardens with a wonderful variety of plants in bloom. As ever, the first thing Ursula did, even before unpacking her cases, was take out her address book and immediately start making calls. By the time I got out of the shower, she had already planned the evening and, of course, gave me strict instructions on what I was to wear. This time, it was a silk shirt and a black velvet jacket.

It was seven o'clock when we arrived at Vermicino, near Frascati, and the residence of Barbara Hislop, which looked less like a real Italian palazzo and more like a Las Vegas recreation of one. Barbara was a wealthy Californian who, after recently divorcing her husband, was keen to make up for the lost time.

When we arrived at her house, she gave me a look of approval before kissing me firmly on the lips. She had known Ursula for a long time and they shared many of the same interests. Barbara's subscription to the spirit of Roman decadence, depicted in Fellini's *La Dolce Vita*, was obvious. In a world full of people wanting to move up the ladder doing as little as possible, just looking pretty was the norm. Cinecittà Film Studios were still booming, thanks to the continuing demand for spaghetti westerns, which made Rome a magnet for young, attractive aspiring actors willing to do anything to achieve fame. Lives were changed like that, and that was the case with Barbara's boyfriend, Sergio Banovic, a Yugoslav whose striking looks had won him supporting roles in movies. He could tell I was star-struck just being in Rome.

'Don't be fooled by all you see here,' he said in a world-weary voice. 'It's all fake.'

'What's fake?'

'Everything. A few streets away from here there's a jeweller who became rich selling fake Gucci Mariner chains, Cartier watches and bracelets. His copies are so good they're indistinguishable from the real thing.' He was determined to disillusion me about Rome and its decadent residents.

'Utterly disgraceful! What did you say the address of his shop was?' I quipped.

'But you should definitely get to Villa Borghese,' he went on, ignoring my little joke. 'That's where the action is if you want to meet men. You don't even have to try very hard, all you have to do is turn up, dress nicely, look a bit lost and they'll find you. I often go when I'm in financial need.'

It bothered me that he thought I would sell sex to men in a park, or that I would appreciate a friendly tip from one hustler to another. But of course, I was a young man who looked like he was being paid by an older woman for his company, which I was, just like he was. I never saw what I did as hustling in the way that he seemed to see it. I saw my relationship with Ursula as transactional. As it so happens, neither she nor anyone else ever paid me for sex.

A few days later we had dinner with Sergio and Barbara in an impossibly narrow cobblestone lane in Trastevere, where space was found for tables, diners, passers-by, and traffic; throughout the evening we had to move our chairs to allow passing cars through. For our arrangement to seem less obvious, Ursula had given me money in advance to pay for dinner, which I did, hoping it might sow some doubts in Sergio's mind about our relationship, as he probably thought it was as phoney as the Gucci Mariner chains he had warned me about.

After dinner, we headed to Caffè Domiziano in Piazza Navona where the crowd was impossibly *dolce vita*. Everyone was dressed in their finest and making sure they were seen. There were a lot of Pucci, Pierre Cardin, and other fashion labels on display, and the buttons of the men's silk shirts were undone to expose their hairy chests. This time I was proudly wearing my fake Cartier watch and an extra-long Gucci Mariner chain tied in a knot.

Sergio's deprecation of *la dolce vita* hadn't put me off and I was dazzled by the glamour of the place, despite the fake labels. We sat at the café with Helmut Berger, Visconti's favourite actor, Austrian actress Marisa Mell, and Argentinian actor Carlos Barbieri who accompanied Jennifer Bramble, all friends of both Ursula and Barbara. It was hard not to be seduced by all that glamour and beauty.

A man came over to the table, greeted Ursula with a kiss on both cheeks, and invited us to join his table. As we made our way over, Ursula explained that this was Emilio Pucci, the man who had revolutionised the world of fashion with his geometric prints. It was clear he was revered from the way that everyone in the café wanted to greet him. The atmosphere became tense when Pucci suddenly corrected what Sergio was telling me about the fountain used in the films *Three Coins in the Fountain* and *La Dolce Vita*. From then on, he ignored Sergio and I became the object of his attention, and while Barbara and Ursula chatted away, Sergio was left to lick his wounds in silence. As we left the bar, Ursula casually announced that she had arranged for me to have lunch at Barbara's the next day.

'She's eager to get to know you,' she added.

'But she already knows me. We just spent the whole evening together.'

'No, I mean to *really* get to know you.'

My mind boggled. What did Barbara want from me? The only thing I could offer was sex. What else could she possibly want?

The invitation itself was strangely formal and accompanied by a series of explicit instructions. A message was left at the hotel for me, asking me to arrive at her house promptly at 12.30 p.m., not a minute sooner or later.

I walked around the baking streets of Vermicino so as not to be early, working up a sweat as I did so, and arrived at the appointed time, happy to get out of the sun. A maid in a blue uniform opened the door. She was very informal and broke into a knowing smile when I introduced myself as though she knew exactly what was to come. 'Signora Hislop is waiting for you,' she said.

I followed her, almost skating across that gleaming, polished, white marble floor. We arrived at a garden designed in a geometric maze that reminded me of the garden in *Last Year at Marienbad*. After negotiating a row of delicately trimmed pine trees, we came across a marble fountain fed by a jet of water from the open mouth of a bronze ogre. Next to the statue, a topless Barbara lay on a sun lounger, the bottom part of her bikini so minimal that at first I thought she was wearing nothing. It was pretty clear that it was indeed sex for which I had been summoned; there was no pretence it was for anything else. Doing away with any small talk, Barbara offered me a drink, which I accepted, and that was it.

Like Ursula, Barbara took the initiative. Beckoning me towards her, she proceeded to kiss me – a sloppy, aggressive exercise. After a while, she unromantically pushed me away, wiped her mouth with the back of her hand, and got up. She covered herself with a camisole and, slipping into her golden heels, she made her way back to the house, with me trotting after her like a slave. When we entered the bedroom, nothing seemed to go her way.

'You're so Catholic,' she said accusingly.

When I returned to the hotel later, Ursula asked me how my afternoon had been, but from the hints she dropped, I realised she had already spoken to Barbara and knew everything.

That night, we went to Jennifer Bramble's party at Vicolo del Leopardo in Trastevere. It was held on a terrace at the top of her three-storey house. The eccentric, upper-class English woman had a reputation for surrounding herself almost exclusively with gay men. Talking with a lisp and grossly overweight, she floated around in an ankle-length kaftan, her trademark.

I had never seen so many men in one place: twenty, thirty, more … I lost count! In this sea of men, I spotted Carlos Barbieri whom I had met at the Caffè Domiziano on my first night. He was a relatively famous actor, known as the Argentinian Tab Hunter; with his athletic build and powerful presence, he was hard to miss. Born in Argentina to Italian parents, he lived in Rome, and although he and Jennifer did not live under the same roof, they were lovers, which was a talking point in itself. They made such an odd couple that people wondered if she had cast a spell over him. I didn't know him personally, I just knew him from his films in Argentina, and when I was introduced to him, I found him to be polite and down to earth. We got on immediately and soon became friends. I wanted someone reliable to guide me around Rome and show me secret places that I would not find on my own. I subsequently saw him often at the Caffè Domiziano, and he always spared a moment to catch up.

At the same party, Ursula introduced me to Eric Hebborn, an English artist friend and owner of the Pannini Galleries. He had moved to Italy because homosexuality was illegal in England and he lived openly with his boyfriend, Graham Smith, in the villa San Filippo in Anticoli Corrado, outside Rome. His home was impressive and boasted a wide range of Old Master sketches and paintings – the only other time I had seen so many drawings by major artists was in Rodolfo Pizarro's studio. Our paths crossed many times over the years and we ended up working together.

Eric had his eye on me from the start, and later on in the evening, he said he'd like to get in touch. Ignoring his request, I tried to discuss art with him but he kept moving the conversation on to more personal matters. Thinking that I'd skilfully avoided his advances, I was irritated when, as we were leaving, I heard Ursula reassuring him that she could arrange for him to meet me in private. That night I finally lost my temper, telling her I was not a sex object; she couldn't just lend me out on a whim without even consulting me first. Ursula ignored every word I said. My outburst simply seemed to amuse her.

As much as Ursula liked to party, she had her limits. One night, we tried to get into Number One, a club on the Via Veneto, near the US embassy. It was a club run by Marisa Mell's boyfriend, Pier Luigi Torri, and was notoriously difficult to get into. We were eventually only allowed in after Marisa's intervention. She took us to the VIP room where we saw the usual princesses, playboys, and models, most of whom were quite openly consuming drugs and indulging in one sexual fantasy or another. It looked like an orgy in Ancient Rome in progress. Some of them were having sex in the velvet-covered armchairs, up against walls, or wherever they found themselves, while others danced with eyes popping out of their sockets. Although I wasn't shocked, I had never seen anything quite like it. As liberal as Ursula was, she didn't like to lose control and didn't like seeing people quite so undignified. Shortly after arriving, she decided to call it a night and we never set foot in the place again.

Rome's heatwave was unbearable that year. There hadn't been the slightest breeze all summer, so we decided to go to Tuscany, along with Barbara and Sergio, to find some fresher air. After a two-hour drive in Ursula's dilapidated Peugeot, we arrived at Il Pellicano, the most elegant hotel in Porto Ercole. Even the car park screamed wealth. There were the Rolls-Royces, the Ferraris, and the Lamborghinis, and in the middle, Ursula's battered Peugeot.

After checking in, Ursula and I followed the porter to a double room. That came as a relief as I was beginning to wonder if she might have booked all four of us into one room. Once we'd unpacked, we all met for lunch, the two women whispering conspiratorially as usual. Then Barbara turned to Sergio.

'I don't think you've been to the islands of Giglio or Giannutri have you?' she said as if reading from a badly rehearsed script.

'Who are you talking to?' he asked.

Me with Ursula Mahler at the swimming pool of Hotel il Pellicano, Porto Ercole, Tuscany, 1971

'I'm talking to you, Sergio. They say those islands are beautiful. Or the countryside around Maremma.'

'Those medieval villages are really something,' added Ursula, with as wooden a delivery as Barbara's.

Sergio got their very unsubtle hint that he should make himself scarce, and without expressing any enthusiasm for either suggestion, he finished his drink, went upstairs, got dressed, and twenty minutes later, reappeared to announce that he was taking the ferry to Giglio 'to see what all the fuss is all about.'

As soon as he left, the atmosphere changed, though a performance of sorts continued. I went for a dip in the pool and returned to our room later on. What happened next is nobody's business and I'm not such a cad as to reveal it.

When Sergio returned, he said nothing about what he must have known had taken place in his absence, and instead waxed lyrical about Giglio, suggesting that we all go on a trip there together. Barbara, who took about as much notice of Sergio's opinions as Ursula did of mine, listened to the account of his day trip with little interest. Needless to say, we never went to Giglio.

Ursula was always arranging things behind my back and never revealed her plans until the very last moment. One evening, some friends of hers appeared at the pool and suddenly we were six. Joe Abulafia and his wife, Prouset, lived in Geneva, and once I got over my annoyance at not being informed of their arrival, I enjoyed their company. Joe was a flashy character who wore a gold Rolex watch and open silk shirts and had an eccentric bouffant hairdo that looked like a wig. He drove a red Lamborghini and regularly supervised and micromanaged the process of polishing the sixty spokes of each of the car's wheels. Everything about him screamed money and midlife crisis at the same time, but I found him likeable. He had made his money in the textile business in Manchester and then became a tax exile in Switzerland. Despite his garish tastes, he was also a cultured man and he treated everyone with courtesy. He also had the good manners never to hint that he knew I was no more than a kept man.

When I told him that I was Argentinian, he mentioned having played polo at Bagatelle. I was so used to people lying about their lives and their achievements that I called my friend Jimmy Dodero, a regular on the French circuit, to verify what Joe said. His story checked out – he was indeed a member of the Bagatelle Polo Club although he had played polo with the sole intention of entering the social scene. Nothing new there, but Joe Abulafia was not a fraud. I began to trust him, but maybe too much.

The next day was muggy, so we decided to head to Porto Santo Stefano for dinner. We stopped at the wonderful Il Moletto restaurant facing the sea, where we had risotto with Norway lobsters al limone, the house speciality, all washed down with several bottles of Pinot Grigio. Joe snatched the hefty bill from the waiter's hand and then proceeded to count out the cash, note by note, on the table as we delicately looked away. After dinner, we went to La Strega discotheque until around 3 a.m. After a short walk, Joe suggested that I come with him in his Lamborghini, relegating his wife to Ursula's old Peugeot with the other three. He sped off through the streets of Porto Santo Stefano, violating all traffic rules, to join the narrow, tight, curvy road that skirted the side of the mountain, the precipice on one side getting higher and higher.

Rather than try and temper his driving, I stupidly encouraged him. For no apparent reason, Joe sang 'My Darling Clementine' on a loop as he sped along, faking a Southern American accent and not getting much further than the chorus:

'Oh my darling, oh my darling
Oh my darling, Clementine
You are lost and gone forever
Dreadful sorrow, Clementine ...'

That was the soundtrack to what followed, which I can only recall in a series of vivid flashbacks. The Lamborghini skidded off the edge while taking a sharp bend at high speed, landing sideways with a loud thud on a protruding rock. We both remained silent for a moment. Then, after a minute or so, Joe asked, 'Are you alright?'

'I'm fine,' I replied.

Joe opened his door, which was level with the road, and climbed out as if emerging from a submarine. He mumbled something as he held out his hand to pull me out. Ursula arrived a few minutes later in her car and became almost hysterical. She began crying and told me how much she loved me. I had never seen her in such a state. I didn't know she was capable of such emotion. We waited for a recovery vehicle by the side of the road from where we watched the sunrise.

The next day, after lunch, Ursula and I returned to Rome as planned. Following the previous night's incident, I was nervous about her driving and was relieved when we arrived. The summer was over, and Ursula decided that Buenos Aires in springtime would be better than spending the winter in Europe. In mid-November, we travelled to Cannes and boarded the SS *Eugenio C* for Buenos Aires. Despite not wanting to return to Argentina, I enjoyed the sea voyage. I met many interesting people on that ship, including women who I later met up with in Buenos Aires, behind Ursula's back, of course.

Once back in Buenos Aires, my family wasted no time in informing me that Ursula was not welcome in their home, that theirs was a decent house and visitors were not accepted 'without a good reference'. Their language became more uncompromising as time went on. At Christmas, my mother said, 'Don't you dare bring that whore into this house.' Once again, I was the black sheep forced to graze in other pastures. But it gave me a good excuse not to see Ursula often, offering me a well-deserved break after the intensity of those months in Europe.

When I saw Linley again, she was outraged that I'd come back with Ursula.

'I told you to air your dirty laundry abroad where no one knows you, and what do you do? You come back with that woman and parade around the city hand in hand with her.'

I told her it wasn't my idea to return but Ursula's, that she'd wanted to spend the warm months in Argentina. I realised it sounded pathetic and showed just how little control I had over my own life, a life that revolved around nothing but the whims and sexual needs of this woman. 'You do realise that, given the slightest chance, she'd leave you for someone else, someone even more convenient,' Linley said, and of course, I knew it was true. For Ursula, our relationship had always been transactional. Even when we'd walked hand in hand on the street, it was so she could show me off; she loved people staring at us, struck by the age difference. It was transactional for me too, partly because I enjoyed the life that the relationship afforded me, and because I didn't mind making love to her friends. But while I can't say that I ever did anything against my will, it was all becoming increasingly stifling.

To get away from the heat in Buenos Aires, we went to Punta del Este on the Uruguayan coast where Ursula had rented a flat in a modern complex. Shortly after we got there, I told her I had to go back to Buenos Aires to see the dentist for a filling. It was a short ferry ride from there across the River Plate to Buenos Aires. 'I'll be right back, darling,' were my last words to her. I had no intention of coming back or ever seeing her again.

It was the first time in my life I had managed to save some money. So I decided it was time for me to travel alone, and England would be the best place to do it.

21

The Heiresses

In 1971, before arriving in Hamburg to start work for Atti Darboven, his German sponsor, Luis visited London to see Lucy Pearson, wanting to ensure her interest in him didn't wane before she became an adult. She was now seventeen, just a year away from having access to that trust fund.

He arrived at Heathrow in the morning and they met for tea. He needn't have worried as her infatuation hadn't diminished one iota. She spoke with teenage naivety of her devotion to him, and he responded accordingly, telling her of his passion for her and how much he thought about her when he was away, and urging her to be patient. An hour later they said goodbye and, brief as it was, his mission had been accomplished. He could put his mind at rest for another few months.

His work on the Darboven estate was not strenuous. His main function was to look after the horses while participating in low-handicap tournaments, most of which were held in Germany. He stood out in Northern Europe because of his dark exotic appearance and was a breath of fresh air for Hamburg's bored housewives. He made sure to take advantage of their interest.

Luis, who was naturally good at languages, got a chance to improve his German, something that was to pay dividends later. He even started reading the German papers and it was in one of them that he learned about the marriage of Christina Onassis to Joseph Bolker, a middle-aged Californian businessman. He could hardly believe it. Hadn't Christina wept bitterly when he left her not so long ago? He got on the phone with her and, in a rare reversal of roles, demanded an explanation. She told him she was free to do as she pleased, that she and Joseph were very much in love. He began calling her all the time, becoming such a pest that she threatened to call the police if he persisted. It made him even more determined to marry Lucy Pearson as soon as she came of age.

Christina's marriage to Joseph was doomed from the start, like so many of her relationships. She confided to Fiona Thyssen, her brother Alexander's girlfriend, that although Joe was a decent and honourable man and they were genuinely fond of each other, they both knew the marriage was a big mistake. It was another consequence of Christina's impetuousness. The marriage played out much like Luis thought it would if it had been him who had married Christina – her father went to great lengths to end it and eventually threatened to disinherit her. Soon after the wedding in Las Vegas, she filed for divorce. According to her, it was to avert the vengeance her furious father vowed to take on Joe.

'I'm too Greek and he's too Beverly Hills,' she told the press, but what she really meant was 'I don't want to be disinherited.'

To put the whole thing behind her, she decided to go to Argentina, almost certainly to see Luis. After a brief stopover in Rio de Janeiro for the Carnival, she arrived in Buenos Aires at the end of February 1972. Luis was back in Argentina at the time, scouting for horses for the forthcoming German season. Christina stayed with her friend Marina Dodero, and no sooner had she arrived than she went to call on Luis. She found herself at a modest block of flats, very much at odds with Luis's tales of his aristocratic background and family wealth.

By this time, his grandfather Vincenzo had died and Aunt Ada had sold the house in Flores and was living in a tiny apartment in Recoleta, 'a shoe box', according to Luis, 'but in the right part of town'. Christina rang the intercom and Ada answered. Thinking it was one of Luis's many unwanted former girlfriends, Aunt Ada told the voice at the other end that she was not welcome. Luis was there but sleeping off a hangover after a long night of clubbing. Undeterred, Christina eventually got hold of him on the telephone. 'I'm surprised to hear from you,' he said. 'Last time we spoke, you threatened to call the police.'

He agreed to meet her at La Biela and a few days later, Luis picked her up to take her to his friend's *hacienda* for the weekend. The property was outside the city with playing fields and a pool by which Christina was invited to relax, enjoy the barbecues, and watch a polo tournament. But this wasn't enough for the spoilt and impulsive Christina. She insisted on riding a pony even though she didn't know how to ride. Not able to control the animal, it bolted and jumped over a wire fence. She fell, luckily landing in a water trough. Although wet through and scared, she emerged without severe injury – just two broken fingernails and bruised ribs – after which she didn't ask to ride any more. On her return to the city, Christina was surprised to be met by a horde of reporters outside Marina's flat. She had purposely taken the precaution of travelling anonymously and not staying at a hotel so she could remain so; it was the ever-disloyal Luis who had alerted the press because he wanted them to write about him and Christina to help raise his profile, something he would make a habit of. Over the two weeks Christina spent in Argentina, her relationship with Luis was momentarily rekindled, the 'couple' appearing on the front pages of most newspapers in Argentina, and reporters and photographers popping up every time they stepped out together, all carefully managed by Luis. Somehow Justine, who was back in New York, didn't find out about this reunion, or if she did, decided to ignore it.

It was during this trip that I met Christina for the first time. I had left Ursula in Punta del Este and spent a few weeks in Buenos Aires before leaving for London. I saw Christina several times during her stay in Argentina, mostly at nightclubs or parties. Marina Dodero organised dinner parties for her, and I was always a guest. Luis made sure that people he wanted to impress in some way were invited, often other polo players who could give him something in return. We usually went to Le Club, which was a fashionable discotheque at the time. Christina loved to dance, and she dragged whoever was to hand on to the dance floor with her. It was both charming and somewhat annoying as she especially loved to dance to slow records. I danced with her cheek to cheek many times. I always felt there was something desperate in the way she kept such a tight grip on me like she was hanging on for dear life.

It was obvious she had a longing for affection that was never satisfied. I saw first-hand her need to be loved, to go through the motions of love, probably because she'd been starved of it growing up. One night when we sat down after dancing, we held hands and made eyes at each other; for a moment, it felt like we were the only two people in the room. It seemed very intense until the music started up again; then she went back to the dance floor with someone else. We had dinner together a few times, just the two of us, but whatever spark had been there that day was never rekindled.

22

An Escort in London

I arrived at Heathrow on the evening of 12 March 1972 and took a cab to what would become my temporary residence for the next two weeks, a run-down hotel in Sussex Gardens, near Paddington Station, an area infested with prostitutes and lowlifes. The stamp on my passport allowed me to stay for three months, though I only had funds for a few weeks – the money I'd stolen from Ursula would soon run out.

As a precaution, I had left a painting with Linley, *The Beheading of John the Baptist*, which my mother had put in storage as she considered it in bad taste. Rodolfo had confirmed that it was a copy of a famous work by Caravaggio on display in St John's Co-Cathedral in Valletta, Malta. My plan was to sell it once I had an address in London to where Linley could ship it.

I started looking for a job almost as soon as I arrived, but what could I do? I was twenty-six and apart from a stint as a salesman of bronze ingots for headstones, I'd never had a proper job. I had brought with me a letter from my long-suffering grandfather who, along with many other things, was President of the Argentinian

Banking Association, and in that capacity had met Dennis Mitchell, Vice-Chairman of Lloyds Bank International when Mitchell had attended an international banking conference in Argentina. So the day after I arrived, I dressed smartly and went to Lloyds' head office in Victoria. I marched up to reception and told the woman behind the desk that Dennis Mitchell was waiting for me, which of course was a lie. After a long wait, I was led to his office, where he greeted me politely but with evident puzzlement. I informed him I had given his name as a reference when applying to open a bank account.

'Thank you for letting me know!' he snapped, not at all impressed.

I handed him the letter my grandfather had given me and asked him whether it might be possible for me to be considered for the bank's training programme, failing to tell him that I was on a three-month tourist visa and didn't have a work permit. He made some polite noises before escorting me to the door. Looking back on that moment, I don't know what I was thinking. At the time, I considered myself very resourceful. I had never applied for a job and wasn't sure how to go about it, but I naively thought that my letter of introduction would be enough and that any other procedures would be dispensed with, just like it was in Argentina. Three days later, I called to find out if there was any news, but his secretary informed me that 'Mr Mitchell' was not available. Mr Mitchell, it turned out, would never be available to take my calls.

By this time, it was clear to me that the only talent I had to offer the world was my good looks, and I began actively searching for my next 'client'. I called Luis who recommended that I make contact with Countess Jellicoe, known as Patsy to her friends. He rang her from Hamburg to recommend me, talking me up as a well-behaved house guest and alluding to my other 'qualities'.

'She'll inspect you from top to bottom,' he told me. 'It's up to you to pay for your accommodation in whatever way seems appropriate.'

I duly phoned Lady Jellicoe and could tell she had already been briefed by Luis. She asked me if I was free that evening, which of course I was. I arrived at a three-storey house in Chapel Street,

Zsa Zsa Gabor (far left) crowning the beauty queen at Oxfam Maytime Fair. With J. Paul Getty (to the right of the 'queen') and me (far right), Dorchester Hotel, London, 16 May 1972.

Belgravia. A maid opened the door and led me to a large room on the first floor. Countess Jellicoe was sitting in a red and white striped armchair. She had just turned fifty-five but she looked older. She was very slim, and had inquisitive eyes and a large unattractive nose which gave her a witch-like look. On a small Queen Anne table next to her was what appeared to be a generous gin and tonic.

She looked me up and down, as Luis had said she would, before extending her hand. 'So, you're Marcelo. Luis has told me a lot about you.'

'Has he really? I hope it was all good.'

She waited a moment and half smiled to herself as if I had intruded on a private joke. Then she invited me to sit down. We chatted for a while: Where was I staying? What did I think of London? The weather came up in conversation, which I discovered was a topic that English people always discussed in a way that generally stated the obvious, providing an opportunity for everyone to agree. It must have been desperation, or over-confidence in what had become my profession, that prompted me to make the first move.

'I'd like to take you out for dinner,' I said, interrupting the small talk. 'That is if you're free.'

As I didn't know the city, it was she who chose a fashionable Italian restaurant in the area, and I found myself in that rather unenviable position of having to watch every single thing I ordered, calculating the prices and making excuses: I'd had a late lunch, I wasn't very hungry, and so on. She may well have understood; indeed she was also restrained when ordering. However, she was very thin, so she probably never ate much anyway. In the end, I had enough to cover the dinner and even a small tip.

'In this country we don't tip. It's considered vulgar,' she said, though I had a feeling the waiter would not have agreed with her. 'Even the word is vulgar. Do you know what the word "tip" also means?'

I didn't, and she explained: 'It's where you dump your rubbish.'

I happily retrieved the measly tip I had left in order not to offend her, and we went back to her house for a last drink. A couple of hours went by when she suddenly looked at the clock. 'You're welcome to spend the night if you don't mind sharing my bed,' she announced.

Once I made it to the bedroom, or to the business that normally takes place in the bedroom, I felt very much at ease. I knew the script and was supremely confident. Her bedroom was spacious, with a dressing table at one end, a sofa at the other, and a large portrait of a woman, who she told me was her mother-in-law, right opposite her bed, though I couldn't understand why she wanted her ex-husband's mother to look down on her from the wall. We both undressed and climbed into bed. 'Now let's rest,' she said, 'we can continue talking tomorrow.'

In the morning, I opened my eyes to see her get dressed. A deplorable spectacle!

'You can move into this house if you like,' she said. 'You see, I'm divorced and need someone to attend parties with. And by the way, you can call me Patsy.' She didn't wait for an answer, just (rightly) assumed that I would be moving in, though for the record I did agree to pay rent – the princely sum of £10 a week.

'Now get dressed and go down to the kitchen,' she went on. 'The maid will make breakfast for you. After that, you can bring your luggage.'

The maid's name was María. She served me coffee, hard-boiled eggs, toast, and a generous helping of moral judgement. While she was cooking, she burnt her fingers and exclaimed '¡La puta madre!', giving away her Spanish origins. I told her I was from Argentina and Lady Jellicoe's new lodger.

'A lodger!' she repeated incredulously.

'I'm going to be taking one of the rooms here.'

'That woman is a whore!' María said, getting right to the point. 'She brings men back to the house to sleep with them. These English women are all whores!'

Ever chivalrous, I came to Lady Jellicoe's defence, telling the maid that she had attended a convent school with my mother and repeating that I was a paying guest.

'Oh, so that's why you spent the night in her bed,' she said sarcastically. She saw right through my barefaced lie. 'It would only have taken a few minutes to make up a bed in the spare room. Paying guest my ass! She's English, for goodness' sake!'

Patricia was only English on her mother's side. Her father was Irish and she was born and brought up in Shanghai. Despite María's condemnation, which she never failed to reiterate, the arrangement worked to the benefit of both of us. Countess Jellicoe had a busy and intense social schedule, and having a male escort was essential for her. Her wide range of contacts included various South Americans, including María Luisa Lobo Ryan who, within a few days of my arrival, invited her, and therefore me, for dinner at her huge house in Thurloe Square.

Our Cuban hostess came from an old Jewish family that had changed its original name of Wolf to the Spanish equivalent, Lobo. Her father had been the greatest of Cuba's sugar barons, and when Fidel Castro came to power, he left the island with his family and most of his colossal fortune intact.

The Lobo Ryan house was the place in London to meet anyone who was anyone in the Hispanic world. Among her guests were Anastasio, son of Nicaraguan dictator Anastasio 'Tachito' Somoza; the niece of the president of Panama, Arnulfo Arias; Alegría Moscoso Plaza, the niece of Ecuador's president, Galo Plaza; the Ortiz Patiño brothers, grandchildren of Bolivian tin king Antenor Patiño, and others of the same ilk.

Although the English guests were a minority that night, I was seated next to a rather pretentious Englishman.

'Charles Wilson is my name. I work in advertising,' he announced, shaking my hand.

'Marcelo Manrique de Acuña,' I replied, which seemed to leave him very unsatisfied.

'In this country, when you introduce yourself, you say your name and describe your occupation,' he said.

'I'm sorry, I didn't realise. I've only just arrived in this country. But I'm afraid I have no occupation to describe.'

'You must have some occupation.'

'I really don't.'

'Well, what did you do before coming here?'

'I didn't do anything there either,' I answered defiantly.

This seemed to frustrate the man no end. He clearly wanted to know if I was worth having a conversation with or whether he would be better off spending his time talking to someone else. It was something I noticed that people consistently did at these gatherings.

I also escorted Patsy to a cocktail party at the home of Mary, Duchess of Roxburghe, ex-wife of the 11th Duke, at 15 Hyde Park Gardens, overlooking the Park. It was there that I met the woman who would change the course of my life. As I conversed with Clare, Duchess of Sutherland, whom I had just met, a woman came over to greet her and remained silently standing next to us until the Duchess eventually introduced her.

'Marcelo, this is Lady Edith Foxwell,' she said with obvious reluctance.

I remembered Lady Jellicoe's advice not to kiss women's hands. She had told me it was vulgar, like tipping, so I shook Edith's instead.

Born Lady Edith Sybil Lambart, she was the daughter of the 9th Earl of Cavan and Adelaide Douglas Randolph, an American heiress. Edith's gleaming red hair matched her vivacious personality, and she had a great physical presence; with her deep blue eyes and pale complexion, she was the quintessential English rose. She was also an eccentric, and I was fascinated by her the moment she included herself in our conversation.

During the ensuing talk, Edith gradually monopolised me to the point that Clare began to feel uncomfortable. 'I'm going to powder my nose,' she announced and never came back.

As soon as we were left on our own, Edith said, 'I have a daughter who I think you might like.'

'How can you know what I'd like? You've only just met me.'

'Something tells me that you might like her.'

'Maybe it's you that I like.'

We were interrupted by her husband, Ivan Foxwell, a relatively successful film producer who had been drinking too much and it showed. He arrived to sound the retreat with little more than a gesture. As soon as he'd turned his back on her, Edith planted a kiss on my lips and asked for my number.

Just as she left, I was approached by another woman. 'Are you the one from Argentina?' she asked.

'I am. However, I'm not the only one. There are lots of us.'

She looked at me for a moment, not knowing whether I was joking or not. 'No, I meant here – at this party. I heard there was someone here from Argentina.'

Clearly, my attempt at English humour had not worked. This lady's name was Patricia, the Hon. Mrs Vere Harmsworth, and we engaged in the usual small talk.

'What brings you to England?' she asked.

I had learned by this time that I should say something – anything – about an occupation or purpose in life.

'I'm an art dealer,' I said, as usual. 'I specialise in Old Masters.'

'Interesting!' was her uninterested response, and once we overcame that formality, she got down to business. 'I'm having a party for Princess Margaret in a couple of weeks. Would you like to come?'

I responded with a big Yes, not knowing that she was the most celebrated hostess in London and that her parties were legendary. Patricia, known as 'Bubbles', was a vivacious, larger-than-life, former Rank starlet and she became my next mentor. Bubbles advised me how to move in these circles, what to say, what not to say, what to wear (she detested all the gleaming jackets that Ursula had selected for me), how to greet people, what flowers to send a hostess after a party to convey the right message ('nothing which may seem romantic, nothing ostentatious'). She enjoyed her role, and I enjoyed mine, playing the slightly naive younger man who needed to be shown the ropes.

Me with Lady Edith Foxwell at her house in Sherston, 1973

So after only a few weeks in London, I had not one but three ladies who I divided my time between, though it was Edith who I was most interested in. Patsy thankfully wasn't home most times when Edith telephoned. It gave us the chance to chat unrestrainedly (albeit with María listening in and making her opinion known). Edith eventually invited me to spend the weekend at her country house in Sherston, Wiltshire. Patsy had already told me about the Elizabethan manor house in the Cotswolds where the Foxwells entertained their aristocratic friends and people from the world of entertainment. Naturally, I accepted on the spot.

She picked me up late one Friday afternoon in her Range Rover, and when we arrived at the entrance to the house, I got out to open the gates. The metallic clang and the sound of the Rover's tyres on the gravel alerted a dog to our arrival, and he started barking. It got louder and louder, echoing across the courtyard, sounding more and more fearsome. I panicked, thinking that some huge guard dog was about to tear me to shreds, and I jumped onto the bonnet of the car, but as I looked down, I saw a very excited dachshund wagging its tail. Edith wouldn't stop laughing, and I had to endure hearing the story over and over again all weekend.

Both the impressive Tudor house and the dog had been wedding presents from Lady Edith's husband, Ivan. Although he'd been unsettled by the attention his wife had paid me at Mary Roxburghe's party, he chose to spend that weekend in London with his actress girlfriend. The house was surrounded by a couple of acres of meadow, a swimming pool, and stables. Edith had a show horse that was her pride and joy, although it never won a prize.

Over the weekend, Edith and I hid our nightly encounters so as not to make her friends accomplices in our affair. She would sneak into my room in the early hours, but during the day, we did our best to restrain our mutual desire. In any case, the news that Edith was having an affair with a young Argentinian became common knowledge, and no one wanted to be involved in the scandal.

When I returned to Chapel Street, Patsy wasn't in a very good mood, partly because Edith hadn't invited her for the weekend and partly because she hadn't been invited to Bubbles Harmsworth's upcoming party for Princess Margaret. She had merely served as a messenger when Bubbles called to confirm my invitation. I had no choice but to act like a victim of circumstances, telling Patsy that I'd accepted the invitations in order not to be rude and because I'd assumed she had been invited too.

'You obviously knew I wasn't invited to the Foxwells this weekend,' she said accusingly.

'I only found out when I didn't see you there. What could I do? Return to London immediately?' I replied.

Although we didn't return to the subject, tension hung in the air between us. From that moment on, I kept my encounters with Lady

Edith secret. I didn't want to fall out with her, and I especially didn't want to have to move out of her house. My newly printed business cards from Smythson of Bond Street, which I was giving out left, right, and centre, had her Belgravia address and phone number on them. Even more importantly, it was the address to which the 'Caravaggio' was being sent. Edith wasn't happy about me living with Patsy in Belgravia; she hated the idea of sharing me. In the short time I had been in England, my life had become ridiculously complicated.

I made my way to Eaton Square for the Harmsworth party dressed to kill. I was wearing a dinner jacket rented from Moss Bros, the renowned dress-wear outlet for formal occasions. As I walked along the square looking for the address, I was approached by a man.

'You're not going to Bubbles Harmsworth's party by any chance?' he enquired.

'I am, though I'm a bit lost.'

'You're not as lost as you think,' he said and invited me to accompany him. There was something familiar about this man, but I couldn't put my finger on it. He was English, in his forties, and wore a pair of thick glasses. He had a very serious, almost dour expression, yet there was a cheeky air about him.

'How do you know her?' he asked as we made our way to her house together.

'I don't really know her. I've just arrived in London,' I said. 'How do you know her?'

I never got an answer. When we arrived at her house at 86 Eaton Square we separated. Two footmen stood at the door, and just behind them was our host, the owner of the *Daily Mail*, the Hon. Vere Harmsworth, in a shimmering black velvet dinner jacket that Ursula would have approved of. I could see that all eyes were on my new friend and I wondered who he was. Then, through the crowd came the guest of honour, Princess Margaret, waving her cigarette holder. 'Peter!' she exclaimed, making a beeline for him, totally oblivious to the hot ash she was scattering on anyone between her and this man I'd arrived with. She greeted him with a kiss, and it was only then I realised he was Peter Sellers. I waited in line to be introduced to her Royal Highness, but she stopped before she got to me and took Peter Sellers off to the party.

I stayed by the entrance, suddenly feeling awkward. Eventually, I followed a waiter carrying a tray of drinks and snatched a glass from him. As soon as I drank it, I wanted another and then another. Not knowing anybody, my tactic was to approach people on their own or who looked lost like myself. This led to my meeting with the indomitable Lord Simon Erleigh, the rightful heir to the Marquess of Reading, who disarmed me with his charm. The next person I introduced myself to was the great Spanish portraitist Alejo Vidal-Quadras, who had painted Winston Churchill. I didn't tell him I was a dealer in Old Masters, just that I was an Argentinian visiting London.

When dinner was announced, we sat at round tables of eight, our names displayed on handwritten cards in sterling silver holders. To my surprise, I was seated at the hostess's table with Princess Margaret's husband, Lord Snowdon, American film producer Ray Stark, and Peter Sellers. The conversation was practically monopolised by Ray Stark, except for the occasional humorous interjection from Sellers. It helped me to feel less excluded; those two did all the talking, everyone else's role being merely to laugh at Seller's jokes or marvel at Stark's accomplishments. The filmmaker was in London following the release of *Fat City* and had been invited to the party at the suggestion of Snowdon, who needed the producer's help with his upcoming TV documentary.

Having been ignored by Sellers for the best part of the evening, I was pleasantly surprised when he later approached and asked if I would like to join him at Tramp, which, he explained, was a discotheque. I was delighted.

I assumed we'd be going together, but he told me he'd meet me there as he had to 'pick up some cats first' – his way of describing women. When I arrived at the club in Jermyn Street and gave my name, the receptionist informed me that Mr Sellers was running late.

Instead, the proprietor, Johnny Gold, welcomed me with a member's application form and told me to make myself at home.

Favoured by film stars, politicians, and even members of the royal family, the club had opened its doors a couple of years earlier to become London's answer to Studio 54, emulating the policy of no dress code – it was common to see people in dinner jackets dancing next to men in shorts and tennis shoes – and was an alternative to Annabel's, the more formal members club in Berkeley Square. In any case, Sellers never turned up, but I had a great time, and Tramp became a regular haunt for me, and for Luis when he was in town.

I was delighted with the whirlwind of parties I had been invited to since meeting Patsy and all the introductions that came with them. But there always seemed to be ulterior motives behind these courtesies; yet again, I felt like I was being passed around. 'Oh, you must meet so-and-so. He's the owner of …', or 'She's the daughter of the Duke of …', or 'He's the Chairman of …'. It was never about someone being nice, attractive, or intelligent; it was always what they possessed or what there was to be gained by meeting them. Of course, I had often been like that myself, or worse, but it was around that time that I started looking for something else in life, something more meaningful.

Meanwhile, the rivalry between Patsy and Edith was heating up and it worried me. I couldn't take sides as they had both been so kind to me. It was thanks to Patsy that I'd met Edith in the first place, as well as Bubbles Harmsworth and all the connections and invitations that came from them. My arrangement with Patsy was more than reasonable as she only charged me ten pounds a week for rent, and I gave her 'extra entertainment', a small price to pay for the number of people I met through her. Therefore, I tried to make Patsy feel as though she was the special one, the real object of my desire, taking her out for dinner, paying her compliments, and making sure that I kept her happy in the bedroom.

However, it came as something of a relief when Patsy announced that she would be going to Iran for a week to lecture on Middle and

Far Eastern Art. Patsy was supposedly an expert on the subject, but the truth was that she gave the same talk over and over again wherever she went. I was so happy at the prospect of a week of freedom that I helped her with her luggage and paid the taxi fare to Heathrow. Now I would have Patsy's house all to myself.

On my return from the airport, I moved into Patsy's bedroom and brought Edith with me. Of course, María couldn't help but notice this intruder and made her feelings known without uttering a word, just tutting and avoiding eye contact.

The morning after Patsy's return from Iran, María knocked on her door at nine in the morning as usual, but this time, she didn't bring the breakfast tray with her. Instead, she came close to the bed, holding something between her thumb and forefinger.

'Look at this,' she said.

Patsy looked but could see nothing. 'What is it?'

'Look!' María insisted.

'What are you talking about, María? There's nothing there.'

María grabbed Lady Jellicoe's glasses from the bedside table and handed them to her. Then Patsy saw what it was: a copper-coloured pubic hair.

'This is the hair I found in your bed, Lady Jellicoe,' María said. 'Your lodger has been sleeping with that red-haired woman while you were away.'

'Here?' Patsy exclaimed. 'In this bed?'

'Yes, in this bed!'

Patsy shuffled around and looked down at the bed. 'I hope you changed the sheets.'

María had purposely not changed the sheets in order to make her revelation all the more dramatic. 'I didn't have time to make the bed,' she said.

'Well, make sure you find time,' Patsy said and asked her to bring breakfast and the morning paper as if nothing much had happened.

Patsy's revenge came at the homecoming party she'd organised for herself. At one point in the evening, she called me over and introduced me to an attractive woman called Zena Marshall who had worked on some of the Bond films and, more significantly, was Ivan Foxwell's girlfriend.

'Marcelo is the young Argentinian who is sleeping with Edith Foxwell,' Patsy explained, knowing Zena would convey the news to Ivan.

Patsy's move was only too successful. Edith and Ivan divorced shortly after. Edith left her marital home to live in her manor house in Sherston while I stayed in London at Lady Jellicoe's house. Despite all this, Edith and Patsy never stopped being friends.

23
The Heiress Comes of Age

It was Saturday 13th May 1972 when Luis arrived unannounced at Lady Jellicoe's house. He rang the bell and María let him in, despite her judgemental attitude towards anyone who walked through the door. But Luis wasn't just anyone. When playing polo at Cowdray Park, he had rented the same room I was now in, and used the place as a pied-à-terre whenever he was in town. And María had a soft spot for him. As he told her about his life in Hamburg, all of her usual prejudices melted away and she hung on his every word. He had a gift for making people feel they were the centre of his world, even though he was usually just boasting about himself.

As usual, I had had a late night and was still in bed recovering when he arrived. Luis had told me he would be coming to London around the middle of May but didn't give me further details. He liked surprising people, to keep them on the back foot. After flirting with María, and helping himself to the contents of the fridge, which was another of his bad habits, he then made telephone calls for more than an hour. He was still on the phone when I walked in.

'I want you to be the best man at my wedding,' he said when he finally ended his call.

'Wedding? Who are you getting married to?' I asked.

'Lucy Pearson.'

'You can't marry her. She's underage!'

'Not any more she's not.'

It was true. Lucy was now eighteen and could legally marry without her parents' consent. Luis had spoken of her many times, and their – or rather, his – intention to marry, but I never thought he would stick to whatever commitment he had made to her.

'Her family don't know yet. You're the only one who knows about it,' he said.

'Does *she* know about it?' I ventured, only half-jokingly.

'She wants to get married more than I do,' he said.

It wasn't a best man he needed; I would be a mere witness. The plan was to get married in secret and announce it to the family as a fait accompli. Luis suggested that Patsy could be the other witness. The plan was that Lucy, who lived with her parents at Cowdray Park, would take the train to London on Tuesday 16th May, and meet Luis at Patsy's house. From there we would all go to Caxton Hall where the ceremony would take place.

On the day, Patsy wore an elegant hat and large tinted glasses that hid her eyes and offered her a sort of disguise, while I stood next to her in a blue suit. Luis, his thick dark hair disciplined by thick brilliantine, entered with his bride whose eyes and mouth reminded me of one of those carved Halloween pumpkins. She was an unremarkable-looking girl with fair skin, translucent eyes and crooked teeth that were constantly bursting out when she smiled, betraying her complete infatuation with her elusive husband-to-be.

Luis, who could never resist the temptation of pretending to be somebody he wasn't, described himself as a stock market investment solicitor on the marriage certificate and gave as his residence Lady Jellicoe's address. After the formalities, Luis invited us to lunch at the Coq Au Vin in Knightsbridge. The restaurant was his new father-in-law's favourite restaurant and was owned by the Hon. Michael Pearson, Lucy's elder brother, heir to the family fortune. Luckily, none of the new in-laws were on the premises, and lunch passed without incident despite the amount we had to drink. The bill was huge. True to form, Luis claimed he had forgotten his wallet, so I was lumped with the bill. As I watched him presiding over the table, performing for his new wife, I recalled the Luis I had first met years ago, the young man who had told me his ambition was to play polo abroad and marry an heiress. Here he was, in London, with an heiress on his arm having accomplished what he had set out to do.

Given the unusual circumstances, they spent their one-night honeymoon at Patsy's and that was it. Marriage certificate in hand, rings on their fingers and the union officially consummated, Luis travelled back to his job in Hamburg and Lucy returned to her parents who were none the wiser.

Fortunately for the newly married couple, Luis's boss, Darboven, unexpectedly rescinded his contract on generous terms, leaving Luis free to join his wife. The reason behind this benevolence was Princess Edda of Anhalt, of the House of Ascania, daughter of the Duke of Anhalt. Having met her a few months before at a cocktail party, Luis introduced her to his employer and they hit it off so well that the coffee king and the Princess got engaged. Darboven temporarily lost all interest in polo and dispensed with Luis's services, his generosity in ending the contract an acknowledgement that he partly owed his new-found happiness to Luis.

As for Luis's marriage, it was only a matter of time before rumours of it reached Lord Cowdray. He had known of his daughter's desire to marry Luis and had vehemently advised against it, suggesting that they perhaps live together first. That way, she would get to know Luis better and, her father hoped, see through him. So, on hearing the rumours of their marriage, he dismissed them as evil gossip.

Rather than ask his daughter for the truth, he sent a clerk from his office to make inquiries at the Civil Registry, where it was confirmed. Lady Cowdray later told a friend it was the only time she had ever seen her husband cry. It was at this point that the British press first heard of Luis. Months later, stories appeared about the young heiress and the Argentinian polo player, spelled 'Louis' rather than 'Luis', who was described as 'an investment consultant', which even in those days meant nothing at all. It was common knowledge that her parents were, at the very least, surprised by the union, and all the stories mentioned Lucy's fortune without further comment.

On 9th August 1972, gossip columnist William Hickey wrote an article in the *Daily Express* under the headline 'Clouds lift for secret coup', confirming the wedding of the young couple. The newly married couple spoke of settling in 'the Argentine', which she was keen to see. Not only would they not settle there, but they never even went there for a holiday, as Luis feared Lucy would also realise how much he had lied about his background. The press noted how little they had seen each other since the wedding, putting it down to his business travels.

Although he seemed to be given the benefit of the doubt, anyone reading between the lines could see that his motives for the marriage were already being called into question.

With an income of her own, they initially rented a flat in South Kensington. She was eligible for a further £35 million settlement at the age of twenty-one, and Lord Cowdray suspected it was this that Luis had married her for. He immediately got his lawyers onto the case to have the settlement delayed. The change in plan provoked Luis to embark on a series of unsuccessful disputes with his father-in-law, supposedly in defence of his wife, arguing that the assets were rightfully hers and, therefore, marital. If there were any doubts about his true reasons for marrying, they were quickly dispelled.

Over time, Lord Cowdray relented somewhat, allowing the couple to move into a house on his estate, ostensibly so that he could offer them a better life but it was also to keep an eye on his son-in-law. A new trust fund was arranged, but as soon as Luis and Lucy agreed to the terms of it, Luis convinced Lucy that they should move to New York, his favoured stomping ground. There he would be able to do as he liked with no one to answer to. Lucy loved the idea and threw herself enthusiastically into the process of searching for a property in New York, which she would be paying for. This was possibly the happiest period of their otherwise rocky marriage. It took them a month to find a house at 165 East 65th Street, on the Upper East Side, next door to the billionaire philanthropist David Rockefeller. Although it was a rented property, Luis felt he had truly arrived in the world.

In an attempt to keep up with his wealthy neighbours, Luis set about working his way through Lucy's money by buying a Rolls-Royce and hiring a chauffeur. But all his efforts were in vain, as he failed to penetrate the closed, elitist WASP society of Manhattan. He found out the hard way that they were bigger snobs than the British. They offered no welcome to an outsider who looked like a Puerto Rican and his socially awkward English child bride. They were an odd couple, Luis and Lucy, and with his ridiculous Rolls-Royce, he was most obviously a fortune hunter.

Feeling discriminated against, he started frequenting La Cabaña, an Upper East Side place that young Latin Americans used to meet in after work. At least he was accepted there. The people who frequented La Cabaña were like him not just because they were Latinos, but also because most of them were hangers-on who lived off rich, well-connected people. Among the principal freeloaders were Alberto van der Mije, Santiago Yatian, Eugene Etcheverry, and Nicholas Simunek. It was with these people that Luis spent a lot of his time in New York. They probably saw more of him than did his wife.

Me (right) with Luis Basualdo, Cowdray Park, 1973

Simunek was an upstart of Czech origin born in London and labelled 'the bouncing cheque'. A well-known social events gatecrasher, he made money on the side by selling gossip to the press, just like Luis. They would go to exclusive clubs and approach members with a drink in their hand in the hope that they'd be offered at least another drink, maybe more.

A millionaire called Bruce Norris enjoyed the company of Latin Americans so much that he always livened up his parties by including them. This opened many doors for Luis and his new friends. Top of Luis's rat pack list was Rudy Chávez, a regular on the party scene and son of the right-hand man of Paraguayan dictator General Stroessner. Thanks to good old-fashioned nepotism, Rudy was his country's New York consul, but he supposedly lived with his wife on Long Island and was rarely seen at his office. Most of the time, he could be found at his pied-à-terre on the Upper East Side, where he would stay overnight on the pretence of getting to work early. Instead, he used it as a bachelor pad where he threw regular parties and slept off the ensuing hangovers. Luis quickly made an impression on Chávez, who gave him unqualified admiration in return.

Another who became a devoted follower was Alberto van der Mije. He had a relatively good job at a bank, but he lived way beyond his means and was always looking for ways to supplement what the bank paid him. Van der Mije had been born in Cuba, the son of a Dutch second-hand car dealer, when buying and selling was allowed in the country. After the revolution, twelve-year-old Alberto moved to New York with his parents and graduated from Georgetown University with an MBA at the age of twenty-two. When Luis met him, he was working for Morgan Stanley. Alberto advised Luis on how to play the stock market, while Peter Bemberg, the millionaire's son, regularly called him at the bank to obtain loans when he exceeded his credit allowance.

Alberto's life was like a roller coaster as he oscillated between excess and deprivation, between luxury and threats from his creditors. On more than one occasion, he sold his blood (literally) for the few dollars that they paid donors before putting on his dinner jacket, still light-headed, to attend a lavish party.

When the legendary El Morocco cabaret reopened its doors in 1972, it immediately became a meeting point for New York's wealthiest and for those seeking connections with them. Alberto was one of the first in line for membership, and to pay for it, he sold his Rolex watch to Rudy Chávez. In addition to the entrance fee, it was crucial to fork out a $50 tip for the Italian maître d', Angelo Zuccotti, so that he would greet you by name and not send you to 'Siberia' – that is, a table in the back. The wily Italian sized people up in seconds and classified them according to wealth, looks, and social grace. Tips could modify his assessment; they financed his son's studies at Princeton University, he told me.

Alberto took full advantage of the club to further his connections. It was there that he met a young French lady by the name of Sybille de Brantes. She was the daughter of a count and niece of Valéry Giscard d'Estaing, who later became president of France. Tall, attractive, and an authentic aristocrat, she took an interest in Alberto, but he realised her interest wouldn't last long. As soon as he went to the lavatory, men flocked to her table.

One of those men was his friend Luis, who later claimed to have had an affair with her. When Sybille called Luis at home, Lucy answered and, immediately suspicious, asked her husband for an explanation. He shrugged his shoulders and blamed Alberto, saying she was his friend. The young Cuban often served as Luis's alibi, and Lucy started resenting Luis for spending so much time with him.

This forced Luis to frequent more discreet places than El Morocco. Instead, he attended parties organised by his old friends Mildred McLean and Mary Sanford, the best hostesses of the two groups that made up New York's social scene. One group was comprised of straight and bisexual men, and the other was mostly made up of gay men, though they sometimes mixed to suit. A poor third place went to Gloria Muller who, after falling on hard times, would throw parties for a fee, mainly for older women looking for a man. It was at one of Gloria's parties that Luis met the women with whom he regularly conducted his extramarital affairs. In short, it was clear that he didn't have any intention of remaining faithful or making any concession to married life. He intended to carry on his bachelor lifestyle just as before, all at Lucy's expense who, although suspicious, never realised the extent of his infidelity. Taking advantage of her youth, naivety, and good nature, Luis managed to be out on the town most nights with one excuse or another. One can only imagine what it must have been like for this young woman, new to the country and the city, spending night after night alone.

24
The Smart Set

Back in London, it was around June 1972 that I met Dai Llewellyn, with whom I would become very close. It happened when Edith asked me to accompany her on a visit to an old friend who lived in Wales. Colonel Sir Harry Llewellyn was the celebrated horseman who, in 1952 with his horse Foxhunter, became an Olympic champion. His wife, Christine, was the daughter of Lord Saumarez.

Well-established in society, the Llewellyns would have enjoyed a quiet life with their three children if not for their mischievous son Dai whose antics were widely reported in the gossip columns. His notoriety began in 1971 on a visit to London when, at an art gallery opening, he met Lady Jacqueline Rufus Isaacs, daughter of the Marquess of Reading, whose name had been linked romantically with Lord Snowdon earlier that year. 'We're just good friends,' Lady Jacqueline said of Dai when quizzed by journalists. Though they never developed a relationship, it was enough to attract the attention of the press. Propelled overnight into the gossip columns, Dai became addicted to his celebrity status, never mind the money he earned from stories about himself and others.

The man dubbed 'The Seducer of the Valleys' or 'Dirty Dai' and portrayed as Britain's ultimate playboy lived in Chelsea, not too far from my South Kensington studio. Charming and charismatic, he seemed to know everybody and everybody claimed to be his best friend. During his short time at Eton, before he was inevitably expelled, his Classics master had named him 'Orpheus' after the mythological character who could charm even the stones. His actual close friends were Old Etonian amateur jockey Sir William Pigott-Brown, Old Harrovian Rupert Deen, and several others of similar background with whom he was often seen sharing a table at club openings where food and booze were free. They all belonged to the best British families and had something else in common: none of them had a job. Sleeping by day and partying the night away was the norm. 'Every day's a party' was Dai's motto.

I shared with him a relentless appetite for the good life, and Dai helped me become a member of both Annabel's and the Clermont Club. However, mixing with the smart set was not enough for me. What I enjoyed most was the seedy life and the buzz that walking up and down the vibrant and iconic King's Road in Chelsea gave me. Fashionable since the 1960s, when it became synonymous with the mod and hippie movements, it was now a key part of the London punk scene.

I regularly visited the Chelsea Potter, a pub full of characters and women of easy virtue. There was also the legendary Club dell'Aretusa, where John Lennon first appeared with Yoko. That was where I met ex-B-movie actress Tessa Welborn, who lived in Paultons Square, off the King's Road.

A worldly woman who sized people up in seconds, Tessa instantly knew that while I name-dropped and was well-spoken, I preferred the company of her sleazy friends. She matched me when it came to name-dropping; she had spent a fortune on parties to promote herself in London society until she realised it was a waste of time, as there was a limit to how far a mixed-race Jamaican could get. Born Marie Therese Prendergast, the daughter of Louis Prendergast, a wealthy Jamaican plantation owner who died when she was a child, she grew up in a prosperous and cultured environment and studied drama at Rochelle University, New York, and the Sorbonne. Shortly afterwards, she spent time in Italy, where she became briefly engaged to Prince Vittorio Massimo, who broke off the engagement when another girlfriend claimed to be pregnant with his child. Vittorio did the 'decent thing' and married her instead. Following the rejection, Tessa tried her luck at acting and landed small movie roles, and when the film work dried up, she used her show business contacts to become a clothing designer. She eventually made a name for herself in the fashion world for being, among other things, the designer of Ursula Andress's white bikini in *Dr No*.

Tessa was always teasing me about how naive and gullible I was, an accusation that I always protested against. At one of her dinner parties, she put me to the test by seating me next to a mature blonde whom she introduced as Lady Caroline. This was a distinguished-looking woman, dressed in a black chiffon silk gown, wearing a necklace and matching bracelet set with what looked like real emeralds. I did everything I could to charm this dinner companion and was indeed besotted by her, or rather her title. I ended up inviting her out on a date, but she made polite excuses not to accept. When dinner was over, I complained to Tessa that Lady Caroline had left without even giving me her phone number.

'You don't want her phone number,' Tessa said.

'Why do you say that? She's my kind of woman. Isn't that why you sat me next to her?'

'Lady Caroline is a man,' Tessa said coolly. 'His name is Group Captain Peter Ridley.'

I had failed her test.

'You have to learn that not all that glitters is gold,' she added.

Ever present at her gatherings was her admirer, the Hon. Garech Browne, son of the 4th Baron Oranmore and Browne and his brewing heiress wife, Oonagh Guinness. Garech's brother Tara, who had been a close friend of Paul McCartney and died in a car crash at the age of

*Me with ex-B-movie actress Tessa Welborn at the
Persian Embassy, London, 1974*

twenty-one, was immortalised in the Beatles' song 'A Day in the Life'. Although Garech was short, balding, with a long beard and ponytail, his voice was like that of a Shakespearean actor. Whenever he spoke, he became the centre of attention.

Other popular regulars to Tessa's gatherings were American sculptor Bayard Osborn and his Cuban wife, Pilar, with whom I developed a close friendship. The couple lived in a converted women's prison in Putney where Bayard had a large studio and bronze foundry.

But of Tessa's friends, the one I took to most was Roger Langdon-Berg, a red-haired, bespectacled, and highly-educated American who dealt in Old Master drawings. Always keen on being the centre of attention, Roger liked to talk and talk until drink got the better of him and he became rude and argumentative. Up to that point, he would shine on these evenings. More to the point, I benefitted from his knowledge of paintings and drawings and was intrigued to know how he made a living from them. So when Tessa mentioned that Roger had a room to let in his flat, I jumped at the chance.

I had been living in a poky South Kensington studio after Patsy kicked me out of her house. Edith and Ivan's divorce scandal and my role in it became too much for Patsy, and I was asked to leave, though I think it had more to do with her not wanting to share me with Edith. I soon moved into Roger's run-down flat in Earl's Court, taking with me the Caravaggio. The fact that my new landlord was gay didn't worry me, though I found his penchant for street urchins somewhat disturbing. When having breakfast in the morning, I usually had to share the small kitchen table with the likes of Mick, Rick, or Nick – they all sounded the same. I kept my bedroom locked at all times just in case.

One afternoon, I happened to walk into the kitchen when Roger was sorting out some Old Master drawings for a client. Right there in front of him were works by Poussin, Giovanni Domenico Tiepolo, Francesco del Cossa, Jan van Huysum, and other artists of that stature. 'These have just arrived from my Roman dealer,' he muttered. That was the story he always told, but the name of his mysterious Roman dealer was never revealed. Whatever he was up to must have been lucrative as he was in a very good mood that day.

'Tomorrow after lunch I'm taking a picture to my restorer,' he said. 'You're welcome to bring along your Caravaggio.'

The next day, we arrived in a taxi, with our respective paintings, at the premises of George Aczel, a picture restorer. When the sixty-five-year-old Hungarian opened the door, we were hit by the reek of turpentine and dammar varnish. Everywhere were racks and easels full of paintings, some newly arrived, some in the process of restoration, and others ready for collection. While I was listening to George's advice on the restoration of my Caravaggio, a man dressed in paint-stained white overalls tapped me on the shoulder.

'Hello, stranger! What on earth are you doing here?'

It was Eric Hebborn, the artist-turned-art-dealer I had met with Ursula in Rome. It turned out that he was Roger's mysterious Roman supplier.

'I wouldn't have guessed you two knew each other in my wildest dreams,' Eric said to Roger.

'He's my lodger,' Roger quickly retorted.

Although Eric was no longer a restorer, George Aczel had called him in for a highly paid job. A client with a 'suspect' Rubens wanted to have it enhanced to try and pass it off as the genuine article. Years before, Roger had come to George with an unattributed painting of a seafaring subject. When he had mentioned it could be a Van de Velde, Aczel knew he was referring to the great seventeenth-century marine artist. 'There's no question about it,' he had declared immediately. 'I can see the seascape in the background. I'm sure the signature will appear during cleaning.' A month later, Roger had collected the fully 'restored' painting, complete with original cracks in the varnish. It didn't take long for the masterpiece to find its way to the mansion of an avid collector. It turned out that the restoration job had been entrusted to the young Eric Hebborn who had just finished his course at the Royal Academy. That was how Roger came to know Eric.

So it was by fluke that Eric and I were to establish a professional relationship similar to the one I had had with Rodolfo Ruiz Pizarro back in Buenos Aires. I began working on commission, and before long, I was sharing some of the profits with him. In return, Eric found a buyer who paid a good price for my 'Caravaggio'.

25

Blackballed

When Luis arrived at Cowdray Park to play the 1973 polo season, he met with a hostile reception. Just short of being booed, he was known as the infamous predator who had seduced Lord Cowdray's daughter when she was still a minor. Avoided like the plague, he turned to me for support, and we saw each other frequently during that time. Despite my lack of interest in polo, Luis insisted on supporting my application for membership at Cowdray Park so he could have an ally there. As for me, I went along with his wishes for purely selfish reasons; meeting young girls and getting invited to parties was the only thing on my mind.

Luis was a man on a mission and toyed with the idea of putting together his own team. But even his wife's generous income wasn't enough. Being a sponsor is an incredibly expensive business; it entails paying for the players' accommodation and expenses and buying and maintaining the horses. To be able to participate, he would have to join someone else's team. Lord Cowdray didn't want him in his Cowdray Park team; Lord Brecknock didn't want him in his Pimms team either. Shipping magnate Eric Moller turned him down for his

Jersey Lilies, and flashy insurance tycoon Ronnie Driver rejected him for his team, San Flamingo. As a last resort, Luis tried his luck with two foreign sponsors who had arrived with their teams aiming to win the Gold Cup. They were Spanish sherry magnate Pedro Domecq with his Spain team, and French millionaire art dealer Guy Wildenstein with his Les Diables Bleus team. However, they both flatly refused to have him, but it wasn't on account of his reputation; it was because they felt he was an overrated player whose performance didn't justify his handicap.

Luis then begged Peter Grace (a newcomer who made a living renting out ponies) to include him in his New Zealand Rangatikis team, but after playing a few cups with him, he was presented with a bill for using Grace's ponies. Finally disengaged from the New Zealander, and still not having the resources to sponsor a team of his own, Luis decided to put together a team of 'friends' on a shoestring budget.

In late May he launched his Golden Eagles team (mauve shirts with a gold eagle on the left side), but unlike established sponsors, he scraped the bottom of the barrel recruiting Argentinians at loose ends like myself. These players without contracts were to play for no remuneration as they tried to attract the attention of potential sponsors. In return, Luis provided them with board and lodging. From then on, he started competing in medium-goal tournaments and, if he was lucky, the occasional high-goal match.

While Luis hustled his way up from the lowest rung on the polo ladder, I moved between London, Edith's house in Sherston, and Cowdray Park. It was during one of those Cowdray outings that I made friends with Beverly Roberts, the daughter of Squadron Leader Alan Roberts, one of the largest shareholders of Unigate Milk and the Kentucky Fried Chicken restaurant chain. The Squadron Leader was the patron of Maidensgrove, a low-goal handicap family team in which he played with his son and two daughters, one of whom (Lavinia) was one of the best female players at the time. On a personal level, Squadron Leader Roberts competed with Luis for the title of most unpopular man in the club; they were both considered charmless and unglamorous. But for some reason, Luis was jealous of my friendship with Beverly.

It was the first time that Luis and I had spent time together since we'd gone our separate ways, and once again, envy and competitiveness showed themselves, just as they had in Miami. 'The Roberts are nouveau riche and so vulgar. Nobody talks to them,' was his constant remark. He kept putting them down, but I ignored him.

Lord and Lady Cowdray gave a party for the club members at their Cowdray Park residence as they did every year, and Beverly thought it would be a good idea to take me as her escort. I made the mistake of telling her that I had been best man at Lucy Pearson's wedding, promoting myself from mere witness. It didn't occur to me that I would actually have to meet Lucy's parents but there they were, greeting their guests as they entered the house.

Beverly, who hadn't understood that their daughter's marriage was a very sore subject for the Cowdrays, went right up to them and gushingly introduced me.

I shook Lord Cowdray's hand firmly and then Lady Cowdray's.

'Marcelo was Luis and Lucy's best man,' Beverly added with a smile.

Lady Cowdray froze, and after a few tense seconds said, 'You're not welcome here.' Her face turned a few shades redder in those few moments before she turned her back on us.

We were rooted to the spot, not quite knowing what to do, but the guests who had just arrived forced us further into the house and we simply continued in the general direction of travel as if we hadn't heard our hosts, or didn't understand. Soon we had drinks in our hands. Eventually, I summoned some courage and approached Lord Cowdray.

'I'm so sorry about that. I was brought here by Beverly. Do you think I should go?'

'Did you not hear what my wife said?' he growled, barely looking at me as he spoke.

I made my way back to where I thought Beverly was to say goodbye, but once again I got caught in the crowd, a fresh glass found its way into my hand, and I just stayed, eventually getting quite drunk and having a good time.

I was enjoying my time away from Lady Edith, who was busy dealing with domestic situations. She was trying to persuade her husband, Ivan, to consent to the marriage of their underage daughter, Atalanta, to Prince Stefano Massimo, an eighteen-year-old part-time photographer, the son of Prince Vittorio Massimo and B-movie actress Dawn Adams. Eventually, Ivan did consent and the young couple were married. None of that had anything to do with me, except that it preoccupied Edith, and in the meantime, I was free to enjoy my social life both at Cowdray and in London.

Luis and I saw a great deal of each other during that season before he went back to New York. When in London we would usually meet at the Clermont Club and then go out on the town together. We often reminisced about our earlier days in Buenos Aires, our plans, and our dine-and-dash escapades. One day after lunch, Luis insisted we stop at John Lobb, the St James's shoe shop by Appointment to the Queen, which made bespoke men's shoes for the British royal family and anyone who can afford their exorbitant prices. Any custom-made shoes that customers hadn't collected, for whatever reason, were sold after a time at a reduced but still very high price. When we went in, we saw a Japanese man trying on a shoe from such an unclaimed pair. Luis sat opposite him and tried a black crocodile shoe on his left foot. As he looked around the floor for the other shoe, he noticed the Japanese man had the matching shoe on his right foot. Luis hid the left shoe from him, and the Japanese gentleman eventually got tired of looking for it and left. Luis immediately put on the matching right shoe, stood up, walked around and made his way towards the exit, leaving his old shoes behind. I hadn't noticed any of this and assumed we were just leaving. It was only when we got around the corner that Luis drew my attention to his shoes.

'You miserable bastard! You've done it again!' I exclaimed.

After all those years, and despite having his wife's immense wealth at his disposal, he still enjoyed the buzz of stealing. Getting one up on the world was his mission, all the more so with an established institution.

Shortly after having drinks at the home of a wealthy stockbroker, Luis spotted a member's handbook from Buck's, the gentleman's club in Clifford Street, Mayfair. He studied the list of names and one of them caught his eye: a certain Luis Barroso, a Peruvian gentleman whom Luis knew visited England very rarely. Pocketing the handbook, he visited Buck's a few days later and walked through the front door as though he owned the place.

'Good afternoon, sir. How can I help you?' the doorman said.

'Good afternoon! Thank you. Nice to see you again,' Luis replied, handing him his coat.

'Sorry sir,' the doorman said in a tone of voice that intimated he didn't have a clue who this man was.

'Luis Barroso,' replied Luis. 'I don't spend much time in London. That's probably why you don't recognise me.'

These doormen were employed precisely to remember faces, but even more importantly, they were employed not to offend.

'Of course, sir. Please come in,' the doorman said, taking Luis's coat and watching him closely, still not convinced he wasn't a fraud and could be trusted.

With his exotic appearance, his sparkling gold Rolex watch, which he made sure everyone noticed, and his polished black crocodile shoes he seemed out of place. He looked more like a pimp walking the streets of Rio de Janeiro than a member of an English gentlemen's club. Despite arousing initial suspicions, Luis became a regular at Buck's Club until one of the members said to him, 'Has anyone ever told you that you look just like that cad who ran off with Lord Cowdray's daughter?' Luis laughed off the observation and made light of the uncanny similarity, but he realised he couldn't continue with the charade any longer and he never set foot in the club again.

The whole question of gentleman's clubs preoccupied Luis. In private, he raged over the hypocrisy of these places and the people they accepted, some of whom he considered to be no better than himself. However, he never lost the chip on his shoulder about not being accepted in them. He had a compulsion to be accepted by the elite. If he were embraced by them, it would confirm his status and the bogus identity he had created for himself.

When he moved to New York, he assumed he would have a better chance of joining an American club because they were less snobbish, but that proved not to be the case. First, he targeted the Knickerbocker Club by persuading his close friends, Argentinian banker Lucio García Mansilla, and Prince Stanislaw Radziwill, the husband of Lee Bouvier, Jacqueline Kennedy Onassis's younger sister, to put him up for membership. Despite their support, when his candidature went to the vote, a significant majority turned him down. Luis later heard that Franklin Forbes Singer, the sewing machine heir, had been among those most vocal in their opposition. Singer allegedly sent a letter to the Knickerbocker's committee stating that Luis Sosa Basualdo was 'an undesirable on both sides of the Atlantic'. The tone and intensity of the rejection made Luis think that a British hand was behind it, maybe even Lord Cowdray's. The advice of his friend Bob Wickser was ringing in his ears: 'You have to join clubs while you're young before you make enemies.'

Luis was still only a young man, but he had made many enemies already, and his marriage to Lucy, although guaranteeing his financial stability, had most certainly branded him an 'undesirable'. Incredibly, he had managed to join the Racquet Club, which was a major achievement because by that time his reputation was so bad that senior members avoided him whenever he appeared. But being a member of the Racquet Club was not enough for him, and his next move was to ask Wickser to put him up for membership in the Palm Beach Everglades Club. Yet again, he was rejected by unanimous decision. He learned that this time, the main objector had been his former boss Dolph Orthwein, who had been outspoken in denigrating him as 'an upstart groom and gold digger'. Claiming the Americans were racists, Luis never wanted to consider that he was blackballed as a consequence of his behaviour.

Luis returned to the UK in 1974. His wife was pregnant with their first child and his relationship with her parents had slightly improved. As ever, they tolerated him for their daughter's sake, but they must have been aware of her unhappiness with Luis's philandering ways, which had become common knowledge.

The day after arriving in the UK, Luis attended a lunch at White's, London's most exclusive gentlemen's club, at the invitation of Commander Jack Pringle, a polo player and soon-to-be teammate. When they retired to the coffee room, one of Pringle's army friends came over to greet him, gave his guest a disapproving glance, and leaned down to whisper something in Pringle's ear. Luis heard every word: 'From the neck down, Lord Chesterfield. From the neck up, Geronimo. The only thing missing is the feather.'

Pringle made no comment and Luis pretended not to have heard, but later on, he complained to his host about his friend's rudeness.

'On the contrary, Luis, his remark was accurate,' Pringle replied gently. 'The idea of a gentlemen's club is to blend in, and you stand out here.'

The comment bothered Luis immensely, so much so that he recounted it to me many times over the years as proof of the snobbery he had been up against. As Luis got older, this obsession to be accepted and the resentment it stirred in him darkened. Indeed, in many ways it fuelled his increasingly spiteful behaviour, not that he needed much encouragement in that direction.

26
A Most Unusual Ambassador

One May morning in 1974, I was awakened by the phone ringing. I fumbled for the receiver and heard a man's voice say in Spanish, 'Marcelo! Is that you, Marcelo?'

'Who's that?'

'Have you just woken up? Do you know what time it is?'

I caught a glimpse of the clock. It was already midday, not early morning as I had assumed.

'Who is this?' I asked, trying to sound more alert.

'Manuel Anchorena!'

It turned out that Manuel was the new Argentinian Ambassador to the UK. At first, I didn't believe him. How could Manuel Anchorena be an ambassador? But he wasn't joking, and to prove it, he invited me to the Argentinian Embassy for lunch the next day. An old friend of the family, Manuel had spent most of his time at his *hacienda* La Corona near Chascomús, 123 kilometres south of Buenos Aires.

A questionable character who had never done a stroke of work in his life or expressed any interest in politics, he decided – perhaps out of boredom or sheer arrogance – that he would stand for the governorship of Buenos Aires Province. President Perón was so amused by the pretensions of this eccentric aristocrat that he indulged Manuel by appointing him ambassador to the Court of St James's.

When I arrived at the embassy in Belgrave Square, Manuel greeted me before leading the way to the dining room where he sat at the head of a long table. Suddenly he became rather formal, as if there was something that he wanted to announce.

'Marcelo Manrique de Acuña, how long have I known you?' he asked as if reading from a poorly written script.

'I don't know. For forever?'

'Exactly. Forever! Always, and even before then. You're an old friend of the family and I want to take you into my confidence.'

He was definitely priming me for something, and for a moment I wondered if he was about to offer me some role at the embassy. Judging by his unlikely appointment, anything was possible.

'In a week, an old friend of mine is coming to work for me at the embassy. He's based in Morocco, and up until now, he's been serving in the Spanish Foreign Legion. He's not really a military person – in fact, he couldn't be less military if he tried – but the reason he joined, well, it's a long story.'

His explanation as to why the man had joined the Legion faltered, and I heard no more about it. The Spanish Foreign Legion (*La Legión Española*), which operated in the Spanish Sahara, was much like its French counterpart but less well known. It was with the *La Legión* that General Franco had cut his teeth.

'The thing is, Marcelo, I offered him a job, but his English isn't very good and that's where I need your help. I'd like you to share a flat with him, somewhere near the embassy. He needs a Spanish-speaking friend to help him out, to make him feel at home.'

As he spoke, my hopes for what I was going to be offered plummeted. He was asking me to share a flat with a journalist, an ex-legionnaire who spoke not a word of English. His name was Alejandro Sáez Germain, and though he was not much of a linguist, he had been a brilliant journalist back in Buenos Aires.

When I met him a week later at the embassy, he was still dressed in the legionnaire uniform he had put on to meet the Spanish ambassador who released him from his military duties. When the ambassador saw him in his uniform and was greeted with a military salute, both men were overcome with emotion and wept freely. However, once Sáez Germain arrived at our embassy, he had to attend to more mundane matters. He changed into a suit and I took him to Rutter & Rutter, a small estate agency in Beauchamp Place, where we were shown a flat in Hans Place that we took on the spot.

The two-bedroom flat on the second floor of the house was at an excellent address, a short walking distance from the embassy, and, best of all, it had a large room ideal for entertaining. Moving to posh Hans Place in the vicinity of Knightsbridge was the icing on the cake for me. However, the set-up made Edith very nervous. She imagined drug-fuelled parties with women everywhere, some of whom might stay overnight and even end up sharing my bed.

The story of how Sáez Germain had joined *La Legión* was far less romantic than Manuel had led me to believe. Alejandro had been on holiday in Morocco where he spent half the time under the influence of hashish; it was in that state that he unwittingly signed himself up for a five-year contract with the Foreign Legion. He was eventually freed due to the intervention of the Spanish Ambassador to London, Manuel Fraga Iribarne, who was in line to become the new prime minister. He made a call to the commanding officer and Sáez Germain was released, having served only two of the five years in his contract.

Manuel Anchorena told me he had given Alejandro a job purely out of the kindness of his heart, but that was far from the truth. He was being given the extremely serious task of negotiating the return of the Falkland Islands, which was becoming a very hot topic in Argentina. Manuel felt that Sáez Germain, with his journalistic skills, could draft the relevant diplomatic correspondence, though as we now know, he was far from successful in this endeavour.

Journalist Agustina Roca, daughter of the president of Argentina's Jockey Club, joined us in Hans Place as Sáez Germain's live-in girlfriend, something which caused her conservative parents a certain amount of concern, as Alejandro had by no means given up his habit of smoking hashish. For someone who didn't know anyone in London and couldn't speak the language, it was amazing how quickly he made contacts to secure an endless supply of the drug. He smoked all day long and the place stank of it. There was also the fact that Sáez Germain and Agustina paraded around the flat in their underwear, if they wore anything at all. As Manuel said, 'He is a very bohemian and eccentric man.'

Manuel Anchorena didn't distinguish himself in his job either; after all, he wasn't a career diplomat. He spent most of his time having fun and trying to get in on the polo scene, offloading most of the work onto his chargé d'affaires. Trying to put a feather in my cap, I arranged for him to meet Luis, and from then on, Manuel was occasionally able to join his team. In return, Luis was invited to embassy parties and allowed to stay overnight to sleep off his hangovers. For the two of them, it was a perfect arrangement, as it was for me. From then on, Manuel and I went every Tuesday and Thursday in the chauffeur-driven ambassadorial car to play practice games at Cowdray Park. With no horses of our own, we were mounted courtesy of Colonel Harper, a not very friendly Somerset-born, Sandhurst-trained officer who had learned the rudiments of polo while serving for the Lancashire Fusiliers in India. Back in the UK, he was employed by Lord Cowdray to run his polo club, where he supplemented his income by renting out ponies.

Manuel had brought his collection of colonial silver to the UK with him, but he was strongly advised against bringing his Nazi memorabilia. He had the silver, which comprised daggers, belts, mates, and other artefacts, nailed to the panelled walls of the embassy's reception room, thus damaging the wood. He also brought the staff from his *hacienda* to work at the embassy, including a gaucho cowhand who always wore a broad black belt with encrusted coins and a matching ornamental silver knife; he was never seen doing much work around the embassy.

Flippant, casual, and a rather dysfunctional character, Manuel was oblivious to whether his antics upset people. To further defy convention, he used to arrive at Cowdray Park with his secretary and sometimes other women he met at diplomatic parties. When the annual Argentinian Ambassador's Cup tournament was due to take place, an anxious Lord Cowdray, aware of Manuel's behaviour, begged him, 'This time, bring your wife please!'

'Who do these English people think they are?' he angrily said to me on our way back to London. 'They think they can treat me like a child. I am the Ambassador of Argentina!'

There was a dinner party one evening at the embassy and, as usual, Manuel wanted to invite fun people. I arrived with Edith Foxwell, Dai Llewellyn and a few strays I had met at polo. Luis, as a matter of principle, never brought his wife to the embassy parties. He was determined to keep her from hearing anything about his humble origins and it was a subject he feared might be mentioned by fellow Argentinians.

The private parties at the embassy were always debauched and out of control. Men openly fondled scantily clad young women, and Sáez Germain shared his best Moroccan hashish with guests. All this prompted the chargé d'affaires, Rafael Gowland, to complain forcibly to his boss, but Manuel simply brushed all complaints aside.

'It's the ambassador's job to entertain people and that's what I'm doing,' he responded. 'Didn't everybody have a good time? Some people never left. I even found a couple sleeping under one of the desks. That's how good a host I am!'

Viewing his mandate as ambassador to the Court of St James's as an extended holiday away from his *hacienda*, he would arrive at the office at eleven o'clock and leave for lunch at one, after which he either went to play squash or, if it was a Tuesdays or Thursday, polo at Cowdray.

Having to pay back political favours, Manuel made a point of employing members of the Peronist Youth Association. One of them was a young man called Luis Fontana, who had just arrived from

Argentina and was asked to assist Sáez Germain in compiling an inventory of embassy property. The pair undertook the task, having agreed in advance to omit various objects so they could sell them later if no one noticed they were missing. The items in question were an antique Russian samovar, a Roman bronze statuette, and a couple of Chinese vases, which they stored temporarily in a small room in the embassy basement. They retrieved the goods late one night when everybody was asleep. 'This will pay for two years' worth of hashish,' Sáez Germain said, and that is exactly how he spent the proceeds. Soon after the items were sold, I opened the door of our Hans Place flat to find a Moroccan delivering two big bags of the drug. While Sáez Germain and his girlfriend were sampling their new supply, I emerged from my room in my jogging gear, ready for my daily run in Hyde Park.

'Whatever you do, you must try this first,' Alejandro insisted, handing me a joint.

Although I had occasionally smoked with him before, more out of politeness than anything else, it was not something I usually indulged in as it made me feel stupid and lazy. But this time when I tried it, a warm wave of torpor came over me so strongly that I had to lie down on my bed. Just a couple of puffs wiped me out for the whole day, and every time I thought my head had cleared, another wave hit me and knocked me horizontal again. I couldn't even take off my trainers; I ended up sleeping with them on all night. How Alejandro ever managed to get anything done, I will never know.

At the end of 1975, Manuel was summoned to Buenos Aires by the new president, María Estela Martínez, widow of the recently deceased Juan Domingo Perón. She told Manuel that his term was over and he could only return to London for a goodbye party. Rafael Gowland, his chargé d'affaires, was now in charge and would not allow him to use the embassy for it, so Manuel hired a private room at Brooks's Club to give a farewell dinner for his close friends.

A few months later, in March 1976, Perón's widow was ousted by a military junta headed by General Jorge Videla. Sáez Germain had also returned to Argentina and I later learned that he was working for a popular Argentinian magazine. Despite his faults, he was a brilliant journalist who wrote beautifully. For Luis and me, Manuel's recall came as a blow. The embassy had become a home from home where we entertained and were entertained, all paid for by the Argentinian government. However, I stayed on at the flat in Hans Place, withdrawing to a quieter life with Edith, who was only too happy to see the end of my 'diplomatic' life.

27
A Walk on the Wild Side

In the late 1970s, London was swinging in a way that was different to the '60s. Although I hadn't been there in the '60s, it somehow felt more liberated and I was very comfortable in the city. Punk had taken hold and shaken the country out of its conservatism. There was a sense of rupture with tradition and ambiguity in sexuality, and although homosexuality was still frowned upon in many quarters, people were much more open about their sexual predilections. You could see it and feel it in the clubs and bars.

One warm summer night, Luis and I went to a trendy restaurant in Egerton Gardens called April and Desmond's, where we soon became regulars. It was run by transexual model April Ashley, who had previously been a sailor by the name of George Jamieson. We were drawn not so much to the food, which was average, but the air of decadence and gender ambiguity that it became known for. One evening while having dinner there, we struck up a conversation with two women sitting at the next table. One of them had a sexy Italian accent and a measured feline way of moving. Not being able to take my eyes off her, I invited her and her companion to come to Tramp with us.

My date's name was Fiammetta, and the more I watched her move, the more fascinated I became. She wore a half-unbuttoned leopard-print blouse, no bra, a short black miniskirt, and the highest stilettos I had ever seen. It was a wonder she could move in them at all. But move she could, not necessarily to the beat of the music, but to a beat of her own, which drove me wild. Luis's date had a more conservative look. She was a Londoner who tried talking posh but gave the game away after a few drinks when she reverted to her Cockney accent.

At first, I was intimidated by Fiammetta, but as the evening progressed and the music slowed down, and inspired by Luis who had become more intimate with his date, I pulled Fiammetta close. Then she put her mouth right up against my ear and whispered, 'Don't you think we should go back to my place?'

Five minutes later we were at Arlington House, next door to the Ritz Hotel, where she entered the building as if she owned it.

'Good evening, Miss Colonna,' the doorman greeted her.

Her apartment was at the rear of the building overlooking Green Park, and the decor was exquisite: expensive furniture, works of art, beautifully arranged flowers in enormous vases. On the wall was a portrait of her that was unmistakably by Lucian Freud. Noticing my curiosity, she said, 'I modelled for it … and for this one.' She pointed to a nude sketch signed by Francis Bacon.

'Are they originals?' I asked.

'Of course,' she responded, amused at my silly question. 'They're both good friends of mine.'

'You're not by any chance related to Princess Vittoria Colonna?' I asked, a few pennies starting to drop.

'Yes, I'm Princess Fiammetta Colonna and Vittoria is my cousin. How do you know her?'

The Colonna family is one of Rome's oldest and grandest. On my first visit to Rome, I met Princess Vittoria Colonna at Gilda's nightclub, and a few days later she invited me to a party at her apartment in the Palazzo Colonna. The friendship didn't deepen into anything more, although I had been attracted by her title and social position.

'Oh, just from a party in Rome a few years back,' I told Fiammetta.

We started kissing and, feeling more confident, I put a hand on her leg, but she lifted it off immediately.

'You're going too fast. I'm a princess, remember? I'm only interested in men who treat me like a lady,' she said so flirtatiously that I was confused by what she meant.

But then she took my hand and guided it between her thighs. For some reason, it was okay when she guided my hand there but not when I did it of my own volition. Either way, I explored her body with my hand, the way she wanted me to. She was another woman who liked to take control, and if I wasn't already turned on, I certainly was by that time. But then, as she moved my hand around her body, I felt something hard between her legs. I froze when I realised what it was. Fiammetta was a prince, not a princess.

I panicked. 'I have to go now,' I announced, trying to get up from the sofa.

But she pushed me back down with some force. 'You're not going anywhere.'

Suddenly that sensual, slightly hoarse voice that had been driving me wild all night had a gruff edge to it. Worse yet, she had the strength of a man and easily overpowered me. She pinned me down on the sofa and tried to continue kissing me. Fortunately, the siren of a nearby fire engine that suddenly rang out startled us both and I managed to get away. I fled the apartment, running down the two flights of stairs and passing the doorman on the way out, who offered me a polite, if rather knowing 'Good night, sir.'

When I called Luis the next morning to give him the news, he brushed it off. 'I thought you knew,' he murmured half asleep.

'How would I have known?'

'Oh, I don't know. Maybe his big hands and his Adam's apple gave it away,' he said, with a snigger.

28
Sarah Comes to the Rescue

Despite my occasional dalliances, Edith and I continued to see each other. I would visit her at her country residence, and when she was in London, she'd pick me up at my Knightsbridge flat. On one of those weekend country visits, she took me to Marsh Court, Dorset, where she had grown up, and even though it had since been sold to the Fox-Pitt family, she knew the new owners well and often visited. The impressive house was surrounded by a few acres of land, in which stood an old hangar where her father had kept his light aircraft. He was a gentleman of leisure who had married an American heiress and flew a plane for his amusement, though he spent most of his time fox-hunting. Edith had told me she often flew with him, and he would ask her to look at the fuel gauge to make sure they were not running low.

When we arrived at the house, we were greeted by Sarah Fox-Pitt, the daughter of the owners, who were in London that weekend. During lunch, I couldn't take my eyes off Sarah. Her wild permed hair seemed at odds with her aristocratic, slightly haughty manner. I found her fascinating. She was the archivist-curator at the Tate

Gallery, but as cultured as our conversation was, it seemed to me to be charged with a mutual attraction. When lunch was over, Sarah escorted us to the door and before she waved us off, she discreetly slipped a note into my jacket pocket with her phone number on it. No further instructions were required; it was all the invitation I needed.

When I called a few days later, I learned that she had given me the Tate Gallery number. I asked for Sarah Fox-Pitt and was immediately put through. With little fuss or the least bit of surprise that I had called, we arranged to meet at her place the next day. I arrived at The Albany, the eighteenth-century Palladian-fronted building in Piccadilly where she lived. It was regarded as one of the most exclusive addresses in London, with the Royal Academy next door and Fortnum & Mason as the local grocer, and only the well-connected could become tenants there. An inquisitive porter in a green tailcoat and top hat greeted me from inside his lodge and asked me a few questions about who I was and who I had come to see before showing me the way to her apartment, or 'set', as they are called. I climbed the steps leading to Sarah's flat where she was standing in the doorway, expecting me.

The luxury inside exceeded the promise of the outside. The place was awash with eighteenth- and nineteenth-century family portraits, Queen Anne furniture, and Persian rugs. She had only one contemporary item: an Eduardo Paolozzi print.

Throughout the evening, I was impressed by her vast knowledge of art and wanted to learn from her. After all, I was a successful art dealer 'in the style of the Old Masters', though I thought it best to keep the true nature of my business out of the conversation. Art, it turned out, was the last thing on Sarah's mind. After dinner at a local Chinese restaurant, she invited me back to the apartment for a nightcap.

'Please help me to get my dress off,' she said. 'I want to slip into something more comfortable.'

She was wearing a Victorian-style, hippy dress that had a seemingly endless column of buttons down the front from her neck to her knees, and I began the tedious work of unbuttoning what felt like a clergyman's cassock. I noticed that she seemed to enjoy my growing frustration. Unable to control my impatience, I ended up ripping the dress from top to waist. A dozen purple buttons came loose and fell on the rug.

'My dress! What have you done? Get out of my house!' she screamed at me.

A couple of weeks later, I got a call from her as if nothing had happened. She invited me to spend the weekend at Marsh Court, which was where we had first met.

We arrived late on a Friday afternoon and were greeted by her father, Major General William Fox-Pitt, a sprightly, old-school military type in his eighties, and her mother, Mary Stewart Sinclair, an old-fashioned lady who set great store by bloodline and lineage. They were perfectly polite and agreeable, but two days later, when we were back in London, Sarah got a call from her father. All I heard, at her end of the conversation, was 'What do you mean bum? Why would you call him that?' My ears pricked up and I realised that I was the subject of their ill-tempered exchange. He seemed to know about my relationship with Edith Foxwell, which was common knowledge in certain circles, and therefore didn't approve of his daughter's involvement with me. She started to defend me, saying that he didn't know anything about me, that I was from a good family, and so on, but he hung up on her. There were to be no more weekends in the country at Marsh Court.

29
Surrendell Farm has a Royal Guest

Although I was two-timing Edith with Sarah, I was often at a loose end at weekends as both of them often made other plans. Sarah was usually at her parent's house where I wasn't welcome, nor could I stay at Edith's when her daughter Atalanta was there because she disliked me intensely. Instead, it was Edith's friend, the young aristocrat Sarah Ponsonby, who came to my rescue.

She had recently bought a sprawling Jacobean farmhouse called Surrendell, set on forty-five acres of land in the Wiltshire countryside, and it quickly became a sanctuary for many of her friends. Prince George Galitzine, Stephen Hurrell, Tessa Codrington, and the actress Helen Mirren would descend on the place at weekends and often stay longer. It became my refuge, and sometimes I stayed for weeks. But Sarah's rustic idyll soon turned sour as she got further and further into debt and her upper-class friends abandoned her. She was forced to take desperate measures to keep the place. Her solution was to make Surrendell a hippie collective, or commune. From then on, instead of being pampered by the hostess, everyone who stayed had to help with the housework and contribute three pounds per day for their upkeep. I didn't like the change as it brought a different type of guest to the house – a less interesting and more ideological type of person – quite apart from the fact I was usually assigned the washing up. The sleeping arrangements were entirely random; we slept wherever we found ourselves. If I was lucky enough to share a mattress on the floor, it was usually next to someone who hadn't washed for days, or I had to fend off unwanted advances from other men.

One of the new intake was Dai Llewellyn's brother Roddy who, after his highly-publicised affair with Princess Margaret, wanted to escape from his recently acquired celebrity status. However, the press, instead of forgetting about him, homed in on the commune and Roddy's current relationship with Naima, a married Moroccan who worked as a Knightsbridge boutique assistant and at weekends did the cooking on the farm, and who by that time had become something of a celebrity herself.

As the days grew hotter, the Surrendell residents wore less and less clothing until it became a nudist colony. The naked cavorting of Roddy Llewellyn and his chums caused consternation among the local population, and friends visiting the commune were shocked to find the convent-educated Sarah Ponsonby and other co-owners also running around without any clothes on. Roddy insisted it was merely a sensible response to the warm weather and that when it turned colder, they would all put their clothes back on. But the stories of Surrendell's decadence were widely reported and made Princess Margaret curious enough to come and see for herself what all the fuss was about. The trouble began as soon as she arrived in her chauffeur-driven Rolls-Royce. There was no room for the driver in the house, so he had to stay in the village. The limousine parked outside a bed and breakfast made it obvious that Surrendell had a special visitor, and so the small community was further besieged by journalists.

The villagers, sick and tired of the attention and the goings-on at the farm, told them that drugs were being consumed at the commune, which of course they were, and soon after, a police inspector, a sergeant, and three other officers visited the farm. It took them no time at all to discover a thriving cannabis plantation in the garden.

It was at this point that I decided it was time to leave, as an arrest or any brush with the law would impact negatively on my residence application. I packed my clothes in a flash and fled. Fortunately, I soon found new accommodation, courtesy of another of Edith's neighbours, Australian Diane Cilento, who had just moved into the area and was living with playwright and screenwriter Anthony Shaffer. A small-time actress, she had become better known after marrying Sean Connery. Two years after her acrimonious divorce from Connery, Diane splashed out on a derelict farmhouse with the proceeds of her last film, *The Wicker Man* (written by Shaffer). The building was in the process of being restored by devotees of Sufism, a mystical branch of Islam to which she nominally subscribed, though according to Edith it was a scam to make them work for nothing.

Meanwhile, Princess Margaret's indiscreet behaviour was taking its toll on the Queen, and MPs were asking for her Civil List payments to end. By the end of the year, Margaret had removed her wedding ring and was preparing for a divorce. It was to be the first divorce in the royal family since 1533 when Henry VIII's marriage to Catherine of Aragon ended in annulment. The divorce was finalised in 1978, and Lord Snowdon remarried that same year. Roddy eventually married fashion designer Tania Soskin, and Princess Margaret never remarried. For Roddy, meeting Princess Margaret gave him much more than Andy Warhol's 'fifteen minutes of fame'. The scandal that dragged him from obscurity played to his advantage, and he occupied many more column inches than his older brother Dai ever did.

30
The Count of No Account

Alberto van der Mije was another of the many freeloaders who used polo to facilitate his social climbing. Eager to compete in the forthcoming polo season, he and his wife, Brenda Lee, arrived in England in 1976. A year earlier, Luis had travelled to Palm Beach to be the best man at their wedding, and so the young couple decided to pay him a surprise visit.

Van der Mije had always wanted to follow in Luis's steps, though lately, his admiration for him had waned somewhat. He was extremely proud of the fact he had been allowed to join the Gulfstream Polo Club (something Luis had never been able to achieve), and it was there that he met Philip Iglehart who, at sixty-two, no longer played polo but was president of the club and did not have a good word to say about Luis. Not wanting to rely solely on Iglehart's negative view of Luis, Alberto hired his ex-groom, Ike Walton, to find out more. But he also relayed various negative tales about Luis and his conduct – his treatment of horses, stealing from other people, lying, and sleeping with other men's wives.

To celebrate Van der Mije's unexpected arrival in the UK, Luis invited me to join them for lunch at Morton's. With white skin, rosy cheeks, and a few extra pounds, Brenda was an American version of the classic 'English rose'. By contrast, there was nothing rosy about her husband who announced his decision to 'start afresh in England' by promoting himself to the rank of Count. Dubbed by Luis 'the Count of No Account', he went on to boast about his noble Dutch ancestry on his father's side and claimed his mother descended from the Cuban hero, General Noel de Betancourt, though it was common knowledge his father had been a second-hand car dealer and his mother's lineage was not worth mentioning.

The couple had booked into Claridge's Hotel and some weeks later, they bought a flat near Buckingham Palace. They had also made arrangements to rent a cottage near Cowdray Park for the polo season. Alberto was convinced that if he followed in the footsteps of his Argentinian idol, he also would reach the peak of 'society'. And although Luis was a little worried that Alberto would queer his pitch, he introduced him to Huntsman, his favourite Savile Row tailor, and Turnbull & Asser, the leading Jermyn Street shirtmakers. But what Alberto needed most was to contact a good shoemaker. This was essential to him as his right leg was one-and-a-half inches shorter than his left following a car crash; hence, he needed a higher heel on his right shoe in order not to limp. By this time, Luis had fallen out with the three most famous London shoemakers: Henry Maxwell, Foster & Son, and, most recently, John Lobb where he had left the premises wearing a new pair of black crocodile shoes, leaving his old pair behind instead of payment. Fortunately, I had a secret weapon that would solve the problem. His name was George Cleverly, and he was an irate and moody Scotsman, rated the best shoemaker in the world, who ran his business from a dingy Mayfair basement. He rose to fame after developing the flattened and chiselled square-toed shoe that Winston Churchill, Humphrey Bogart, Fred Astaire, and Clark Gable made famous. He took clients strictly by recommendation, and I had been recommended by my close friend, Baron de Redé.

But behind the apparent cordiality, a rivalry was developing between Luis and Van der Mije. Trying to keep up with him, Luis bought a Daimler and hired his neighbour, Edgar Quijo-Duggan, a hard-up Old Etonian, as a part-time chauffeur. First, he took Edgar to Moss Bros to hire a suit for the occasion, and then ordered him to drive them all to Ascot. When they arrived, Luis, the 'Count', and their respective wives sat down to drink champagne only to find no one was interested in talking to them. To their amazement, it was only when Edgar the chauffeur joined them that people flocked to greet him. They were suddenly the centre of attention. Friends of the chauffeur kept coming over to say hello while Alberto and Luis paid for several bottles of champagne, happy to rub shoulders with Old Etonians and aristocrats. To carry on the charade, Luis encouraged Edgar to drink.

'I can't drink. I'll lose my driver's licence,' he protested sarcastically.

'Don't worry about that,' Luis replied. 'Lucy will drive. What do you think wives are for?'

For that year's polo season, Luis managed to recruit the very talented Australian player Sinclair Hill, thanks to whom the team won the prestigious Warwickshire Cup and other trophies. Luis tried to avoid 'Count' van der Mije as much as possible as his clumsy attempts at social climbing were rapidly making the Cuban an embarrassment. Trying hard to pass himself off as an English gentleman, he took to wearing a tweed jacket with a matching cap and brown brogues. He completed this unconvincing ensemble with a pipe that was permanently clamped between his teeth, even when he was talking.

31
Charles Keeps His Word

Luis decided it was time for a clean start and moved his base to the Guards Club at Windsor Park. From the beginning, it was noted in the changing rooms that Luis never wore underpants, something the other players found offensive. Underpants or no underpants, however, he aimed at the Prince of Wales who he had set his sights on some time ago. Although the club mainly comprised army officers who didn't particularly welcome foreign players, Argentinians were tolerated as they were known to be the best players.

Having engaged a professional of Sinclair Hill's calibre, Luis had all he needed to lure the Prince this time. When the Golden Eagles team beat Charles's team, the heir to the throne exclaimed, 'You wretched man, Basualdo, I should play for you!' This throwaway half-joke was exactly what Luis had been waiting for. 'That can be arranged, sir,' he replied.

With a top professional such as Hill, and Chamaco Herrera as a spare player, the Golden Eagles team was highly competitive, only narrowly losing the final of the Royal Windsor Cup.

Les Diables Bleus, winners of the 1974 Deaville Coupe D'argent. Left to right: Guy Wildenstein, Dicky Cernadas, Fernando Merlos and Luis Basualdo.

Following the award ceremony, the two finalist teams were invited to tea with the Queen and Prince Charles. While everyone was enjoying a cup of tea in the clubhouse, Luis bypassed Ronnie Ferguson and Gee Lee, the 'rottweilers' whose task was to keep people away from Charles, and approached the Prince.

'I meant what I said, sir,' Luis said with a smarmy smile. 'We'd be delighted for you to join our team in the forthcoming season. I'll be hiring Sinclair Hill again, and it'll be an even stronger team with you in it.'

'What an excellent idea, Basualdo,' Charles replied, though it was difficult to gauge whether he was serious or not.

In the meantime, they played friendly matches and began to form a bond. Charles was twenty-eight at the time, three years younger than Luis, and he was nowhere near as experienced and confident around women as Luis. When it came to women, the hierarchies were inverted. According to Luis, Charles couldn't get enough of his stories of romantic conquests and encouraged him to elaborate on them.

Marcelo Manrique de Acuña

Golden Eagles team, winners of the Warwickshire Cup, Cirencester Polo Club, 1976. Standing (left to right): Luis Basualdo, Sinclair Hill; Kneeling (left to right): E. Horswell, D. Gemmell.

Golden Eagles team, winners of the Spring Cup at Cowdray Park, 1977. Left to right: Russell Corey, Sinclair Hill, HRH Prince Charles, Luis Basualdo.

Golden Eagles team, winners of the Alitalia trophy at Guards Polo Club, Windsor, London, 1977. Left to right: Hector Crotto, Russell Corey, Luis Basualdo, HRH Prince Charles.

Golden Eagles team, runners up in the Warwickshire Cup at Cirencester Polo Club, 1977. Left to right: Russell Corey, Luis Basualdo, HRH Prince Charles.

The heir to the throne kept his word, and from the beginning of the 1977 season, Charles played as a guest in Luis's Golden Eagles team. Also as promised, Luis hired Sinclair Hill for a second time running and included American Russell Corey, to whom he owed many favours. The team started successfully, with Charles scoring the winning goal in the Alitalia Cup in the presence of the Queen. But when Russell congratulated the Prince by patting his shoulder, he was severely reprimanded by Major Ronald Ferguson.

Golden Eagles went on to compete in the Jubilee, Tatham, and Spring Cups. This time, Luis had provided his team members with good horses. As an extra incentive, he also arranged to have a small number of attractive female grooms, partly to impress the Prince, but mostly to cement his own playboy reputation.

Lord Brecknock, the patron of the Pimms team which had won the Gold Cup on several occasions, had fallen on hard times and was not only forced to withdraw from his polo activities but also to put his mansion, Lodsworth House, up for rent. Luis immediately took the opportunity to become his lodger, and he invited his sister, Marité, and his old mentor, Beto, to stay as his first guests. But ultimately the impressive manor house offered Luis a suitable base from which to conduct his charm offensive on the future king, who was to become a regular visitor.

At the time, the Prince was dating Lady Sarah Spencer, who was looked on with favour by his family as a potential bride, so much so that he came to the Cowdray Polo Ball hand in hand with her. But at a certain point in the evening, he asked Luis, who had become his confidante in these matters, about a particular woman who had caught his eye. Her name was María Eugenia Garcés Etcheverría and she came from a wealthy Colombian family. When she arrived in England, she became involved with Juan Manuel Santos, a young diplomat from her country who worked in London for the International Coffee Organisation. Luis had his eye on the Colombian himself, but he had to put the Prince first. When Charles asked for a discreet introduction, a last-minute change to the seating plan meant that the heir to the throne was sitting next to her.

Cirencester Polo Club, 1977. Left to right: Luis Basualdo and HRH Prince Charles talking to Lord Vesty.

South America team, winners of the Coronation Cup, 1977. Left to right: HM Queen Elizabeth, E. Moore, H. Crotto, G. Pieres, Luis Basualdo.

She was dressed in a sparkling blue, backless, mid-length dress, the flattering outfit a perfect complement to her pulled-back dark brown hair, while around her neck she wore a double row of pearls. She certainly looked fit for a prince. They engaged in small talk, Charles directing a few clumsy lines about how beautiful she looked, and as soon as the band started playing, he took her by the hand to the dance floor.

'Should I call you Charles or Sir?' she asked timidly.

'Call me Arthur,' he replied, which, of course, was his third name.

Arthur and María Eugenia danced the night away while Luis busied himself by distracting Lady Sarah. As the party started to wind down, Luis was keen to drive María Eugenia back to London himself despite the amount of alcohol he'd consumed. But Charles insisted on driving her home and, despite Luis's protests, he prevailed. María

Eugenia sat in the front seat of his Aston Martin while Lady Sarah and the bodyguard were crammed into the backseat.

As a result of this flirtation with María Eugenia, the Prince's courtship with Lady Sarah wound down, as did María Eugenia's relationship with her compatriot Juan Manuel Santos. She and the Prince saw each other for a while, but it didn't last. Her Catholicism may have been a reason, though it was clear that Charles was determined to have a good time one way or another before taking his marriage vows.

Years later, Luis would elaborate on this relationship, selling a widely publicised story to Annette Witheridge, a New York journalist, which was subsequently published in the *Sunday Mirror* in January 2002. He claimed that he procured women for Prince Charles, carefully selecting them from the villages around the Cowdray estate and taking them shopping so that they looked presentable before meeting the future king. But this is yet another of Luis's fabrications. I know that because I saw a great deal of him during that time, whether at Cowdray Park playing polo or in London at the clubs. Although he boasted about his relationship with the Prince, he was not in any sense his 'wingman'. The Prince, although happy to play in Luis's team and socialise with him at a superficial level, did not engage with him otherwise.

32
Luis, the Family Man

It was around this time that Luis developed a taste for cocaine, which would become a permanent feature of his life. When we went clubbing, whether to Tramp or elsewhere, often in the company of Dai Llewellyn, Luis would disappear and return even more animated than usual, telling stories that neither Dai nor I took seriously.

Amid this hedonistic and debauched period, Luis was selected for the 1977 Coronation Cup, South America's annual international polo competition against England. The man in charge of the selection was Eduardo Moore, the best Argentinian player on the English circuit, who was not aware that Luis had put on weight and hadn't been training. On hearing the news of Luis's inclusion, Héctor Barrantes, who had also been selected, strongly opposed it. 'It's him or me,' he said angrily. He had neither forgotten nor forgiven Luis's cruelty to his horses, one of which had had to be put down. This put Eduardo Moore in an awkward position, but he eventually decided to exclude Barrantes from the team and replace him with the one-eyed Héctor 'Juni' Crotto, an extraordinary player with the same handicap as Barrantes. The other team players were Gonzalo Pieres and Luis.

A frustrated Barrantes could only watch from the stands as the Argentinians beat the English team.

The Coronation Cup was presented by the Queen to the winners, and champagne was served in the clubhouse. But instead of having a celebratory drink or two, Luis got so drunk that Eduardo Moore insisted on taking him home. However, Luis blatantly refused and instead made his way to the home of John Horswell, the owner of Sladmore Art Gallery, where there was a party. Luis ended up staying the night and sharing a bed with a woman he met there. When he finally returned home the next morning, he found his house empty. His wife, children, and even the nanny had gone. Only Sam and Dickens, their white English bull terriers, were there to greet him, left behind by Lucy who considered them to be as threatening and diabolical as their owner.

Lucy had been desperately unhappy with Luis for some time. He came and went and did as he pleased, with little or no consideration for her or their two children. His daughter Charlotte was born in 1974 and was the light of Lucy's life. Luis had held her up in the air like a trophy as we stood together dressed in our polo kit before a practice match that July, not long after she was born. 'You see this?' he exclaimed. 'This is worth at least $200,000 in any divorce settlement.' As always with Luis, it was hard to know if he was being serious or whether he was just trying to shock. At the time I allowed myself to think it was the latter, but as it turned out he was serious, and naming the figure of $200,000 would prove to be prophetic. Charlotte's birth brought Luis and Lucy together for a while, but he soon found excuses not to be at home again. He was either in Argentina or travelling elsewhere for his mysterious investment consultancy business.

His son Rupert was born in 1976, and soon after showed signs of autism and was confined to a care home in Florida. Lucy eventually became well aware of her husband's philandering ways and she began to despise him, just like her parents always had. She even found out that Luis had met up with Christina Onassis in Buenos Aires a couple of months before he had married her in the London registry office.

His failure to return home the night of the Coronation Cup win was the last straw for Lucy.

As Luis made his way through the virtually empty house, the telephone rang. When he picked up the receiver he heard the familiar beeps of a public phone; a coin was thrust in at the other end, followed by his wife's voice. She informed him that she was at Heathrow about to board a flight to the United States. Luis pleaded one excuse after another for yet another night of absence, but she had heard it all before. She told him that she was filing for divorce; he wasn't to bother coming after her. She hung up and that was it.

Luis assumed that he could still win her back, but for him, the question was whether to put his marriage and family before his commitment to Prince Charles and the team. He had made arrangements to ship his horses on a ferry for the forthcoming polo tournament in Deauville, northern France, and whatever the consequences, he wasn't going to miss his date with the Prince.

While Luis, his sister, and Beto took a flight to Deauville, his neighbour and part-time chauffeur, Edgar Quijo-Duggan, drove his car over with a heavy load of luggage. He had the task of delivering the clothes and mallets to the rooms of Luis's team members at the Royal Hotel.

Following the break with his wife, and no longer having access to her bank accounts, Luis was broke. His own money was long gone, and he had to go to great lengths to pay for the transport of his horses, his grooms, and the accommodation in Deauville. However, although the Golden Eagles team didn't win any cups, the trip was a social success.

María Eugenia Garcés Etcheverría also arrived in Deauville, purportedly to watch the polo, but the press assumed it was to see Charles. If so, her ploy initially seemed to fail as Charles arrived arm in arm with Czech-born aristocrat Angelika Lazansky von Bukowa, who later married the 6th Earl Cawdor. But Angelika didn't stay in Deauville for long, so María Eugenia's mood improved when she again became the Prince's date for the weekend.

Luis Basualdo with his first wife, Lucy Pearson, and their daughter, Charlotte, at the Gold Cup Polo at Cowdray Park, July 1975

Reading about María's visit to Deauville, a disappointed Juan Manuel Santos finally understood that he had lost María Eugenia to Charles. Thirty years later, when Santos became President of Colombia, he met Prince Charles in London during an official visit and surprised the then heir to the throne by saying, 'I know you well, your Royal Highness. You stole my girlfriend from me!'

It soon became public knowledge that Lucy had flown back to New York and that Luis had preferred to join the Prince at Deauville rather than save his marriage. Without the financial support of his wife, he couldn't afford to keep his Golden Eagles team running and he had no choice but to tell Charles he wouldn't be playing the next season. Charles then accepted an invitation from French millionaire Guy Wildenstein to join his Les Diables Bleus team for the following year. By trying to cosy up to the Prince, Luis was left with no family, no wife, and no money. In the end, he also lost Charles – if he ever had him.

Luis had taken to drinking heavily, and when the Deauville season drew to a close, he began courting wealthy clients and offering his horses for sale. By a stroke of luck, Alex Ebeid, the Cirencester-based Egyptian sponsor, took pity on him and bought the whole lot, buckets and brushes included. It was a reprieve, but Luis had to curb his expenses dramatically, so as a last resort, he went to Palm Beach to stay with his friend 'Count' Alberto van der Mije. However, his wife Brenda, who had never liked Luis, wanted him gone as soon as possible, accusing him of being a bad influence on her husband, which he was. So as a parting gift, Alberto put him in touch with a neighbour who needed a six-goaler for his team.

His name was Fred Fortugno, Pennsylvania's mushroom king and polo sponsor who played with his sons Paul and Gene in his Mallet Hill team. It was a dramatic fall from grace for Luis who, one year earlier, had his own team with the Prince of Wales as one of his players. Now he was the fourth member of an obscure family team, wearing the silly green jacket and white bowler hat that was the Fortugno uniform.

He wasn't paid much but he was housed in a motel, with full board and the use of an old Ford Fairlane. The little money he saved was enough for him to make his way to New York where he booked himself into the cheap and central Pickwick Arms Hotel and set about trying to get his life back together.

He called his banker friend Lucio García Mansilla, who invited him for lunch and introduced him to the powerful Argentinian banker Luis Oddone, also a polo enthusiast. When Luis boasted of his royal connections, the banker Oddone was all ears, eager to hear all Luis's anecdotes about the British royal family, especially Prince Charles. Luis happily obliged, exaggerating their friendship, but avoiding telling him the reasons for his exile and the fact that he was penniless.

Oddone confirmed that he was thinking of sending a team the following year to the UK and asked Luis to manage it. He, like so many others before him, saw polo as a way to further his social ambitions, and Luis's relationship with the Prince held a great deal of potential in that regard.

It was at this time – while Luis was staying in New York – that his wife Lucy filed for divorce on the grounds of cruelty, flagrant debauchery, and adultery. However, what promised to be a field day for the press did not materialise. To avoid his son-in-law's antics being aired in the open, and his own name dragged through the mud, Viscount Cowdray offered Luis a £200,000 pay-off to keep the whole sordid story out of the courts.

The proposal was most enthusiastically accepted. Part of the deal was that Luis was denied custody or access to his children, Charlotte and Rupert, which was hardly a sticking point, as he had seen so little of them anyway. Luis was to be erased from the children's lives, even to the extent of changing their surname to Pearson. Unfortunately for Luis, he didn't get the chance to enjoy the money as a long line of creditors were waiting to be paid. There were rumours that he had to resort to selling cocaine from his New York flat. When I confronted him about that on the phone, he replied, 'Hell no, I only cut it!'

Thirty days later, he was admitted to the Betty Ford Center for rehabilitation treatment. When Luis unexpectedly arrived back in the UK in April to play the 1978 polo season, very few people were happy about it, not least the Pearsons who hoped they had seen the back of him.

Luis made declarations to the press claiming that thirty thoroughbred ponies had been delivered to him for the forthcoming polo season and that he was receiving a generous salary from banker Luis Oddone to run his polo team, La Elvira. 'Everybody assumed I wouldn't have a team this year. I told Prince Charles in Deauville last August that it was unlikely,' he explained.[7] But despite this public display of confidence, he was turned down by Cowdray Park ahead of the Gold Cup, the most desired trophy in the tournament. Cowdray's excuse was that he had been late in applying, and they had already received the required maximum of ten entries. Instead, however, La Elvira was included in other, less prestigious, tournaments. Taking advantage of the fact that Oddone was absent, Luis told everybody that La Elvira was his own team.

When Luis showed up to play his first match at Guards Club in Windsor with his new team, Prince Charles thought he was seeing a ghost. La Elvira won several cups, and Luis even managed to get Charles to play friendly matches with him on a few occasions. On the surface, it all seemed like the good old days – Luis even got an invitation to Charles's thirtieth birthday party at Buckingham Palace where he was seated next to a certain Lady Diana Spencer – but the Prince's relationship with him had decidedly cooled.

Oddone was disappointed not to have Charles in his team as more than an occasional guest player. In an attempt to further ingratiate himself with the Prince, he told Luis to give Charles a polo pony as a belated birthday present and allow him to select it himself. There were eighteen to choose from, and after taking the most promising one, Charles entered the field for the first chukka against Cowdray Park. But from the outset, he looked decidedly uncomfortable on the horse, and within minutes he was back at the stables. 'I can't play on this donkey,' he exclaimed, unaware the press was nearby. His words were widely reported and Oddone's plan failed spectacularly.

Luis telephoned the banker to tell him the horses he had sent were worthless. What he hadn't realised was that the 'donkey' in question had been sold to Oddone by none other than Captain 'Negro' Carlos Enrique Jáuregui, a noted polo player and infamous member of the military junta's death squads, responsible for the deaths of thousands of people. He was not someone to be messed with, and after Oddone complained to Jáuregui, quoting Prince Charles and Luis's verbatim, a furious Jáuregui swore revenge.

33
Bad Company

While Luis dedicated himself to regaining the Prince's good opinion, I got on with my life. It was in 1978 that I met Marcus Emerson, a young red-haired man who played polo at Cowdray Park. He very kindly lent me his ponies to play practice games and also invited me to stay weekends at the modest weekend family flat in Haslemere. The Emersons ran a business called Marcus Flowers, headed by Marcus's father, Stan, a thin, active forty-something who got up at the crack of dawn to head down to Covent Garden Market to buy flowers which his wife, Brenda, supplied to the leading London hotels and restaurants. I first met the Emersons when they visited Cowdray Park to cheer on Marcus who was competing in a polo tournament. On that occasion, they were accompanied by Stan's business partner, Jock Campbell-Muir, who arrived in a vintage Rolls-Royce with a middle-aged blonde woman who looked like the raunchy actress Barbara Windsor.

According to Marcus, Campbell-Muir had been in prison in Spain for drug trafficking after getting caught red-handed entering the country in a small vessel crammed with cannabis. He now smuggled

BMW parts into the UK with his father and was a vintage car dealer on the side.

Our paths crossed again, either coincidently or by design, when I was invited to dinner at the Emersons' London flat. Both Campbell-Muir and the Emersons seemed to be impressed that I had been the best man at Viscount Cowdray's daughter's wedding, which I assumed Marcus had mentioned because I certainly had not, and also by my 'friendship' with Lady Edith Foxwell. It was Stan who proposed that I enter into business with them by buying vintage cars in Argentina and shipping them to the UK, offering me a twenty per cent commission on each deal. Needless to say, I had little interest in travelling to Argentina in search of old cars; I had even less interest in entering into any kind of partnership with these people as they were clearly not to be trusted. I told them that I thought their proposal was interesting (another word I had learned that could have several meanings), and that I would let them know if I was planning on visiting Argentina. The conversation then turned to my status in the UK, and maybe because of the amount I had drunk, I confessed that I had still not settled my residence. When I first arrived in the country, I had been given three months on a tourist visa, which I had to renew by travelling abroad, usually to France, and getting a fresh tourist visa stamp each time I returned to the UK. But immigration officers were asking more and more difficult questions every time I came back. Jock's eyes lit up at this news.

'Say no more,' he said, 'I'm in touch with a government minister who could get you a British passport no problem.'

In the short time I had known Jock, I had decided not to trust him, more by instinct than anything I could put my finger on. However, he seemed confident that it could be done and I could think of no other solution, so I arranged to meet his contact the next day. Our agreed meeting place was a drinking club called The Maisonette, on Hertford Street by Shepherd Market. I entered an unprepossessing doorway and climbed a rickety flight of stairs, thinking that perhaps he had selected this as an anonymous rendezvous, but it turned out to be Jock's regular haunt from which he conducted his shady business dealings. I found him inside sitting on an armchair reading a newspaper.

'Hard luck, my friend,' he said before I'd had a chance to even greet him. 'My contact was unable to come. You know how these government people are.'

I had no idea how they were, but he wanted me to think he did.

'When can I meet him then?' I asked.

Taking off his glasses, Jock became business-like, the shadiness that I had always suspected in him now only too obvious. 'I guess you've taken into account that it won't be cheap.'

At that moment, we were approached by a mature woman who introduced herself as Jock's partner. Her name was Ruby Lloyd, formerly known as the Queen of the Night, and widow of an Irish gangster who had left her this house on Hertford Street that she'd converted into The Maisonette. Ruby could drink anyone under the table, even me, and that evening I stupidly tried to keep up with her. After losing count of the whiskies I had knocked back, I went to the gents for a break. It was pokey and dank, the red linoleum on the floor was torn and the porcelain sink was chipped in the corner. I raised the toilet seat and while taking aim, I lost my balance. I grabbed hold of one of the pipes and, in the process, ripped it clean off the wall. I crumpled onto the tiny floor, a section of pipe still in my hand as the rest of it sprayed the entire place with water. In my drunken state, I believed I could somehow put it all back together again and tried to do just that. My ridiculous endeavours were soon interrupted by Jock bursting in.

'What the fuck have you done?'

'It's okay. I think I can fix it,' I called out over the sound of the gushing water. I was soaked from head to foot.

Ruby came to my rescue and escorted me back to the bar.

'You must be feeling a little tipsy,' she observed. It was she who wore the pants there, so Jock had to swallow his anger and stick an 'out of order' sign on the bathroom door.

Despite that incident, I began to frequent The Maisonette, which was one of the many drinking clubs popular in London at that time. It was the law that pubs had to close at 3 p.m., reopen at 6 p.m., and close for the night at 11 p.m. For that reason, out-of-hours 'private' drinking clubs became fashionable. They were exciting places to be as they drew a variety of people. The most pretentious and aristocratic people could mix with villains and, of course, drugs were freely available.

It was at The Maisonette that I met Bobby McKew, better known as the Chelsea Scallywag, an Irishman who had recently been released from prison after being convicted as the mastermind behind the best counterfeit Swiss banknotes in recent times.

'We were going to launder the Swiss francs through the casino of a friend of mine because it's impossible to trace the origin of cash in casinos,' he told me. I was surprised by how candid he was about his activities. 'But my partner changed too many of the notes in one go, the bank became suspicious and our cover was blown.'

There was something about The Maisonette that had a confessional quality, as if whatever was said within those four walls would not be repeated or even remembered outside. I was intrigued by how Ruby got away with so many infractions without being penalised. Serving drinks well after hours was the norm, as was all-night gambling. The reason for her impunity, I discovered, was Wally Virgo, the dashing commander of Scotland Yard's Major Crimes Squad. Handsome and slim, with a trimmed moustache and trilby hat, Commander Virgo, who was awarded the Queen's Police Medal, the highest award an officer can earn, ended up convicted on corruption charges and sentenced to twelve years in prison. Before his downfall, he was in overall control of nine squads, including the Flying, Drugs, and Vice Squads, and for years, he had been receiving payments from drug dealers, pornographers, and club owners. His conviction was overturned on appeal and he was soon back drinking at The Maisonette as if nothing had happened. Once out of the police force, he acted as a consultant for people requiring advice on how to circumvent the law and became a very powerful player in London's seedy underworld.

I also learned that my friend Tessa Welborn had acquired The Little House, another drinking club in Shepherd Market. Tessa loved pink champagne, and what better business for an alcoholic than owning a drinking club? The Little House, a dive located in a mid-eighteenth-century house, had operated as a 'members-only' club since 1928. Although its clientele was supposedly more select, like all drinking clubs, its atmosphere was seedy. From the first-floor windows, one could see the whole of Shepherd Market, where well-dressed prostitutes stood in doorways trying to attract the attention of wealthy clients walking from Mayfair to Green Park tube station.

A few days after my disastrous introduction to The Maisonette, Jock rang as though nothing had happened.

'My government contact is too busy to deal with your situation, but I managed to get somebody else just as good.'

We arranged to meet at the club, where I turned up, sober, at the appointed time. Jock introduced me to his friend, Samuel, a debonair-looking black man who from the preliminary exchange of pleasantries appeared to be American.

'So what is it that you do?' I asked.

'I sip,' he replied, raising his gin and tonic to his lips. 'Like this,' he continued, his little finger in the air as he tipped the glass back.

After another couple of questions brought similarly unhelpful replies, I thought it would be wise not to ask any more. Jock found our exchanges very amusing in a forced kind of way, but suddenly he turned very serious and motioned to a table in the corner, away from the bar and any eavesdroppers. Once he was sure we couldn't be overheard, he got down to business.

'The problem with a British passport is that the loopholes are closing and the passports are increasingly expensive to get hold of. Samuel here is a very old friend of mine. He's also a Vietnam veteran who served in the Marines and was decorated for his service. His record is impeccable, and the reason I tell you all this is because he is now the US Honorary Consul to the UK, which takes me to the business you're interested in – your American passport.'

All this time Samuel said nothing and carried on nonchalantly sipping his drink.

'My American passport?' I protested. 'It's a British passport I need!'

'American passports are much easier to obtain and they're just as good as they require no visas to enter the UK,' Jock said. 'I want you to think it over and then bring two photos and eight hundred pounds. In a week you'll have your American passport.'

In the first instance, I wasn't sure if I would ever see either a passport or my money again, and secondly, I was afraid that any passport they provided would not get through a customs control check. The whole thing seemed off, but I didn't want to upset Jock or Samuel by revealing that I didn't believe their story. Instead, I tried to hedge.

'Why don't you give me your telephone number,' I suggested. 'I'll give you a call in a couple of days with my decision.'

Samuel, who had been casually sipping the whole time, froze at my suggestion. 'You don't need my phone number for anything,' he said menacingly. 'All you need do is bring Jock the cash and the photos. Now, if you'll excuse me, I have business to attend to.'

With that, the Honorary Consul downed the last of his drink and left.

In the end, I didn't pursue the matter. I informed Jock that I didn't have the money, which was sort of true, but the real reason was that if I accepted their terms, I would likely become a resident, but only as a guest of Her Majesty's Prisons.

34
Hashish and Ashes

It was unusually cold and misty for the time of the year when Luis and I met in London in August 1978. The city looked beautiful. As Monet had observed, London wouldn't be as beautiful without the fog, and it was a day that proved his point. Things were going well for Luis with his sponsor Oddone, but he was drinking too much, which he blamed on his divorce, and he blamed the loss of his family on his loyalty to the Prince of Wales, something even he could not possibly believe. He told me about a recent meeting he had had with his old friend Fulco di Santostefano who had steadied the social ladder, so to speak, when he started to climb it back in New York.

 The two old friends had not seen each other in a long time, but they bumped into each other at a cocktail party in London and Fulco was so pleased to see him that he invited him for lunch. Luis appeared at the appointed time and place, but there was no sign of Fulco. After waiting forty minutes and drinking a few glasses of Pinot Grigio, he decided to order a plate of spaghetti *alle vongole* and wash it down with some more wine to appease his anger at being stood up. A few days later, he received a call from an Italian gentleman by the name of Mario Salvo.

'Terrible news, Signore Basualdo, our friend the Duke of Verdura died a couple of days ago. Would you like to join me and another friend in carrying his 'hashes' back to Sicily?'

Shocked by the unexpected news, Luis said 'Yes' without further thought. Arrangements were made, and a few days later he arrived with the two Italians to catch the midday flight to Sicily.

When Salvo went through customs, the officer on duty pointed at the shiny box he was carrying, and asked, 'What have you got there?'

'Hashes—'

'Hashish? You are under arrest!'

We were led to a small cell where we spent the night and it was only when the Italian Consulate intervened the following day that we were released.

'I thought they were going to lock me up for good, ashes and all!' Luis said.

According to him, he had volunteered to travel to Sicily with Fulco's ashes out of loyalty to an old friend, but I knew the real reason was that he could never resist the social opportunities of a grand funeral. Luis added this story to his stock of amusing anecdotes, however, the fear of being investigated was a shadow that hung over both of us. I had particular concerns of my own about it.

The Times had just published a very damaging story about my friend and associate Eric Hebborn, labelled – unjustly – an infamous art forger. It revealed that Hebborn's main activity was the production of drawings in the style of famous artists, and I was immediately concerned that I would be named as one of the dealers who had placed his work on the market.

Eric had been 'imitating' the style of artists such as Corot, Mantegna, Rubens, and Jan Brueghel on a large scale since he arrived in Italy. Setting aside the ethics of his work, what he created fooled even the most renowned experts. The quality of his work had been my justification for getting involved in selling these outstanding drawings to 'reputable' dealers, and I had done very well out of it. Eric was grateful to me, which made it an ideal arrangement while it lasted. I felt I had nothing to worry about as I always pleaded ignorance of what I was selling, and the dealers, in turn, thought they were taking advantage of an idiot by offering me less than the market price.

But now it appeared that Hebborn might be investigated by the authorities and his connections traced. That could mean I would also be investigated. *The Times* article specifically questioned the authenticity of a group of Old Master drawings bought by two former directors of the Colnaghi Gallery in London. As a result, Colnaghi's new directors decided to contact the owners of the suspect drawings and get them back for further examination.

It had all begun when the Pierpont Morgan Library in New York questioned the authenticity of a drawing Colnaghi had sold them in 1970. The drawing in question, *Page Boy* by Francesco del Cossa, had been acquired by the gallery at a Sotheby's sale. It had originally passed the scrutiny of three lots of experts: Sotheby's, Colnaghi's, and, finally, the Pierpont Morgan Library itself. It took months of patient detective work to provide sufficient evidence that it was a forgery, yet there was no general agreement as exhaustive scientific tests on paper and ink could not prove the drawings were forgeries.

Eric was a true master of masking, which is essentially copying the style of artists to perfection and leaving the experts to decide the attribution. It was an ideal situation as no one knew any better, and the law only punished misrepresentation. In an act of damage limitation, and to maintain their prestige, Colnaghi decided to indemnify all the clients. But fearing legal action, they did not name Eric in the statement. Instead, they pointed the finger at the salesmen who had offered them the drawings with no evidence of their provenance. In some cases, that salesman had been me. It seemed it was only a matter of time before the trail led to my door.

Experts from the Metropolitan Museum of New York insist to this day that the works it acquired, cited in *The Times* exposé, were genuine. It was the same for the National Gallery of Denmark, which had bought its masterpieces from Hans Calmann, a dealer of some standing and prestige who specialised in Old Master drawings. The British Museum, on the other hand, kept some of the drawings they bought but took the precaution of labelling them as Eric Hebborn's. The conclusion reached was that it was the distributors who were unreliable, and most of the money was made at Eric's expense. Even Sotheby's Old Master expert Julien Stock acknowledged that Hebborn was a master of his craft who delighted in outsmarting experts like him. Eric was never arrested since he never signed his work and always left the authentication task to the 'experts'. But the twist in the story was that following the scandal, dealers inundated him with commissions for new work.

A few years later, an article defending Eric's drawings appeared in Rome's *International Daily News*: 'Done on authentic paper of the 15th–16th centuries with ink and carbon above any suspicion, they are effectively the work of a true artist who has been able to fit himself into the style of the various masters he has imitated, and therefore no responsibility marks the experts of the auction houses who examined them before the sale.'[8]

Between 1978 and 1988, Eric made at least five hundred new drawings most of them found their way to the mansions of reputable collectors. He took pleasure in attacking the art world, its cliques, and its experts, not just through his work but more directly in his bestselling book *Drawn to Trouble*, in which he makes clear that he had never been a forger. 'I only provide drawings in the style of Old Masters,' he writes. 'The false attributions are made by dishonest dealers.'

Hebborn was murdered in Rome in 1996, allegedly by the Mafia, for whom he had (allegedly) been commissioned to copy the style of famous artists. His death brought a definitive end to my activities as an art dealer, but by then, I was only selling very occasionally. The article in *The Times* and the ensuing scandal, although it did not incriminate me, was my wake-up call.

By then, my mother had died, and I inherited a sizeable amount of land in the district of Balcarce. Situated about 400km southeast of Buenos Aires, it is mainly a potato-growing area where most of the local landowners sell their produce to the processing plant of McCain, the multinational supplier of French fries based in Balcarce.

Following my mother's death, I had to engage in unpleasant and protracted legal proceedings against my siblings to take full possession of my share, but eventually I succeeded. The cash this generates was and is enough to keep me going. For someone living hand to mouth for the best part of his life, this was the first time I had had a steady, honest income. It came as a great relief, as by that time, relying on my 'charms' for a living would have meant depending on rapidly depreciating assets.

35
Back in the Saddle

Wherever Luis went, he made friends and enemies in equal measure. One of those most certainly in the enemy camp was Captain 'Negro' Carlos Enrique Jáuregui. A rather shadowy figure, he was being prosecuted for crimes against humanity for his part in quashing opposition during the so-called *Proceso de Reorganización Nacional*.

On Perón's return to power in 1973, the government created the Triple A (Argentinian Anti-Communist Alliance), one of the first right-wing death squads. This organisation began kidnapping and killing members of leftist militant groups and expanded their attacks to anyone considered a leftist subversive or sympathiser. Amnesty International estimates that up to 30,000 people disappeared at that time.

As well as complying with his military 'duties', Jáuregui also spent time as an eight-goal polo player in the UK, and it was through polo that he and Luis crossed paths at the Guards Polo Club in Windsor, of which Prince Philip, Duke of Edinburgh, was president until his death.

Luis, who had joined the club with the sole intention of gaining access to the Prince of Wales, was careful not to frequent the club too often whenever Captain Jáuregui was in the UK. The captain had had it in for Luis since Charles had commented, within earshot of journalists, on the 'donkey' of a pony given to him as a belated birthday present by Luis. The pony in question had been supplied by Captain Jáuregui. As much as Luis went out of his way to avoid 'Negro', in the small world of polo they were bound to meet sooner or later.

This happened during a cocktail party thrown by a fellow player in his Ambersham home. Luis and eight-goaler Ezequiel 'Pilo' Fernández Guerrico were among the first guests to arrive, but they were soon followed by Captain Jáuregui and his sponsor, Harold Bamberg, the German-Jewish refugee owner of British Eagle independent airline who named his polo team Eaglesfield after his airline. The mere sight of the captain was enough to send Luis into a panic. He jumped out of a window, fell into the garden, and made a fast exit through the gates that he had so confidently entered one hour before. Pilo, who assumed that Luis got a ride home from someone else, eventually left the party. As he made his way towards his car, he thought he heard hissing: 'Psst! Psst!' He looked around and saw nothing. He kept walking and heard the voice again: 'Psst! Here!' Then he saw Luis lying flat on his belly in a ditch behind his car, his cheek pressed to the ground.

'What on earth are you doing, Luis?'

'Has he left?' Luis asked, still cowering in the ditch.

'Has who left?'

'Jáuregui.'

'You're such a coward!'

Luis demanded that Pilo open the back door of the car so he could slide into the seat unnoticed. For the whole journey, Luis stayed cowering in the back as though Jáuregui might appear at any moment and exact his revenge. It was a pitiful sight and from that moment, Pilo, who had been close to Luis, distanced himself from him.

There was worse to come towards the end of the 1979 season when Luis was still on the crest of the wave. His sponsor Oddone, the Argentinian banker, was arrested and jailed on charges of embezzlement in what was a huge financial scandal in Argentina.

Oddone, who had started with nothing, had become one of the country's leading bankers and businessmen in less than two decades. His bank was valued at $500 million, and with forty-eight branches, it was the sixth-largest bank in Argentina at the time. Almost overnight, the entire operation collapsed, along with Oddone's fortune and Luis's source of income.

Luis Basualdo with heiress Pilar Irisarri at Chez Castel, Paris, October 1980

It would not be easy for Luis to find another sponsor especially someone as generous as the disgraced banker. It was also around this time that Luis was accused of making unwanted sexual advances to a female groom and assaulting another player. He therefore decided that the best course of action would be to disappear for a while to Deauville, hoping it would all blow over. In his absence, the Guards Polo Club expelled him 'for bringing the game into disrepute.'

The Hurlingham Polo Association (HPA) also recommended a permanent ban from playing polo in England. The recommendation was made official in a telegram. The allegations centred around a female groom who, together with her husband, accused Luis of asking her to commit unnatural sex acts. Quite what the acts were was not disclosed, although the matter was reported in the press. As if that were not enough, he was also accused of being involved in a physical altercation with another member, and, though unrelated, there was at the same time an ongoing dispute with a commodity brokerage, Doxford's, which sent bailiffs to the clubs to serve Luis with a writ.

In the meantime, in January 1980, the *Daily Mail* ran an article under the headline 'Luis on the carpet': 'Now the Latin smoothie has been carpeted by polo's governing body, the Hurlingham Polo Association, for alleged naughtiness. He will have to face a disciplinary hearing sometime next week to answer a variety of charges including lack of attention to his string of ponies. Says the association secretary, Colonel Alec Harper: Mr Basualdo says that he will be attending, but until then the whole thing is *sub judice*.'[9]

Luis promptly appealed against the HPA decision and on 7th January 1980, he made his way to the Naval and Military Club in London to face the Disciplinary Committee of the Hurlingham Polo Association. He arrived late for the hearing but just in time to hear Arthur Lucas, chairman of the committee, addressing the Windsor Club representatives: 'You can ban him from playing at Guards Club, but you cannot ban him from playing in the UK. And that is final!'

Lucas's dictum was conclusive. Voting against were Major Ronald Ferguson, vice-president of the HPA and manager to the Prince of Wales, and his deputy and honorary secretary, Colonel Harper, Cowdray Park's polo manager. Both were against professionalism in the sport and objected to Argentinian nationals like Luis invading their territory. Realising Luis had been made a scapegoat, Lord Patrick Beresford and others seconded Lucas in the motion.

The president of the HPA, Douglas Riley-Smith, asked a somewhat crestfallen Luis if he would have a glass of sherry at the bar, perhaps his way of saying, 'Nothing personal, old chap.' A sheepish Major Ronald Ferguson joined them, saying, 'I swear I had nothing to do with that, Luis. You are your own worst enemy.' Like many others, he had always hated Luis for marrying Lord Cowdray's daughter and having Prince Charles's ear. Yet Ronnie's vote showed his resentment. Year after year his team had lost in the finals of England versus South America, and to top it off, his first wife had run off with an Argentinian professional. Luis chose to view the ban from the Guards Polo Club but not from elsewhere as a great victory. However, the reality was rather different because now, no club in England would have him as a member. As a last resort, he tried to join a club in Scotland by asking an acquaintance, Drummond-Moray, to put him up for membership, but his request was refused as the Scotsman was related to Ronnie Ferguson. Luis blamed Ferguson for being the chief architect of his downfall. However, his former father-in-law, Lord Cowdray, had more power in the polo world, and he had never forgiven Luis for how he treated his daughter Lucy.

36
The Falklands War

It was 3rd April 1982. I was having breakfast at a café in Portobello Road, where I was a regular, when I caught a glimpse of someone's newspaper. It was *The Sun*, and the headline, which took up most of the front page, read 'ARGENTINA INVADES THE FALKLANDS'. I remember the date vividly.

I bought the paper to find out what had happened. Immediately, my old fear of deportation arose again. I saw myself as I had been in Miami, except in a different country. It was not just paranoia. A few days later, an acquaintance who worked at the Argentinian Embassy told me that given the growing hostility towards Argentinians in the UK, they were considering advising Argentinian nationals to leave the country. The language used by the popular press reflected a new climate of hostility. Suddenly, all Argentinians were enemies; we were the 'Argies' who had invaded these far-away islands in the South Atlantic, where brave British lads were heading to take them back. The scenes at Portsmouth as crowds waved goodbye to the aircraft carriers HMS *Hermes* and HMS *Invincible* were reminiscent of the Second World War. A man in the crowd held up a sign that read

'Death to dirty Argies'. *The Sun* later led the story of the sinking of the Argentinian cruiser *General Belgrano*, in which 323 Argentinians died, with the headline 'GOTCHA!' This was the language of war, and for the first time since settling in the UK, I felt very unwelcome.

The hostility was noticeable everywhere, even from people whom I had known for years. A friendly neighbour, who walked his Red Setter every afternoon and with whom I often had a friendly chat, now crossed the road when he saw me. Worse still, the man in the kiosk on the corner of Westbourne Grove stopped serving me altogether. All this came at a time when I had finally found some emotional and financial stability. Despite her family's disapproval, my relationship with Sarah Fox-Pitt had become quite serious and we enjoyed a comfortable life together now that I was solvent. This harmony was suddenly threatened by the war and I increasingly felt that I should leave England immediately, at least until the war was over. It was certainly not my plan to return to Argentina, as I had always had an ambivalent relationship with my country of birth. Britain was my adopted homeland, my refuge, the place where family memories did not haunt me. Sarah suggested that my best option was to go to Paris and I agreed.

Acting on impulse, my first thought was to book a room at the Hôtel Brighton in the Rue de Rivoli, where I had previously stayed with Ursula. Then I remembered my friend Alexis von Rosenberg, Baron de Redé, whom I had met when I stayed in Paris that first time with Ursula. He had a soft spot for me and had previously put me up at his residence.

'Marcelo! This war is terrible. How are you?' he exclaimed down the phone as soon as he heard my voice.

'That's why I called. I don't think I can stay in London, not the way things are. It's just not safe here.'

'Then you must come here, Marcelo. At once. Today!'

'That's exactly what I was thinking of doing. I wondered if you could recommend a reasonably priced hotel for my girlfriend and me.'

'Marcelo, please don't insult me. You must stay here at Hôtel Lambert. I insist you stay here.'

It was what I had been angling for and we left for Paris right away. He had already arranged for us to have dinner at Le Privilège, the new club owned by Fabrice Emaer, Paris's 'King of the Night'. It was members-only with an interior inspired by the designs of Jean Cocteau. 'No riffraff, if you know what I mean,' Alexis assured us.

Sarah and I understood perfectly and happily got into his car to pick up Marie-Hélène Rothschild, his other guest. When we arrived at the club, Fabrice came out to personally welcome us. He had set aside one of the best tables in the place; seated at the table next to us was Yves Saint Laurent, who not only remembered me but stood up to greet me as soon as he saw me. Dinner and champagne were ordered, but just as we finished our first course, I felt a stream of cold liquid, which I later discovered was champagne, being emptied onto my head.

'Dirty bastard,' a woman growled.

At first, I couldn't see who it was as the alcohol had got in my eyes. When the fog cleared, I saw a defiant Ursula Mahler. Fabrice quickly intervened to prevent things from escalating and ordered Ursula to leave. But when he realised that she was one of Yves Saint Laurent's guests, he decided to let her stay. Alexis laughed it off and suggested everyone raise their glasses to toast my champagne baptism. Sarah, however, was not amused and demanded an explanation.

'She's somebody I met a long time ago,' I said, without volunteering any further detail.

Marie-Hélène Rothschild was delighted by the spectacle. She was pleased to learn that I'd broken up with 'that cheap woman' whom she had never liked. Despite that episode, we had a very enjoyable stay in Paris. Alexis was the perfect host and we both became very fond of him.

It was 15th June when, sitting with Sarah in the Café de Flore, I read in the *Daily Mail* that the war was over. We had a big celebration that evening and caught a flight back to London the next day. Despite the sense of rejection I had felt in the UK during the short war, on returning to London I learned that I had been elected a member of Turf Club, one of London's leading gentlemen's clubs. This came as a complete surprise to me, especially since many of the members were serving or former army officers.

My proposer had been the billionaire meat baron Lord Vestey, who owned a considerable amount of land in Argentina and had two Argentinian players in his Stowell Park polo team. My admission to the club made me confident that London could remain my permanent home. Also, our stay in Paris had strengthened my relationship with Sarah. However, although I genuinely wanted to put my days of being a kept man behind me, occasionally there was still an itch, which I occasionally scratched.

One evening I received a call from Viscountess Rothermere's secretary, Violet, who wanted to know if I would be free the next day 'to escort her ladyship to a fashion show'. I had met Patricia Harmsworth – Bubbles – when I first arrived in the UK. I did not hesitate in accepting the invitation and arrived punctually at her house in Eaton Square which I already knew from the party she had given for Princess Margaret in 1972. Knowing I was in for a long wait, I made myself comfortable on the sofa in the drawing room. The room was in a kind of Louis XIV style, but with gleaming white marble floors and Greek statues dotted about the place. For all its grandeur, there was something homely about it and I felt quite at ease. One of the paintings on the wall caught my eye: a magnificent still life by the eighteenth-century French Master Chardin, which in almost any other home one would have assumed to be a reproduction. I got up to admire it in detail, at which point the door opened and Bubbles came in wearing nothing but a pair of oversized Yves Saint Laurent sunglasses and a Shirley Temple wig with a big black bow. She kissed both my cheeks. 'Hello, Marcelo,' she said. 'I like punctual men.' No sooner had she entered the room, than she left it again.

The secretary Violet came in and told me to ignore Lady Rothermere's antics, adding that she wore wigs because of frequent attacks of nerves that caused her to pull her hair out. None of that bothered me as I had already heard so many stories about Bubbles. It was therefore not surprising that she was not ready on time. Needless to say, we missed the fashion show and so we went straight to Annabel's. Once she was bored of Annabel's, the chauffeured Bentley took us to Tramp where we carried on until closing time. Not having had enough, Bubbles decided we should go to a seedy, illegal belly-dancing joint in an Edgware Road basement, where drinks were served with lamb kebabs and pitta bread.

When we walked out into the bright sunlight of the next day, I knew I'd had my fill of Bubbles for a long time. Ever restless, she contacted me the following week to invite me to her Jamaican home, explaining that she needed to treat herself 'to some time off from the social whirlwind of London and sunbathe with friends'.

I declined the offer and later found out that the guests she had invited were landed with a hefty bill for staying at her property. It made me realise that I was tired of pandering to rich women and reminded me how much I valued my happy, stable relationship with Sarah, which I didn't want to jeopardise. I was finally ready to settle down.

37
Homme d'Affaires

After Luis's sponsor, the banker Oddone, was jailed on charges of embezzlement, Luis found himself yet again in a serious financial predicament. It was the story of his life. Even though he often described himself as an investor and stockbroker, he was never any good with investments. Every financial endeavour he ever got involved with had ended either in disaster or in court.

Although he constantly bragged about having a knack for business, he always seemed to lose more money than he ever made. He was cagey about his losses whenever I brought them up and became defensive or changed the subject. Nigel Dempster often chronicled these misadventures in his Diary in the *Daily Mail*. In 1978, in a story headed 'Luis is a loser yet again', he detailed a writ issued by commodity brokers M. L. Doxford & Co. in which the company claimed they were owed over £16,000 by Luis following a series of failed investments.[10]

In October 1978, another story appeared about a judgment brought against him by the legendary drummer Ginger Baker for £4,000. The unfortunate musician, who had met Luis at a party, got into business with him as an investor in a polo club that existed only on paper as no games were ever played there. Luis got as far as registering his new club with the Polo Association, giving an address at the Northamptonshire estate of Lord Rothschild's sister, Miriam. Did he do this to emulate his ex-father-in-law by having his own club, or was it another of his scams? The club only had two members – him and Ginger. After a year, Ginger decided he'd handed over enough money to Luis and the project ended. Luis sought damages from Baker, claiming he had kept some of his ponies and refused to let him off the hook.

Rather than resolve the trivial dispute amicably, Luis took him to court and won the case with disastrous consequences for Ginger's estranged wife, Liz. The court case took a few years, and in 1984, the *Daily Mail* revealed the disastrous consequences that Ginger's wife endured after the judge ruled against him.[11] While Baker absconded to Italy with his new wife, the court gave Luis the right to force the sale of Ginger's mock Tudor house in Harrow to recover the outstanding debt. Liz and her two children had to find alternative accommodation, although they moved back as squatters a few days later.

Under the headline 'Luis – an ex-polo player with a hole in his pocket', a Dempster's Diary of 18th October 1979 was about the ongoing Doxford affair.[12] With the amount still outstanding, the firm finally took him to court to recoup their losses.

Luis failed to appear at any of the hearings, claiming either that he was out of the country or that he hadn't been informed of the court's date. This time Luis was threatened with prison if he didn't turn up for the next hearing. Later that same month, Dempster reported: 'A polo-playing friend of Prince Charles escaped being sent to jail yesterday for contempt of court … The threat was lifted after Argentinian businessman Luis Basualdo promised the High Court that he would attend a special hearing about his finances.' When Luis failed to attend yet again, Mr David Prebble, Doxford's counsel, issued a jail order against him, but the judge adjourned the hearing because Luis went into hiding.

Luis Basualdo with Clare Lawman at the Prix de l'Arc de Triomphe, Longchamp, Paris, 1981

When Luis surfaced again, this time in Paris, there was a new woman in his life. Her name was Clare Lawman, a tall, slender, elegant English girl, who Luis later said was the only person he'd ever truly been in love with. It was always hard to know what Luis really felt about anything, but for once he might have been telling the truth. When I saw them together, they seemed to be genuinely besotted with one another, though of course, he would be unfaithful to her, as he was with all his girlfriends.

After his recent financial problems, Luis had tightened his belt by having only one dish when he went out for dinner. One evening, when Luis and Clare had arrived for dinner at Le Relais in the Hôtel Plaza Athénée and were trying to decide how best to economise, who should walk in but Christina Onassis. She was with a friend and they invited themselves to sit with Clare and Luis. The couple, who up to that point had been prepared to hold back, now chose freely from the menu in the expectation that Christina would foot the bill. Luis flattered Christina, remarking on how well she looked, although she had put on a lot of weight since he had last seen her, and he allowed her to monopolise the conversation with stories of past times and her relationship with him, ignoring the fact that he was there with a new companion. Not only did Christina pick up the bill, but she also extended an invitation to them to join her skiing that year. Over the next few months, the three of them became almost inseparable, and even Clare, whom Christina only grudgingly tolerated at first, became quite close to her. Wherever Christina went, Clare and Luis went too, and when she decamped to her private island of Skorpios for the summer, so did they.

Christina Onassis (left) with Clare Lawman, Paris, 1982

After her father died in 1975, Christina inherited his businesses, his ships, and his properties, including the private island of Skorpios where she had spent summers as a child. She now held court on the island with guests that she assembled, pampered, and tyrannised. They had to acquiesce to her every whim, staying up till the early hours, going dancing on a nearby island, watching films in her private cinema, which she might stop halfway through because she didn't like it or wanted to do something else. This erratic behaviour was exacerbated by her increasing abuse of barbiturates.

'We were all on Christina time,' Luis said when I saw him after his stay. After a few weeks of putting up with Christina's caprices, the couple felt restless and decided it would be better to move on and get away from her. But even the suggestion that they might move to another part of the island was enough to set her off. Christina, who had complex medical and psychological problems, tried to emotionally blackmail the couple, saying that their move would be detrimental to her nerves and general health, and insisting that she needed regular companions on doctor's orders. According to Luis, it was at this point that Christina first proposed the idea of paying for his company. They haggled over a price, Luis wildly exaggerating the amount of money he would forfeit by not being able to play polo as a professional. Christina had no idea that he did not, and could not, play any longer. In the end, they settled on a monthly retainer of $30,000.

The role itself was very undefined. In many ways, what she was paying for was his emotional support and his availability: a man at her side in whom she could confide, particularly about her relationships. This she pursued with increasing frenzy, moving from one object of obsession to another. While Luis was still claiming poverty to his creditors in Britain, the French press reported that he was employed by his ex-lover Christina Onassis in Paris as her homme d'affaires earning a five-figure salary. The story was picked up in December 1982 by the *Daily Mail*, which reported: 'Thrice married Christina Onassis, 31, who inherited a £250 million shipping fortune, has

Luis Basualdo leaving bankruptcy court in London, March 1984

appointed the handsome but bankrupt Argentinian polo player Luis Basualdo as her personal companion, at a salary said to be in excess of $200,000 a year.'[13]

Back in the UK for his day in court, Luis was officially declared bankrupt on 8th March 1984 for monies owed to commodity brokers Doxford and Co. Sometime after this, I met him with Dai Llewellyn for a drink at Annabel's, and when the time came for the bill to be settled, he insisted that he pay for it, which was quite unusual for him. He handed the barman a personal cheque in the name of 'Luis de Souza'. When I quizzed him about it, he replied, 'I've reverted to my own name with its original Portuguese spelling.'

What he had done was open a bank account under a false name. It turned out that Luis had saved money from his employment with Christina and had some left over from his divorce settlement, but he had decided to go bankrupt rather than pay his debts.

The renewed association with Christina gave him insight into her affairs and allowed him to exert a certain amount of control over aspects of her private life and financial affairs, at least until 1984 when she married Thierry Roussel, the playboy son of Henri Julien Gaston Roussel, President and General Manager of Roussel Uclaf Laboratoires Pharmaceutiques. At that point, Luis was informed that his services were no longer required. In the meantime, he had got to know members of her extended family, particularly her stepbrother, the Marquess of Blandford.

Jamie Blandford was the son and heir of the Duke of Marlborough, who Christina's mother, Tina, had married in 1961 after she divorced Aristotle Onassis. After some initial suspicion, Christina became very close to the family, living with them at their country estate in England, and those were happy years for her. She remained particularly close to her stepbrother whom I often bumped into at Annabel's and other places and found to be very affable. Over time, Jamie developed a heroin addiction, something that was widely reported in the press. Luis, who was no stranger to drugs and addiction himself, knew only too well how vulnerable Jamie was and saw an opportunity. It took very little effort for Luis to get close to Jamie and gain his confidence. I saw Luis in his company on many occasions during this time and realised the two of them had become inseparable. What I later found out was that Luis was grooming him for a scam that was far bigger than anything he had attempted to date, and which would seal his reputation not just as a bounder but as a criminal.

Jamie Blandford, the Marquess of Blandford, with Luis Basualdo at the Business Connection Concert, Hippodrome, London, June 1985

Having planned everything meticulously, he suggested to Jamie they go on a trip together and Jamie agreed. The first stop was to be Cadaqués on the Costa Brava, where the Guinness family had a house, and where Luis said he would introduce Jamie to the beautiful Daphne Guinness, whom he was very keen to meet. From there, they went to St Moritz where Luis claimed he had some banking matters to attend to.

Luis requested a personal appointment with the manager of Credit Suisse, where he had an account, as did Christina. When the manager arrived, he introduced himself and Jamie who he had brought along.

The two men were taken to an office where some paperwork was put before them to sign. Whatever business Luis had with the bank, it had nothing to do with his companion. However, Jamie was asked to sign something 'as a witness', and because of his fragile state, he did not understand what he was putting his name to. Only a couple of months before he had been arrested for breaking into a pharmacy in search of heroin. He had mistakenly come to trust Luis over the previous months and duly signed the documents that were put in front of him.

After a few days in Switzerland, Luis announced that he needed to go to Austria where he had some other financial matters to attend to, and once again asked Jamie to accompany him. They took a train across the border to the small town of Landeck where Luis took Jamie further into his confidence, flattering him by asking for his advice on where he should open an account. Luis eventually opened an account at the Tirol Bank, making it seem to the befuddled Jamie that it was done on his advice when it had been part of Luis's plan the whole time. He then told Jamie that when he mentioned to the bank manager that he was travelling with the son of the Duke of Marlborough, the manager had insisted on meeting him. Luis then introduced him to the manager, speaking in the basic German he had learned in Hamburg so Jamie wouldn't understand what was being said. The manager asked Jamie to produce his passport, which Luis explained was to prove that he was indeed the son of the duke, something which, according to Luis, had impressed the star-struck manager. Jamie duly produced his passport and signed another document, thinking that he was acting as a witness to confirm Luis's identity. He was in fact opening a joint account with Luis.

When quizzed later on about the events that took place, all that Jamie could recall was something about a telephone password that had to be recorded for the bank to send money, but Luis kept the password to himself; in any case, most of the talk had been in German. Jamie would come to regret his failure to understand what happened that day.

38

The Strange Case of Christina's Missing Money

By the middle of 1985, Luis was back in the United Kingdom with big plans for the future. This time, his ambition was to become a country squire. While his girlfriend Clare stayed in London most of the time, he decided to join the Beaufort Hunt in Wiltshire. David Somerset had just inherited the dukedom of Beaufort and the 52,000-acre Badminton estate that came with it. The Beaufort Hunt attracted a large turnout (or 'field') partly due to the frequent presence of Princess Anne, Prince Charles, Princess Michael of Kent, the Earl of Suffolk, and others of the same ilk.

To get closer to this exclusive group, Luis seduced American heiress and resident Didi Saunders and moved into her Easton Gray Manor House, even though he was still in a relationship with Clare. He started by sharing Didi's bed, but when their relationship deteriorated, he moved out to a cottage on the estate. To ensure he could safely stay, he persuaded her to sign a lease that prevented her from evicting him. Over time, Luis became acquainted with Didi's handyman, Ludovico Sanok, a Second World War Polish Army veteran, who lived with his wife in the nearby town of Tetbury. In addition to taking care of repairs in the house, Ludovico became the driver of Luis's spacious BMW for a few extra pounds, Luis insisting he wore a grey chauffeur's uniform.

Luis Basualdo shooting and hunting on the Badminton Estate, 1985

While he waited in vain for a polo club to accept him as a member, he appeared at the Beaufort Hunt meets wearing a top hat and immaculate hunting attire. His presence there did not go unremarked. Not only had his bad reputation preceded him, but he also spread what was considered vicious and ungentlemanly gossip about other members. Princess Michael of Kent was among the first to complain about his presence and she requested that he be ejected from the hunt. Others added to the call for his exclusion, to the point where the Duke of Beaufort had to agree to ban him.

Luis later took revenge on Princess Michael by spreading the stories he'd read in the press that the Princess had plagiarised the work of others for her history books. When it was heard that Didi Saunders had put Easton Gray Manor up for sale, residents breathed a sigh of relief, thinking Luis's lease would be cancelled and they would see the back of him. However, their relief was to be short-lived: Luis had enjoyed living there so much that he decided to acquire a country house in the vicinity.

By early October 1986, he was viewing the most desirable properties in Gloucestershire, informing estate agents that he would

Left to right: Model Shelley Smith, Sir Gordon White, actress Cheryl Ladd and Luis Basualdo at the Prix de l'Arc de Triomphe, Longchamp, Paris, 1984

be paying in cash. The agents didn't think to ask where the money would be coming from, although he had been very publicly declared bankrupt not so long before. He had even stated to the press at the time, 'All I have are the cufflinks I am wearing'. Later that month, the *Daily Mail* published the latest on Luis: 'There is chilling news for the socially prominent who turn out regularly with the Duke of Beaufort's Hunt – Argentinian born Luis Basualdo has been looking over properties in the area, and is proposing to buy a manorial house with 11 loose boxes and paddocks.'[14]

It was around this time that Christina received a call from her office in Monte Carlo informing her that her account at Credit Suisse in St Moritz, usually in credit to the tune of one or two million dollars, was almost empty. Although Christina squandered money thoughtlessly much of the time, usually on prospective lovers or husbands, she could also be quite particular about it and those to whom she had given it. This was one of those times, so she confirmed with the bank that she had not used the account for some time and demanded an explanation. Further investigation revealed that for over a year, more than a million dollars had been transferred from her account to an account at the Tirol Bank in Landeck held in the name of 'James Spencer'. She was aghast to learn that her own stepbrother Jamie, with whom she had always had a good relationship, had stolen money from her. But when the recording of the telephone password, which operated the account, was played to her, Christina immediately recognised it as the voice of Luis Basualdo.

Later, on 12th December 1986, another article was published by the *Daily Mail* stating, amongst other things, that Christina's stepbrother, the Marquess of Blandford, was being investigated in a case of fraud perpetrated against his stepsister.[15] Jamie's situation looked even worse when his bank balance was found to have recently gone far into the black. However, it was later confirmed to be due to the maturing of a trust fund established by his great-grandmother, American heiress Consuelo Vanderbilt.

Luis Basualdo with brewery heiress Daphne Guinness at a reception, 1985

During those months, Luis only visited his Wiltshire cottage whenever he had appointments with estate agents, the rest of the time he spent in London. When he read the news of the investigation in the press, he decided it would be best for him to stay away from the countryside and wait in London for the heat to die down. On one of his rare visits to Wiltshire, he went to Tetbury to collect saddles and polo mallets from his faithful servant Ludovico. As soon as Ludovico opened the door, Luis could see he was a changed man. He looked gaunt and anxious.

'Mr Basualdo!' he exclaimed. 'Where have you been? Everyone's been looking for you.'

'Looking for me?' Luis asked nervously. 'Who's been looking for me?'

'Everyone.'

'Well, I'm here now.' Luis tried to sound nonchalant, as if he didn't know what Ludovico was talking about, but Ludovico soon told him.

'The police came here. They accused us of stealing money from Christina Onassis. They put us in prison and ransacked our house. It was a nightmare. They asked about you. They asked where you were. They couldn't find you on Mrs Saunders' estate!'

'Don't worry, Ludo, I assure you it's all a misunderstanding,' Luis said reassuringly. 'Leave it all to me. I know exactly how to deal with this.'

He put a fifty-pound note in Ludovico's hand and turned back towards his car, still muttering empty assurances. Then he drove back to London and never returned.

The reason the police had come knocking on Ludovico's door was because Luis had opened a joint account in his and Ludovico's name at a local

Luis Basualdo with Lady Henrietta Spencer-Churchill, daughter of the Duke of Marlborough, at a society wedding, 1985

Luis Basualdo at the Derby, Epsom Downs, 1986

bank in Tetbury. This he did, ostensibly so that 'Ludo' could pay bills in his absence, but Luis never gave Ludovico a cheque book and there were never any bills to pay. It had been just another account to siphon money from Christina's account. A few days after the Tetbury account had been opened, it was credited with $700,000 from Christina Onassis's bank in Austria. The bank statements went to Luis's address in London, so Ludovico was none the wiser. Luis had opened this account in their joint names so that he could blame Ludovico if the crime were to be discovered.

The investigation was closing in on Luis. It was clear that he had been behind the scam and that Jamie and Ludovico were unwitting pawns. The police looked for him, but as Luis had no fixed address, they weren't able to find him. But Luis had left a clue as to his whereabouts. A few months earlier, we had met for drinks at Annabel's and to show off his new-found wealth, he drove me home in a new Mercedes. After dropping me off, he was arrested for drunk driving and taken to Paddington Green Police Station where they kept him overnight. He was summoned to attend court the next day but absconded without a trace, as he usually did. When filling in the forms the night before, he had given the Ritz Hotel as his address. When the officers investigating the scam located the drunk driving file, they decided to pay him a visit at the Ritz.

Two plain clothes officers went to the hotel on a freezing December day and asked the receptionist if he knew a Mr Luis Sosa Basualdo; the receptionist said that he knew him well. Luis did not have a room at the hotel then, but he had previously had one of the butler's rooms, which he paid little money for just so he could give the prestigious Ritz as his address. He used to tip the porters so they would keep his mail even though he was not living there. The receptionist explained to the officers that while neither he nor the other staff knew where Mr Basualdo was at that precise moment, he came to the hotel almost every evening to pick up his mail.

At around eight o'clock that same evening, Luis arrived at the hotel with Clare Lawman and immediately noticed something wasn't right. The doorman standing by the front steps, who usually smiled and bowed, acted as if he didn't know him. Despite that, Luis went to reception, picked up his post, and sat down on his usual chair to sift through it. It was at this point that Detective Inspector Robert Townley and Sergeant Ralph Taylor appeared and stood in front of him. They asked him to confirm who he was, before requesting that he accompany them to the station. Luis sheepishly stood up and he and Clare were escorted to a car parked at the side of the hotel. First, they drove to Clare's flat in Knightsbridge where the police expected to find part of the money stolen from Christina's account, but after an exhaustive search, they found nothing. They were sure Luis was guilty, but there was very little that they could do until the requested extradition order from Austria arrived. They asked

Luis to hand over his passport, which he did and because the drunk driving charge was still outstanding, they were able to take him into custody and keep him overnight. The next morning, they took him to Marlborough Street Magistrates Court, where he pleaded guilty to the drink-driving charge, was fined £200, and banned from driving in Britain for twelve months. Luckily for Luis, the extradition papers had still not arrived by the time his court case was over, so the police had no choice but to release him.

'It goes without saying, Mr Basualdo, that you mustn't leave town without telling us,' DI Townley said.

According to the statement that Luis gave Nigel Dempster for his article, there was no indication of any wrongdoing on his part. 'I telephoned Christina at the Hilton Hotel in London because I heard my name was being mentioned in connection with this matter,' he said. 'She told me to forget it and the only conversation we had was about family matters.'

That wasn't true. When I met Christina later, at Luis's request, she was furious with him and accused him of being a thief. He also said, 'The police at Rochester Row interviewed me but they said there was no reason I couldn't leave the country.'

It was another barefaced lie, as the police had confiscated his passport. A week after his detention, Luis answered the phone at Clare Lawman's flat. It was DI Townley inviting Luis to report to Rochester Row police station. 'It's just for a quick chat,' Townley said, casually playing down his real intentions, but Luis suspected that the extradition papers had arrived.

Luis had handed his American passport to the police, but what they didn't know was that he had an Argentinian passport under his mattress. They had never found it when they searched Clare's flat. Retrieving the hidden passport, Luis packed what he could get into one suitcase, said goodbye to Clare, and left. Fearing that he would be stopped at the airport, a cautious Luis phoned me, omitting to say the police were after him. I gave him a lift to Euston Station, where he caught the next train to Glasgow. From Glasgow, he boarded another

Joan Collins with Luis Basualdo (centre) and Nigel Dempster (right) at the Derby, Epsom Downs, 1986

train to the south-west tip of Scotland, from where he took the ferry to Larne in Northern Ireland. Once there, he made his way south in a farmer's Land Rover, which was pulling a trailer of cattle. They crossed the border into the Irish Republic (no passports required), and a few days later, a very dishevelled, sleep-deprived, and muddy Luis arrived at the Aer Lingus desk at Dublin airport. He purchased a ticket to Buenos Aires, via Amsterdam and Madrid, paying in cash so he didn't leave a trail.

His suspicion that he was about to be arrested was correct. In the early hours of the following morning, DI Townley and Sergeant Taylor arrived at Clare's flat in Egerton Gardens with an arrest warrant. When they discovered that Luis had fled, they took Clare back to the station instead. After a four-hour interrogation, during which she consistently denied knowing his whereabouts, she was released. Over the following days, they continued to put pressure on her, believing she must have known where Luis was hiding. They quizzed her on several occasions to 'help them with their enquiries', but Clare stuck to her story, pleading ignorance of everything. In the end, the police stopped harassing her. Clare was simply a naive girl who loved Luis and never questioned anything he said or did. What baffled DI Townley was not Clare's apparent ignorance, but what an attractive young woman from a good family was doing with a scoundrel like Luis Basualdo.

I didn't want to see Clare after this episode, nor did she want to see me. Both of us had been tainted by our involvement with Luis and all we wanted was to forget about the whole affair. Clare soon put Luis behind her, marrying Charles Holland not long after (although they later divorced).

The police also came knocking on my door and I was taken to the station for questioning. The interrogation seemed to go on forever and I was exhausted after I was released. They kept asking me the same questions over and over again: where was Luis? Where was he going? I told them that Luis had said he was taking a train to visit friends in Scotland and that's all I knew. After a while, I got the idea that they already knew how much or how little I had been involved. It was then I realised they had bugged Luis's conversations with me. Thankfully, nothing happened, possibly because bugging was illegal.

Luis landed in Buenos Aires on 24th December 1986 and took a taxi to the small flat in Recoleta that his Aunt Ada shared with his sister Marité. At the time, his mother, who had recently been widowed, was also staying there. 'I've come to spend Christmas with you all,' he announced with his usual high spirits when he buzzed the intercom. It had been a long time since the family had spent Christmas together.

Luis Basualdo with Clare Lawman at Ascot, 1986

39
A Game of Cat and Mouse

Luis had never been such an attentive and exemplary son, nephew, and brother as he was that Christmas of 1986. He lavished attention on his family and friends; in return, he felt protected and safe back in Buenos Aires, away from the strong arm of the law. By New Year, however, the positive feelings were fading and he began feeling isolated and bored. It was at this point that his cocaine habit became uncontrollable.

Despite his time in rehab, and being perennially restless and incapable of responsibility, he had never really given up drugs. Cocaine and alcohol were always around wherever he went, and it was not in his nature to resist temptation. In all the time I had known him, he had never turned down a drink, a line of cocaine, or whatever else was on offer. Although he drank little in the early days, as he aged, he increasingly overindulged in everything. His other vice was sex, particularly with prostitutes, and he indulged in that without restraint during his time in Argentina. As much as he was drawn to the high life – or at least the appearance of the high life – he was also drawn to seediness.

From the safe distance of Buenos Aires, in a country with which the UK was not on friendly terms following the Falklands War, he started playing tricks on DI Townley. He regularly called him on his direct line from a Buenos Aires call centre, claiming to be back in London. He had taken a leaf out of Ronnie Biggs's book: the Great Train Robber used to call Inspector Jack Slipper, pretending to be in the UK when he was actually calling from Brazil. Luis's greatest fear was to be extradited to the UK and put on trial. He therefore took the precaution of substituting his Basualdo surname for his mother's last name of Bissoni, which appeared in his new Argentinian passport. He also replaced the American passport seized by the London police by claiming he had lost it, and with his new one, he travelled to Europe.

Determined to keep taunting Townley, he called him on his arrival in Paris. Not content with that, he purchased another passport under a different name from a bent police officer and came to London, calling Townley from the hotel he was staying at. The detective refused to speak to him, a mistake on his part for if he had traced the call, he would have caught him.

He was desperate to see Clare, but after the trauma of her arrest and being hounded by the police, and knowing the wealth of evidence against Luis, she had finally decided to move on. If she had wanted to be with him, she could have gone to Argentina, but she never did. Luis also contacted the press, saying that he would be returning to the UK for Ascot. When the press approached the detectives working on the case for a comment, one of them was quoted as saying, 'My God, that man has got a nerve! … If he thinks he's going to Ascot I'm afraid he'll be very disappointed. He's not. He's going to the nick.'

But despite these diversions, Luis hated being stuck in Argentina, and as a result, he became increasingly bitter, lashing out at anyone and everyone, including me … especially me. He would bring things up from our days in Miami, as though he still harboured grudges. His favourite taunt was to remind me of my deportation, and he spread rumours about me, telling anyone who would listen that I was a thief and that when we shared a room in Miami, I would steal money from him. He also told friends that I was not an art dealer, merely a stallholder in Portobello Market. It was nasty and petty, but very much in his nature.

Despite these cat-and-mouse games and his apparent nonchalance about his fugitive status, the reality was that Luis was a pariah, with no more access to money. His career as a polo player was well and truly over; he would never get sponsored again as he was too old. His main concern was Christina Onassis's decision to take him to court. She had been devastated to discover that the two men she was closest to, her stepbrother and Luis, had conspired to steal from her.

The way Christina took revenge on the people who had wronged her was through the courts. First, she travelled to London to demand an explanation from Jamie. Jamie stood his ground, rejecting all her accusations. She knew he had a drug problem but thought it impossible that he could have signed all those documents in complete ignorance. Still vivid in her mind was his arrest for breaking into a pharmacy in search of heroin. In the end, Christina did not believe his account of events and she never forgave him. It was a sad end to the relationship that had weathered many personal tragedies.

On the other hand, Luis, who was always confident he could bluff his way out of any situation, decided on an offensive strategy. He asked me to make contact with Christina directly and to mediate on his behalf – or rather to find out exactly what she had in store for him. I accepted Luis's request, partly out of curiosity and partly from an unhealthy temptation to play a role – even if it was a minor one – in the forthcoming drama. After making some enquiries, I discovered that Christina was staying at the Hilton under the name 'Madame Bloom'. I called the hotel and managed to get through to her suite. When I gave my name, all I could hear was silence at the other end.

'Don't put the phone down,' I pleaded, thinking she was about to do just that, but she stayed on the line. 'Don't think I'm taking sides, because I'm not,' I went on. 'I have a message from Luis.'

'You can tell that piece of shit that the only place I ever want to hear from him is in a court of law,' she said angrily. I could feel her almost spitting down the line.

'I think you might want to hear what he has to say.' I paused for effect.

'Well?'

In keeping with the dramatic nature of this whole episode, I told her that I could only deliver the message in person, and Christina, who was never one to shy away from drama, agreed to meet. When I arrived at Cecconi's restaurant for our meeting, Christina was already there, seated, wearing the biggest sunglasses I had ever seen and attracting more, rather than less, attention. She was cold with me – no peck on the cheek, no small talk, just straight down to business.

'So what's this story that Luis wants you to tell me?'

I repeated the story exactly as Luis had given it to me, although I knew it was completely untrue: 'Luis wants you to know that initially the account was opened because you wanted to pay certain expenses into it without your husband's knowledge.' Her husband at the time was Thierry Roussel.

'What kind of expenses? What are you talking about?'

'The black beauties,' I said, leaning in and speaking in hushed tones.

She almost choked on her Diet Coke. 'Is that what you came here to tell me?'

'He said you told him that you wanted to make a monthly payment to Jamie for his expenses,' I said quietly, 'and also to reimburse him for the amphetamines he bought for you in New York.'

'One million, two hundred thousand dollars for personal expenses! Tell him he can fuck off! And tell him I know that this story is another one of his lies.'

The fact was that Christina knew more than I did. She had already had an interview with a detective who briefed her on Luis's involvement and how he used Jamie and Ludovico Sanok in his scheme. There was little I could say to that. It was quite obvious that her version of events was far closer to the truth. Luis's story was nothing more than a not-so-veiled threat to Christina that if it went to court, his defence would involve revelations of unpleasant details about her private life. The threat did not work. I tried to direct the conversation to when we first met in Buenos Aires in early 1972, but she remained icy with me and left me with the bill, as she often had in the past.

Luis called me late that night, eager to know how the meeting had gone.

'If I were you, Luis, I would forget about that woman,' I said.

'How can I forget her when her lawyers are breathing down my neck?'

'Forget the idea that she'll ever forgive you.'

'Why? What happened? Didn't she believe you?' he asked, as though the story I had spun her was mine and not his.

'Her exact words were "fuck off",' I told him and went on to give him a blow-by-blow account of the meeting, conveying her general outrage and everything the police had told her. 'It's not looking good,' I added.

We ended the call with him announcing that he was going to phone her himself, which is what he did. He called the Hilton and asked to be put through to Madame Bloom. 'It's Luis Basualdo calling,' he clarified.

According to him, the Christina who answered the phone was a surprisingly smoother and calmer version of the one I had met, but it was all a game.

'Ah, Luis! I wondered when you were going to call.'

'You greet me as if you hadn't denounced me and tried to get me imprisoned.'

'Forget about it. I've already asked for the charges to be dropped,' she said.

'I did everything you asked,' Luis said. 'I gave Jamie money and paid your doctor in New York for your black beauties, and your way of repaying me is to have me prosecuted. I had to take refuge in Buenos Aires because of you.'

'I was very upset.' Her little-girl-lost pretence continued. 'I thought you and Jamie were taking advantage of me,' she went on. 'Jamie swore to me that he had nothing to do with it. He said it was all to do with you and I believed him.'

It was all an act, and he probably knew it. It was typical of their bizarre co-dependent relationship, which in recent years had become weirder due to their increasing use of drugs. Christina had her uppers and downers, which made her paranoid and needy in equal measure, exaggerating her natural eccentricity; Luis had his cocaine habit, which made him even more shameless, irresponsible, and desperate.

Luis's attempts to threaten her with unsavoury revelations should she pursue him in the courts backfired spectacularly. She was not only ready for the fight, but she decided she would be there in person to see the whole case through.

At various times in her life and often for no particular reason, she would decide to make a new start in a new place. She had done this when she met her first husband and moved to Los Angeles. When she later married a Russian businessman, she declared that she would move to Moscow at the height of the Cold War, although the idea of the world's richest woman decamping to the world's greatest communist power was grotesque. She ended up staying in Moscow for little more than a few days. So her decision to move to Argentina was no real surprise. She did have a history with the country. Her father, Aristotle, had lived there as a young man and made his first fortune there. But the prospect of witnessing Luis's court case in person was too good to pass up. However, what she probably didn't realise was that in Argentina, the litigants are not present at a trial; the whole process is conducted via lawyers.

With extensive experience as an international adviser on business transactions, Christina's lawyer, Emilio Cárdenas, promptly got down to business. Luis, in turn, was represented by Victor Sassoon, a lawyer with a reputation for chicanery, who made good on Luis's threat to air her dirty laundry. He argued that Christina had asked his client to open a secret account, behind her husband Thierry Roussel's back, so that she could obtain drugs to fuel her habit and that the account was opened with her full authority and knowledge. With money from that account, Luis paid a doctor in New York who supplied him with the highly addictive amphetamine pills known as 'black beauties', on which Christina had increasingly come to depend. The money was also used to meet the debts incurred by her stepbrother Jamie Blandford's drug addiction.

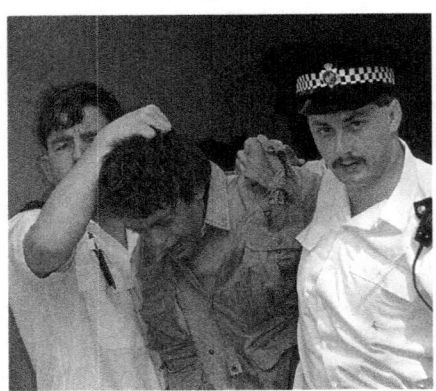

In short, Sassoon argued that Luis had been caught in the middle of Christina's and Jamie's sordid drug addictions. It was all reported in great detail in the press, day after day. Then, on 19th November 1988, when it seemed things could get no more dramatic, Christina Onassis was found dead in a half-filled bathtub at a friend's house in Tortuguitas, on the outskirts of Buenos Aires.

Jamie Blandford arrested for failing to pay maintenance to his first wife, June 1993

A couple of days later, a post-mortem revealed that she had died from a heart attack caused by acute pulmonary oedema. With no evidence of suicide, drug overdose, or foul play, the body was cleared for release to her family. Her ex-husband, Thierry Roussel, arrived in Buenos Aires within twenty-four hours to seal the black coffin with an elaborate silver rim, and she was laid to rest overnight in Avenida Figueroa Alcorta's Greek Orthodox Church.

Christina's body was then flown to Athens for what turned out to be a state funeral. Held in the St Photini church, it was declared a day of national mourning. Hundreds of wreaths were waiting for the daughter of the world's largest ship owner. It seemed the whole of Greece was mourning the death of its favourite little girl. With the funeral over, she was taken to the family vault on the island of Skorpios, where her father and brother were buried.

Luis claimed from Buenos Aires that he was very sorry to hear of her death, though I doubt he meant it. He naively thought that her death would mean that he was off the hook, but he was wrong. Christina's team didn't give up the fight, making sure to see the proceedings through to the very end. It took three years for the case to be heard and the court to reach a verdict. The irony was that Luis was forced to spend much of the money he had stolen from her on legal fees. Finally, in November 1992, the Argentinian court found Luis guilty of all charges.

However, the same court that condemned him, denied the request for his extradition. A further extradition request was made to the Argentinian Foreign Ministry. Following those two refusals, Credit Suisse bank officials appealed to President Carlos Menem himself, but he too refused to have Luis extradited. Luis had taken the precaution of joining the president's 'youth association' and it worked.

40
Ducking and Diving

During the three years of the trial, Luis was free to come and go as he pleased, thanks to a passport under a different name. Eventually, he sold his apartment in Buenos Aires and decamped to New York where he married Jan Leach, the daughter of a financier and a well-known New York socialite. Jan had fallen for Luis's high profile and married him on that basis. He, for his part, had assumed he was bagging another heiress. The fact was, neither of them had money. They had each deceived the other into thinking marriage would improve their circumstances. Jan lived in a cramped studio apartment which they had to share. It was now that Luis once again let himself go, taking cocaine and drinking like a fish. He became bloated and looked tired most of the time. This put the new marriage under a lot of pressure. By the time it came to its inevitable end, it had barely lasted a year.

As a parting gift, Jan booked him into rehab at the Betty Ford Center. Meanwhile, in an attempt to keep his name in the public arena and earn some pocket money, he continued selling stories to the press about his various affairs and escapades. These included his plan to become a lord by purchasing the title 'Lord of the Manor of Brindley and Burland' in the county of Cheshire. He never paid the invoice, so the title was never his. He even spun a story that he had contracted AIDS so that it could be followed with various denials and, eventually, more articles with photographs of his negative test result.

With two failed marriages behind him and no money, he started attending parties in New York given by a socialite called Gloria Muller. These gatherings were held for society ladies who wished to be introduced to suitable gentlemen. He had gone to these parties when still married to Lucy Pearson, but then it had been just for fun. This time, he was not there to fool around; he was desperate. With no means of supporting himself and his polo days over, his only hope was to put his remaining attributes to use and get his hands on a rich woman.

Luis Basualdo with his second wife, Jan Leach, and Alberto van der Mije, Meadowbrook, 1991

It was at one of these parties that he bumped into Martha Reed, the New York socialite whom he had first met in the late sixties during one of his stays in the city. Her family had sold their Chicago pasta business, Ronco, to Coca-Cola for forty million dollars, and when she reconnected with Luis, she had been a widow for two years. At sixty-one, she was fourteen years his senior, so Luis felt he had no time to waste. He quickly moved into her apartment on the twenty-first floor of the Ritz Tower on Park Avenue. The relationship was transactional, but the balance was all in Luis's favour.

Without shame, he ruthlessly exploited his benefactor. Martha owned another apartment on the seventh floor of the same building, which Luis often retired to, claiming he wanted to read in peace. Instead, he would invite girls back for drinks and put the date-rape drug Rohypnol in the ice cubes he served in the drinks. His trick

Luis Basualdo and second wife Jan Leach, New York, 1991

went on for some time without any major problems until one day he invited a young English lady who enjoyed drinking. When nothing happened after a second drink, Luis thought that maybe this time he'd forgotten to put the drug in the ice, so he decided to take her to dinner at Nello's, the fashionable Italian restaurant on Madison Avenue. They were joined in the restaurant by his partner in crime, the Cuban Alberto van der Mije, but just after they ordered starters, she collapsed. An ambulance was called, and on the way to New York University Hospital, a worried Luis gave Alberto three hundred dollars to keep quiet if the police questioned him. He need not have bothered because when they arrived at the hospital, Alberto jumped out and fled the scene. Luis, in turn, gave a false name, paid in advance for the woman's treatment, and also absconded. Eventually, Martha learned the truth about his love of 'reading', and she put an end to their relationship and the blank cheque that came with it. He had lived off her for seven months.

Soon after the split, an article appeared in the gutter press in which Luis claimed that Martha had fooled him into believing she was a multi-millionairess in her fifties when in reality she was in her seventies and had barely a million to her name, adding that her late husband, Stass Kropotkin, was a liquor salesman in Manhattan and not a Russian prince as she had claimed. It was a cheap and nasty form of revenge that showed Luis's worst side. He had stooped very low, and it was at this seedy and shameful level that he spent the rest of his life. Meanwhile, Martha took herself off to Marrakesh for a seven-month sabbatical to lick her wounds.

Luis Basualdo with pasta heiress Martha Reed, New York, 1993

In November 1993, his friend Lucio García Mansilla decided to lend Luis a hand. Lucio was a successful Argentinian financier who, for some strange reason, had a soft spot for Luis. Feeling sorry for him, he gave him enough money to start afresh. But as usual, Luis decided that instead of making good use of the money, he would spend most of it in one go moving into an eleventh-floor apartment in Helmsley Carlton House, an exclusive 'white-glove service' building on the Upper East Side of Manhattan.

His new lease gave his name as 'Count Héctor Bissoni'. He chose his new home to be near his old friend, another bogus count, Alberto van der Mije, who had divorced his wife and was living the life of a man about town on the proceeds of the divorce. The arrival of Luis in the exclusive condominium was of no advantage to his Cuban friend.

Alberto had convinced the staff he was a genuine count and most of the Hispanic staff called him 'Señor Conde'. Having two Latinos in the same condo, both claiming to be aristocrats, made people in the building wonder whether either of them was the genuine article.

Despite his treatment at the Betty Ford Center, Luis was soon back on drugs, if he had ever been off them. The way that Luis talked about his time at the rehab clinic was very revealing. For him, it was principally an opportunity to meet vulnerable, wealthy women in comfortable surroundings, not a chance to change his life for the better. Cocaine heightened his already frenetic exuberance and masked any disappointment he felt about how things had gone in recent years. Although he did not seem to eat much, his daily champagne intake made him put on weight and gave him a bloated appearance. His hair had turned grey as he no longer bothered to dye it, and it was permanently greasy.

Needless to say, yet again he was living beyond his means at the Helmsley Carlton House. As a downer from his cocaine-fuelled highs, he would take a strong, antipsychotic tablet that enabled him to sleep for days at a time. On one occasion, the housekeeping staff, unable to get access to his room for three days and fearing the worst, decided to call security, and eventually, someone came up to force the door open. They found Luis sprawled naked on the bed and immediately assumed he was dead. But Luis eventually opened his eyes and, outraged that his privacy should have been invaded, angrily demanded that they leave his apartment. It was just one of a series of problems the management had with Luis and his unsavoury guests, and it led Helmsley Carlton House to cut off his credit in an attempt to force him to leave; he was already several months in arrears. The manager informed him that in future, they would require cash payments in advance for room service, laundry, and other services.

In what was probably another drug-fuelled psychotic episode, Luis locked himself in the bathroom with a gun and turned on the taps, flooding the floors below. Drugged out of his mind, for a whole night he refused requests from the doorman and neighbours to open his door. The police were eventually called and broke the door down. Seizing his weapon and restraining him, they took a naked Luis out of the building, tied to a stretcher, howling at the top of his voice and begging onlookers to help him. One of his neighbours took pity on him and covered his naked body with a blanket. He woke up in hospital and was discharged the next day. Since he had been admitted naked, the hospital provided him with clothes left behind from recently deceased patients. Wearing pyjama trousers, a sleeveless vest, and a pair of sandals, he was out on the street, looking like a vagrant. He called Lucio García Mansilla and was lucky to find him at home. He collected Luis and lent him some clothes.

When Luis arrived at Helmsley Carlton House, he was denied access to his apartment or his effects until he settled a $300,000 bill for the damage caused inside the building. The matter was dropped after Lucio intervened, insisting that the police had entered without a warrant and no drugs were found in the flat. In any case, Luis had no money. Once again, Luis was homeless, and although Lucio had helped him in the past, he now understood that his friend was a never-ending liability.

A born survivor, during his stay at Helmsley Carlton House, Luis had developed a relationship with diligent Good Samaritan Cristina Zilkha (neé Monet), a former singer and Harvard drop-out who had previously been married to Michael Zilkha, the heir to England's Mothercare retail empire. She was a useful ally who was willing to champion his cause, and on Luis's behalf, she visited the local police precinct, but found there was no mention of police involvement.

Soon after, Luis moved to Cristina's flat where, according to him, she loved being tied up and slapped in the face during sex. The practice ceased to be fun and games when in a fit of jealousy, he hit her on the head with the telephone handset and she had to be taken to Manhattan's Beth Israel Hospital. Luis quickly left the Upper East Side duplex and went into hiding. Cristina later commented to the press, 'He's no gentleman. His mother left home when he was nine for the local doctor, and he hates women.'

Not long after the incident, when visiting the Racquet Club, he was told by the porter that a couple of FBI officers had been making inquiries. When they were informed that he wasn't on the premises, the officers tried to seize his mail, which a zealous receptionist prevented. Not only were the police after him in connection with the Onassis-Credit Suisse affair but so were other hard men. With poverty hounding him, he decided his best bet was to keep a low profile.

41
Biting the Hand That Fed Him

For the next few years, Luis travelled backwards and forwards between Buenos Aires and New York, staying with friends until he was no longer welcome before moving on to the next place. On one such stay in New York, he paid a visit to his old girlfriend Justine Cushing. While chatting about old times, he suddenly collapsed on her kitchen floor and had to be taken to hospital. With no money and no medical insurance for his treatment, Justine felt sorry for him and let him stay in her flat. She did so even though her life was complicated enough. She was in a relationship with a man called Paul Schneider, who was terminally ill and staying in a nearby hospice, so Luis would be the second patient she had to deal with. The only condition she gave Luis while staying with her was that he was never to answer the phone, as Paul regularly called her from his deathbed.

Luis moved into Justine's flat at the end of August 2002 and stayed there for the next three years. Some say Justine took Luis to live with her for altruistic reasons, but others say it was her undying infatuation for him. According to him, they had sex only occasionally. At some point during his stay, Luis suggested that they open a joint account to cover household expenses. Although Justine knew what Luis was like and how he operated, she agreed to open the account. However, too many things were happening in her life for her to monitor transactions.

Luis Basualdo with Justine Cushing in her flat in 2002, before he absconded

Taking advantage of her situation, Luis intercepted her bank statements, reprising his old trick of moving money from her current account to the joint account and, later, to his personal account. He also spent freely on all her credit cards. Justine eventually became aware that money was going missing and demanded an explanation from him. Of course, he denied any knowledge or responsibility for it and promised he would help her get to the bottom of the situation. Incredibly, she believed him. That same night, as Justine slept, he rifled through her bag, took her ATM, card and withdrew the remaining funds in the joint account. On his return to the apartment, he put the card back in her bag and got back into bed with her.

When Justine finally came to terms with the truth, she calculated that Luis had stolen $250,000 from her. Once again, she confronted him, but this time he admitted that he had taken the money. She contacted the police, and he was brought to the police station at 67th Street and Lexington Avenue for questioning. Luis tried to talk her out of pressing charges by offering to pay back $100,000 of the amount he had stolen. He eventually did that after she issued a legal claim against him.

In May 2005, an affidavit was issued by Justine's lawyers, Messrs MacLaughlin & Stern, against Luis who, upon notification, fled to Argentina. He did not return for the court hearing and instead sent a letter to her lawyers alleging ill health. This left American Express and other credit card companies with no choice but to continue pursuing Justine to settle the outstanding bills. As the investigations continued, it was discovered that he had taken almost $150,000 more than she had calculated, so the total was just shy of $400,000, only a quarter of which she got back. With a prison sentence looming over his head, four years lapsed before he ventured back to New York.

Back in Buenos Aires, with the money safe in his pockets, his alcohol addiction worsened, causing him severe liver damage. In desperation, his sister had him confined to a clinic for eight months of detoxification. He emerged fifty pounds lighter, sporting 'a peacock's jowl and protruding frog eyes', according to one of his old friends. With his new slender image, he settled in an apart-hotel building in Rodríguez Peña Street in the Recoleta area of the city.

Lonely and short of money, with his old friends scattered or dead, he reverted to his old habits. He was back on the antipsychotic pills that put him to sleep for days at a time and he became reliant on Cialis for regular sexual encounters.

42

An Honest Man

Maybe it was watching Luis degenerate into a seedy shell of his former self that prompted me to consider my own situation. I certainly came to see his life as a cautionary tale, but there was more to my urge to course-correct than that.

My first step towards respectability came when I inherited the land from my mother. I had seen how Luis squandered every penny that had come his way, and I did not want to end up like him. Although I had always been around money, I had never had any of my own. For my entire life up to that point, I had always been short of cash, sometimes living hand to mouth, and often living off other people, usually the women in my life. It was only in middle age that I experienced what it was like to have money of my own and realised what I had been missing.

I enrolled in a history of art course at the Victoria and Albert Museum and it was there that I met the woman who I would marry and to whom I am still married. It was she, as much as anyone or anything else, that put me on the right path. She constantly reminded me to stop being so vain, because that was what I had been all those years: vain, self-regarding, judgemental, philandering, snobbish when I had little cause to be, and dishonest, for as much as Eric Hebborn insisted that he created art 'in the style of' the Old Masters and neither of us ever claimed them to be originals, I was the one who was responsible for his drawings finding their way to the mansions of reputable collectors. All this came to a head in a vision of hell that appeared to me at that time and which led to my conversion. From that day, I changed my life drastically. All those Christian principles that I had been brought up with, which my Irish nanny, Anne Dowd, had reinforced in her gentle and spiritual way, were reawakened in me.

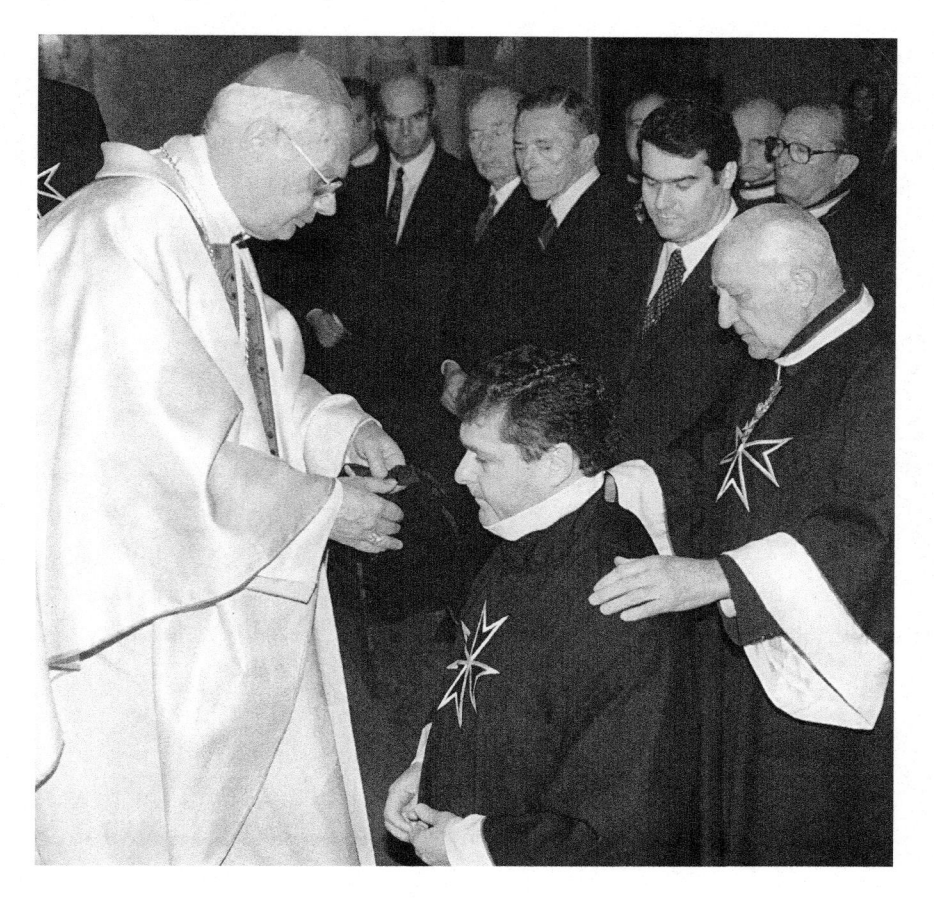

Me taking the solemn vows of the Sovereign Military Order of Malta on 24th June, the feast day of St John the Baptist, its patron, Buenos Aires, 1993

I had not set foot in a church for the previous thirty years, but I decided to try and save my soul by going to confession. I told the Franciscan priest what I had been doing for a living, still being somewhat economical with the truth. But when he understood that even if I was not deceiving with false claims, dishonest dealers were taking the opportunity to do so and he severely reprimanded me. When I insisted that I hadn't hurt anybody, his reply was, 'It's not what you do to them, but what it does to you. You deliberately set up a trap!'

I also bought myself into the supposedly prestigious Sovereign Military Order of Malta, which was good for my image but not for my soul. Regarded by some fools as the most exclusive club in the world, the Order was a disappointment to me. I was disillusioned by seeing notorious scoundrels in full religious garb pretending they were something they were not. One of the rules applying to a member of the Catholic Order of Malta is that they should not be in a relationship with a woman without being married. That was what finally prompted me to ask for the blessing of the Church.

In 1993 I married my peaches-and-cream, down-to-earth English rose, which also allowed me to become a British citizen. The ceremony took place at St Mary of the Angels in Bayswater in the most unusual circumstances. The priest in charge at the time was Father Michael Hollings, a former Coldstream Guards officer who was awarded the Military Cross for bravery in North Africa and Italy. Regarded by some as a saint and by others as an eccentric, he kept an open house where he fed 'the gentlemen of the road', as he called the poor, and the 'street ladies', as he called prostitutes.

'Don't worry,' he assured me. 'I'll sort out everything for you – witnesses and the lot.'

When we arrived at the appointed time of 5 p.m. for the private ceremony, he wasn't there. I went upstairs to his office and found Father Hollings fast asleep. He awoke with a start, rushed into the church, grabbed a man by the arm who was lighting candles there, and said, 'He will be your witness.' The man happened to be a vagrant who couldn't read or write. His name on my marriage certificate is given as 'Emmanuel Christmas' and he signed with a cross.

After the parties and the titles and name-dropping and the vacuous pursuit of the crests of this and that family, I understood the Lord was giving me a sign to embrace humility. However, I still found it a little embarrassing having to explain to family and friends why there was a strange old man with wild hair and a beard in our wedding photo.

43
Our Last Meeting

I was jet lagged and still fatigued when the winter sun streamed through the gap in the heavy silk curtains of my luxurious room in the Alvear Palace Hotel in Recoleta. I opened my eyes to find that I had slept through most of the morning and had almost missed my lunch appointment with Luis. It was July 2013, and thirty-seven years had passed since my mother's death, but I was still litigating with my siblings over properties she had left in her will. Even after such a long time away, I had not shaken off my bad memories of Buenos Aires and my life there, and I resented being in the city, especially for unpleasant legal reasons. After a quick shower, I dressed and walked the few blocks to meet Luis at our old haunt, La Biela. It had been a long time since I had seen him in the flesh and we had a lot of catching up to do. When I arrived, he was already sitting at a table waiting for me.

I was shocked at how much he had aged since I had last seen him. He looked greasy and unkempt, and everything about him was grey. His clothes were inelegantly loose on his body as if they were hand-me-downs. It was hard to believe this was the same man who had hobnobbed with royalty, seduced infatuated heiresses, and who, at his peak, had enjoyed substantial wealth. Even his trademark treasured gold Rolex had gone. He used to make a point of consulting it frequently, not to know the time but to draw other people's attention to it and reassure himself of his wealth and status. When I innocently enquired what had become of it, he told me that it had long gone under the hammer at a local auction house. What had not changed was his characteristic optimism; even in the face of such obvious adversity, he pretended that everything was all right. He tried hard to hide his obvious resentment. Jealous of my freedom to come and go as I pleased visibly consumed him, so I edited the account of my life, focusing on its dramas and downsides, rather than the comforts and blessings I truly enjoyed.

When lunch was over, I made my way to La Recoleta cemetery to pay my respects to my parents, as I had not attended either of their funerals. Luis volunteered to come with me. It had been a long time since I visited the family mausoleum and I got lost, but Luis knew the way and without any hesitation, took me straight to it. When I asked him how he knew where it was, he flabbergasted me by saying he had attended the funerals of both my parents. It seemed like a touching act of respect and courtesy, but it still sent a shiver down my spine. I recalled his Aunt Ada's words, 'He never misses a good funeral.'

The conversation naturally turned to funerals, to the ones that he had not been able to attend (due to his outstanding arrest warrants), and we talked about the friends and lovers and foes we had lost.

Lady Edith Foxwell had died in 1996 and neither of us had attended her funeral. Her two daughters had always seen me as a gold digger and hated me, so I stayed away. However, I did go to Dai Llewellyn's funeral, whose death in 2009 seemed like the end of an era as he was someone who brought joy to a lot of people. Both Dai and Edith were intermediaries between the aristocracy and the real world. They were comfortable in their skins and in any setting, and never judged people by their backgrounds or titles, which taught me a valuable lesson as to the real meaning of class.

Luis Sosa Basualdo is laid to rest in the Etcheverrigaray family mausoleum in La Recoleta cemetery, Buenos Aries

We also talked about Rita Lachman's passing. That seemed to make Luis perk up a bit, as her fall from grace had been as spectacular as his. She and her husband had split up, and after messy legal proceedings, she came away with a fraction of his vast wealth, which she then frittered away. She ended up in London and was evicted from her flat after failing to keep up with the rent. She died in an old people's home two years later and was buried in a North London cemetery, the funeral costs paid by a Jewish benevolent fund.

Luis seemed to identify with her fall from grace, although we didn't dwell on it as he had always been suspected of stealing her ring. Luis would also have been living in squalor were it not for his sister Marité. He had been thrown out of the Rodríguez Peña apart-hotel due to endless disturbances caused by the prostitutes he brought back. Marité came to his rescue yet again and installed him in another apart-hotel in the Recoleta area.

It was during this meeting that Luis also shared with me the possibility of inheriting his sister's $9 million fortune, left to her by her late husband. It seemed more of a forlorn hope than a possibility. I wondered if Marité was aware that she too had a price tag, and that he was speculating on who would be the first to die. I had not seen Marité in years, but she had always been measured in everything she did. I suspected she enjoyed very good health.

Given Luis's penchant for excess and the visibly sorry state that I found him in, it seemed clear to me that he had very little hope of outliving her, or any of us. He was no longer drinking alcohol, claiming it made him put on weight, but his cocaine intake had increased considerably. He would get a buzz by cruising around Buenos Aires's less salubrious areas at night, hunting for prostitutes. On top of cocaine, he was taking thirteen pills a day, to fight depression among other things.

We also discussed the sensational two-page article he had penned about Prince Charles for the *Sunday Mirror*, for which he had received a tidy sum. Under the headline 'I helped Charles bed dozens of girls ... even the local butcher's shop assistant', it recounted Luis's role as a royal pimp by appointment and described how he introduced humble Sussex village girls to the heir to the throne for sex.[16] Of course, none of it ever happened. It was all in his imagination.

'How could you betray a man who can't defend himself?' I asked him.

'It was payback time,' he responded. 'I subsidised his polo for a whole season and never got anything out of it.'

To add insult to injury, in the same article Luis added a copy of a thank-you letter from Prince Charles praising him for his kindness in having him as a guest in his polo team. All these royal shenanigans supposedly took place in 1977, which happened to be the year of the Queen's Silver Jubilee. The Prince of Wales would have been so busy with royal engagements that he'd hardly have had time for sex in Sussex even if he had wanted to. Also, during that time, I saw Luis regularly and often stayed with him; I never saw or heard anything to suggest any such thing was occurring. All the lies and inaccuracies were put straight by Luis's American teammate, Russell Corey. A gentleman to his fingertips, he had played in Luis's team along with Prince Charles that year. In his book *Golden Eagles*, he describes in detail the trophies they won together and the other events that took place at the time. Full of praise for everybody, he sent a copy to Prince Charles, who sent him back a complimentary thank-you letter.

Luis's absence was noted at the London wedding of his twenty-six-year-old daughter Charlotte Pearson to journalist Charles Methven. But it was for a good reason, as Luis himself revealed in a piece in the *Daily Mail* in 2001: 'I have not seen Charlotte in a long time, and I didn't even know she had become engaged. I won't be at the wedding.'[17] He had seen very little of his daughter over the years, apart from the odd occasion in New York when he stayed with his ex-wife Jan Leach in her cramped studio. A close friend of the family told me he rarely visited his son in his Florida care home. The pain was too much for him to bear.

He was, however, delighted to hear about the divorce of his first wife, Lucy Pearson, from the younger, handsome Sandhurst-educated

Charles Fraser. A high sheriff of West Sussex, a steward of the Hurlingham Polo Association, and a trustee of Arundel Castle, he was a pillar of the establishment. 'Another gigolo down the hatch,' he gleefully remarked and I caught a flash of his cheeky grin in what was otherwise a somewhat melancholy encounter.

It was the last time that I saw Luis. We would speak on the phone and he would write me letters, then emails as the years went by, giving me accounts of his adventures, sometimes full of bravado, sometimes loaded with bitterness about the past and how things had turned out for him.

For all our ups and downs and our many unpleasant exchanges and rivalries, Luis always kept in touch. Strangely enough, he always communicated with me in English, not Spanish. It was as if he wanted to maintain his connection with England, however tenuously. Yet despite all this correspondence, I had the sense that he didn't value my friendship. He never asked about me or what I was doing, or asked after my wife or our plans. He only kept in touch because he wanted to be informed of the latest gossip, needed my help, or wanted someone to listen to him dwell on the past and his regrets. When he was in good spirits, I hardly heard from him at all.

Luis's life was always going to end badly. His last few years in Buenos Aires were rather pitiful. There's nothing sadder than an old gigolo trying desperately to defy age. In December 2020, he was rushed to hospital after collapsing at his home due, it was later discovered, to an internal haemorrhage. He fell into a coma and did not regain consciousness.

Luis was his own worst enemy. Everyone who knew him knew that about him. Despite his many successes, and his access to great wealth, he didn't know what to do with it. He always wanted more – more acceptance and more money, like the addict that he was. It was this ambivalent relationship with the upper classes in Argentina, the United States, and the United Kingdom that was his undoing. On the one hand, he sought to be accepted by them, but on the other hand, he sought to destroy them, to bring them down somehow and reveal their hypocrisies and shallowness. He loved the chase and the challenge, he relished his plots to defraud and humiliate, whether it was selling on duff horses to polo sponsors, tricking Lucy Pearson into a sham marriage, or ripping off Christina Onassis by ensnaring her helpless stepbrother. It was his betrayal of Justine Cushing that finally showed me he was incapable of any genuine feeling for another human being. Justine had shared with him whatever she had at a time when he was at his lowest ebb, when he was physically vulnerable and practically friendless, and to thank her, he stole $400,000 from her. I am no psychologist, but this complete lack of empathy for other people was what set Luis apart. He simply did not care about the harm he did to other people, and as close as you got to him, you never really got to know him, or could ever count on him.

As for Clare Lawman, whom he often said he so devotedly loved, he absconded leaving her to face a criminal investigation that aimed to charge her as an accessory. In all the conversations I had over the years with him, he never accepted responsibility for any of his actions. He always cited circumstances or events or other people who were to blame for how things had turned out: it was Cowdray who had ended his polo career; it was Prince Charles who had broken up his marriage; it was the snobbery in the UK that had excluded him. Those cases where he was unequivocally to blame he never mentioned.

As we stood at the entrance to the cemetery and said goodbye, I knew it would be the last time I'd see him. It had been a difficult encounter; his bitterness and sadness weighed heavily on me throughout the meeting and I felt happy to be leaving him. Luis excited many different opinions from those who came across him, varying mainly according to the harm he had caused them. Even those close to him knew very little about him. When Luis was asked by a tabloid if he minded being referred to as a bounder, he had replied, 'They can call me what they like, I don't care. The important thing is that I've avoided boredom, which is the greatest sin of all.'

Endnotes

1. Obituary, Luis Sosa Basualdo, *La Nación*, 10th December 2020.
2. Stephanie Linning, 'My father, the polo-playing Casanova', in *Daily Mail*, 5 July 2021, https://www.dailymail.co.uk/femail/article-9757335/My-father-polo-playing-Casanova.html.
3. Personal letter from Luis Basualdo, Waldorf Astoria Hotel, New York, to the author, 26 October 1966. The 'April in Paris Ball' took place on 29 October 1966; there were too many balls in April, so it was moved to October.
4. When Luchino Visconti was adapting the book for the screen, he hired Fulco not only to advise on the way the Sicilian nobility dressed, talked, and danced, but also to do the choreography of the ball scenes.
5. Cárcano's sister, Stella, was married to Lord Ednam, and his other sister, Ana Inez, was the wife of Sir Jacob Astor, whose father, Lord Astor, played a prominent role in the Profumo Affair, the biggest sex scandal of the twentieth century.
6. Personal letter from Linley Sánchez de Bethancourt to the author, 3 March 1971.
7. '£100,000 shock for the world of polo', *Daily Mail*, 10 May 1978, p. 5.
8. *International Daily News*, 12 March 1980.

9. 'Luis on the carpet', *Daily Mail*, 4 January 1980, p. 66.
10. Nigel Dempster, 'Luis is a loser yet again', *Daily Mail*, 14 October 1978, p. 4.
11. Nigel Dempster, 'Family of rock star evicted', *Daily Mail*, 28 May 1984, p. 1.
12. Nigel Dempster, 'Luis – an ex-polo player with a hole in his pocket', *Daily Mail*, 18 October 1979, p. 9.
13. 'Christina O's tame bounder', *Daily Mail*, 2 December 1982, p. 20.
14. 'Huntin', shootin', fishin', boundin',' *Daily Mail*, 14 October 1986, p. 27.
15. 'The strange case of Christina Onassis's missing money…', *Daily Mail*, 12 December 1986, p. 82.
16. 'I helped Charles bed dozens of girls … even the local butcher's shop assistant', *Sunday Mirror*, 20 January 2002.
17. 'Luis left out', *Daily Mail*, 20 June 2001, p. 34.

Acknowledgements

I am grateful to the *Daily Mail*'s editor-at-large, Richard Kay, for helping me in my research, and to Stéphane Giusti, film director and screenwriter, for his invaluable advice. I would also like to thank Averill Buchanan, who in addition to editing and producing the book, also guided me through the book publication process. Last, but certainly not least, I wish to thank my close friend, the late Luis Sosa Basualdo, who shared with me a great deal of information without realising I was writing a book about his life and who would be relishing the attention.

Photographic credits

Some of these photographs, collected over the years, are from my own collection; others were given to me by Luis himself. Every effort has been made to trace and contact other copyright holders before publication.

Front cover: Luis Basualdo at the 1986 Derby, Epsom Downs Racecourse, Surrey. Photo: Desmond O'Neill | Desmond O'Neill Features

Back cover: Luis Basualdo with HRH Prince Charles at Cowdray Park, 1977. Photo: Mirrorpix | Trinity Mirror/Alamy Stock Photo

p. 7: The Ortiz Basualdo Palace in Plaza San Martín, Buenos Aires, c. 1910. Photo: Public domain, courtesy of Archivo General de la Nación, Argentina/Wikimedia.

p. 11: Me with Leticia Arrighi, Buenos Aires, 1963. Author's own collection.

p. 35: The impressive Harbour House condo complex, Miami, Florida. Photo: Miami MLS® | Miami MLS®

p. 35: Harbour House swimming pool. Photo: Miami MLS® | Miami MLS®.

p. 38: Me with fellow beach boy, Harbour House, 1966. Author's own collection.

p. 38: Me with fellow beach boys, Harbour House, 1966. Author's own collection.

p. 83: The 1969 Yale team tour to Costa Rica. Courtesy of Luis Basualdo.

p. 96: Royal Windsor Cup, 1969. HM Queen Elizabeth presents the runners-up trophy. Courtesy of Peter Orthwein.

p. 101: Luis with Justine Cushing, Cowdray Park, 1970. Courtesy of Luis Basualdo.

p. 109: Me with Cecilia Tiscornia, Mau Mau discotheque, Buenos Aires, 1971. Author's own collection.

p. 111: Me with Cecilia Tiscornia, Africa discotheque, Buenos Aires, 1971. Author's own collection.

p. 139: Me with Ursula Mahler at Hotel il Pellicano, Tuscany, 1971. Author's own collection.

p. 150: Zsa Zsa Gabor crowning beauty queen, with J. Paul Getty and me, London, 16 May 1972. Photo: Ray Bassett | Ray Bassett

p. 155: Me with Lady Edith Foxwell at her house in Sherston, 1973. Author's own collection.

p. 166: Me with Luis Basualdo, Cowdray Park, 1973. Author's own collection.

p. 173: Me with Tessa Welborn, London, 1974. Author's own collection.

p. 203: Les Diables Bleus, winners of the 1974 Deaville Coupe D'argent. Courtesy of Luis Basualdo.

p. 204: Golden Eagles team, winners of the Warwickshire Cup, Cirencester Polo Club, 1976. Photo: Mike Roberts | Mike Roberts

p. 205: Golden Eagles team, winners of the Spring Cup at Cowdray Park, 1977. Photo: Mike Roberts | Mike Roberts

p. 205: Golden Eagles team, winners of the Alitalia trophy at Guards Polo Club, Windsor, London, 1977. Photo: Mike Roberts | Mike Roberts

p. 206: Golden Eagles team, runners up in the Warwickshire Cup at Cirencester Polo Club, 1977. Photo: Mike Roberts | Mike Roberts

p. 207: Cirencester Polo Club, 1977. Luis Basualdo and HRH Prince Charles talking to Lord Vestey. Author's own collection.

p. 208: South America team, winners of the Coronation Cup, 1977 with HM Queen Elizabeth. Photo: Michael Chevis | Michael Chevis

p. 213: Luis Basualdo with first wife, Lucy Pearson, and daughter, Charlotte, July 1975. Photo: Desmond O'Neill | Desmond O'Neill Features

p. 230: Luis Basualdo with Pilar Irisarri, Paris, October 1980. Courtesy of Luis Basualdo.

p. 240: Luis Basualdo with Clare Lawman at the Prix de l'Arc de Triomphe, Paris, 1981. Photo: Alan Davidson | Shutterstock

p. 241: Christina Onassis with Clare Lawman, Paris, 1982. Courtesy of Luis Basualdo.

p. 243: Luis Basualdo leaving bankruptcy court in London, March 1984. Photo: Mirrorpix | Trinity Mirror/Alamy Stock Photo

p. 245: Jamie Blandford with Luis Basualdo at the Business Connection Concert, London, June 1985. Photo: Alan Davidson | Shutterstock

p. 248: Luis Basualdo shooting and hunting on the Badminton Estate, 1985. Both photos: Ludovico Sanok | Courtesy of Luis Basualdo.

p. 249: Shelley Smith, Sir Gordon White, Cheryl Ladd and Luis Basualdo at the Prix de l'Arc de Triomphe, Paris, 1984. Photo: Alan Davidson | Shutterstock

p. 250: Luis Basualdo with Daphne Guinness, 1985. Photo: Alan Davidson | Alan Davidson

p. 251: Luis Basualdo with Lady Henrietta Spencer-Churchill, 1985. Photo: John Walters | Daily Mail/Shutterstock

p. 252: Luis Basualdo at the Derby, Epsom Downs, 1986. Photo: Desmond O'Neill | Desmond O'Neill Features

p. 255: Joan Collins, Luis Basualdo and Nigel Dempster at the Derby, Epsom Downs, 1986. Photo: Alan Davidson | Shutterstock

p. 257: Luis Basualdo with Clare Lawman at Ascot, 1986. Photo: Alan Davidson | Shutterstock

p. 264: Jamie Blandford, arrested for failing to pay maintenance, June 1993. Photo: Alex Lentati | Daily Mail/Shutterstock

p. 267: Luis Basualdo with his second wife, Jan Leach, and Alberto van der Mije, Meadowbrook, 1991. Courtesy of Luis Basualdo.

p. 268: Luis Basualdo and second wife Jan Leach, New York, 1991. Courtesy of Luis Basualdo.

p. 269: Luis Basualdo with pasta heiress Martha Reed, New York, 1993. Courtesy of Luis Basualdo.

p. 274: Luis Basualdo with Justine Cushing in her flat in 2002, before he absconded. Courtesy of Luis Basualdo.

p. 277: Me taking the solemn vows of the Sovereign Military Order of Malta on 24th June 1993, Buenos Aires. Author's own collection.

p. 282: Luis Sosa Basualdo is laid to rest in the Etcheverrigaray family mausoleum in La Recoleta cemetery, Buenos Aries. Both photos: Juan Pablo Capilla | Juan Pablo Capilla.

About the Author

Marcelo Manrique de Acuña is the *nom de plume* of Marcelo Álvarez Prado, a British national, born in Argentina in 1945. An unruly and wayward young man, he left home at an early age for a life of adventure, becoming a well-known figure on the international social scene. Related by birth to British nobility, and a Knight of the Sovereign Military Order of Malta, he settled in London where he eventually married an English lady and made a living as an art dealer. *The Bounder and Other Scoundrels* is a memoir of his life as it intersected with that of his good friend, Luis Sosa Basualdo.

Name Index

Page numbers in italics refer to photographs

Abulafia, Joe 140–1
Abulafia, Prouset 140
Aczel, George 174–5
Ada, Aunt, *see* Bissoni, Ada
Agnelli, Emanuele Filiberto 'Lele' Nasi 11
Anchorena family 79
Anchorena, Florinda Fernández de 132
Anchorena, Manuel 183–9
Andrésen, Björn 122
Andress, Ursula 172
Anhalt, Princess Edda of 164
Anne, Princess 247
Arias, Arnulfo 153
Armstrong, Charlie 83, 84, 95
Armstrong, John 95, *96*
Arrighi, Leticia *11*
Ashley, April (George Jamieson) 190
Astor, Vincent 84

Baker, Ginger 238–9
Bamberg, Harold 229
Banovic, Sergio 134, 135, 136, 139–40
Barbieri, Carlos 135, 137–8
Barrantes, Héctor 80, 81, 100, 210–11
Barroso, Luis 180
Beaufort, Duke of, *see* Somerset, David
Bemberg, Otto 102
Bemberg, Peter 102, 167
Beresford, Lord John (8th Marquess of Waterford) 95
Beresford, Lord Patrick 95, 231
Berger, Helmut 135
Bethancourt, Raúl Sánchez de 114
Bigger, Chacho 18
Biggs, Ronnie 259
Binger, Jim 47, 49, 53, 54
Birrell, Aida 60

Index

Bissoni, Ada (Luis's Aunt Ada) 2, 4, 6, 17–18, 146, 256
Bissoni, Amanda Teresa (Luis's mother) 1, 2, 103, 259
Bissoni, Vincenzo (Luis's grandfather) 2, 4, 18, 146
Blackstone, Bernie 34
Blanco, Jorge 4
Blandford, Jamie (Marquess of Blandford) 244–6, *245*, 250, 252, 260, 261, 262–3, 264 (*264*)
Bolker, Joseph 145
Bouvier, Lee 181
Bowie, David 122
Bramble, Jennifer, 135
Brantes, Sybille de 168
Browne, Garech 172–3
Browning, Ricou 43–4
'Bubbles', *see* Harmsworth, Patricia
Bukowa, Angelika Lazansky von 212
Burgos, Guy 50–1, 52

Campbell-Muir, Jock 217–19, 221–2
Cárcano, Michael 99–100, 289 n.5
Carden, Sandy 81, 84
Cárdenas, Emilio 263
'Caroline, Lady' (Group Captain Peter Ridley) 172
Castellane, Georges de 132
Cernadas, Dicky *203*
Charles, Prince (Prince of Wales) 202–209 (*205*, *206*, *207*), 212–13, 214, 215, 216, 223, 228–9, 231, 232, 239, 247, 283–4, 286
Chávez, Rudy 167, 168
Chiappe, Françoise 112
Christian, Virgil 47, 53–4
Cilento, Diane 198
Clara, Aunt, *see* Unzué, Clara Leloir
Cleverly, George 200
Codrington, Tessa 196

Coleman, John 74–5, 79, 80, 81, 98, 99
Collins, Joan *255*
Colonna, Princess Fiammetta 190–2
Colonna, Princess Vittoria, 191
Connery, Sean 198
Corey, Alan 74
Corey, Russell 74, *83*, 84, *205*, *206*, 284
Cowdray, Lady 164–5, 178
Cowdray, Lord (John Churchill Pearson) 79–80, 107, 164–5, 176, 178, 181, 186, 187, 215, 232, 286
Cranwell, Fernando Castro 5
Crotto, Hector *205*, *208*, 210
Cushing, Alexander 84
Cushing, Justine 84, 100–101 (*101*), 102, 104, 105, 106, 146, 273–5, 274, 286

Dagwood, Linley 113–16, 117–18, 120, 142–3, 148
Dalí, Salvador 122
Darboven, 'Atti' Albert 99–100, 102, 144, 164
Davis Junior, Sammy 36
Deen, Rupert 171
Dempster, Nigel 78, 238, 239, 254, *255*
Dodero, Jimmy 125, 141
Dodero, Marina 105, 145, 146, 147
Dowd, Anne 9, 277
Driver, Ronnie 177

Ebeid, Alex 214
Edinburgh, Duke of, see Philip, Prince
Efthymios, Dora 132
Elizabeth, HM Queen 96, *208*
Elsmore, Dorothy 63, 66
Emaer, Fabrice 235

Emerson, Marcus 217, 218
Engelhard, Susan 98
Erleigh, Lord Simon 158
Etcheverría, María Eugenia Garcés 207–209, 212–13
Etcheverrigaray, Marité Sosa de vii, viii, 1, 2–3, 4, 5, 6–7, 17–18, 31, 66, 207, 256, 283
Etcheverry, Eugene 166

Fabri, Martin 70–1, 73
Fairbanks, Beatrice Murray (Beatrice de Holguin) 49–52, 53, 54, 73
Fazio, Manuela 2
Feldman, George 92, 93
Ferguson, Major Ronald 203, 206, 231, 232
Fontana, Luis 187–8
Foreman, Ruth 39–41, 44, 65
Fortugno, Fred 214
Foster & Son (shoemaker's) 200
Fox-Pitt, Major General William 195
Fox-Pitt, Sarah 193–5, 196, 234–5, 236, 237
Foxwell, Ivan 154, 156, 161, 174, 179
Foxwell, Lady Edith 153–4, 155–7 (*155*), 159, 160, 161, 170, 174, 177, 179, 185, 187, 189, 193, 195, 196, 198, 218, 281
Fraga Iribarne, Manuel 185
Fraser, Charles 284–5

Gabor, Zsa Zsa *150*
Galitzine, Prince George 196
Gemmel, D. *204*
Getty, J. Paul *150*
Getty, Paul, Junior 122
Gold, Johnny 159
Goldberg, Ruth 38–40, 42, 58, 66, 119
Gordillo, Donald 82–3

Gould, Anna, 132
Gould, Jay 132
Gowland, Rafael 187, 188
Grace, Peter 177
Grangére, Desirée de la 14–15, 94
Grangére, Gustave de la 14
Guébriant, Diane de 132
Guébriant, Wanda de 132
Guerra, Tommy 29, 30, 87, 88, 89
Guerrico, Ezequiel 'Pilo' Fernández 229
Guerrico, Fabián 117, 118, 119
Guinness, Daphne 245, *250*
Guinness, Oonagh 172
Gutiérrez, Benny 46, 47, 55

Hall, Mary Vanderveer 75, 98
Harmsworth, Patricia ('Bubbles') 154–5, 156, 157, 159, 236–7
Harmsworth, Vere 157
Harper, Colonel Alec 186, 231
Haynes, Amanda 100, 102
Hebborn, Eric 138, 175, 224–6, 277
Henry Maxwell (shoemaker's) 200
Herrera, Antonio 'Chamaco' 99, 202
Hill, Sinclair 201, 202, 203, *204*, *205*, 206
Hislop, Barbara 134, 135–7, 139–40
Holguin, Beatrice de, *see* Fairbanks, Beatrice Murray
Holguín, María Beatriz de 49
Holland, Charles 256
Hollings, Father Michael 278
Hopper, Dennis 122
Horswell, E. *204*
Horswell, John 211
Hurrell, Stephen 196

Iglehart, Philip 46, 199
Iglehart, Stewart 25, 26, 46, 60, 62
Iribarren, Martín 97–8

Index

Irisarri, Pilar *230*
Isaacs, Lady Jacqueline Rufus 170

Jamieson, George, *see* Ashley, April
Jáuregui, Captain 'Negro' Carlos Enrique, 216, 228–9
Jellicoe, Lady Patricia (Patsy) 149–52, 154, 155, 156–7, 159–61, 162, 163–4, 174
John Lobb (shoemaker's) 179, 200

Kelly, Grace, *see* Monaco, Princess Grace of
Kennedy, Jackie, *see* Onassis, Jacqueline Kennedy

Lachman, Charles 75
Lachman, Rita 75–6, 125, 126, 127, 283
Ladd, Cheryl *249*
Langdon-Berg, Roger 174–5
Laurent, Yves Saint 122, 124, 128, 235
Lawman, Clare 240–1 (*240, 241*), 247, 253–4, 255–6, *257*, 259, 286
Leach, Jan 266–7 (*267*), *268*, 284
Lee, Brenda 199–200, 214
Lee, Gee 203
Lewis, Marty 35, 37, 42, 57
Livanos, Tina 103
Llewellyn, Colonel Sir Harry, 170
Llewellyn, Dai 170–1, 187, 197, 198, 210, 244, 281
Llewellyn, Roddy 197, 198
Lloyd, Ruby 219, 220
Lucas, Arthur 231
Lugar Nuevo, Count and Countess 52

Mahler, Ursula 117–20, 121–132, 133–4, 135–6, 137, 138–40 (*139*), 141, 142–3, 146, 148, 155, 157, 175, 234, 235

Mansilla, Lucio García 181, 214, 269, 271
Marentette, Danny 106
Margaret, Princess 155, 156, 157–8, 197, 198, 236
Marlborough, Duke of 51, 244, 246, 251
Marshall, Zena 161
Martínez, María Estela 188
Massimo, Prince Stefano 179
Massimo, Prince Vittorio 172, 179
McKew, Bobby (Chelsea Scallywag) 220
McLean, Mildred 168
Mell, Marisa 135, 138
Menditéguy, Charlie 24, 26
Merlos, Fernando 17, 18, *203*
Methven, Charles 284
Meyer, Betty, 42–4
Michael of Kent, Princess 247, 248
Mije, Alberto van der 166, 167–8, 199–201, 214, *267*, 268, 269–70
Mirren, Helen 196
Mitchell, Dennis 149
Moller, Eric 176–7
Monaco, Princess Grace of (Grace Kelly) 72
Moore, Eduardo *208*, 210, 211
Moscoso Plaza, Alegría 153
Muller, Gloria 168–9, 267

Norris, Bruce 167

Oddone, Luis 214–16, 223, 230, 238
Onassis, Aristotle 102, 244, 263
Onassis, Christina 78, 100, 102–6, 123, 145–7, 211, 240–2 (*241*), 244–5, 250–4, 260–5, 286
Onassis, Jacqueline Kennedy 72, 181
Orthwein, Dolph (Adolphus) 46, 47, 55, 66, 181
Orthwein, Peter 55, 81, *83*, 84, 95

Orthwein, Stephen 55, *96*
Ortiz Basualdo family 6–7, 12, 13, 16, 22, 46, 47
Ortiz Basualdo, Luis 68, 97

Palacio, Luis 71
Patiño, Antenor 153
Pearson, Charlotte (Luis's daughter) 211, *213*, 215, 284
Pearson, John Churchill, *see* Cowdray, Lord
Pearson, Lucy 107, 144, 145, 163–5, 166, 168–9, 176, 178, 180, 181, 201, 211–12, 213 (*213*), 215, 232, 267, 284, 286
Pearson, Michael 164
Philip, Prince (Duke of Edinburgh) 95, 228
Picasso, Paloma 128
Pieres, Gonzalo *208*, 210
Pigott-Brown, Sir William 171
Pizarro, Rodolfo Ruiz 87–92, 93, 108, 112–13, 138, 148, 175
Polignac, Princess Ghislaine de 126
Ponsonby, Sarah 196–7
Prebble, David 239
Prendergast, Louis 171
Prendergast, Marie Therese, *see* Welborn, Tessa
Pringle, Commander Jack 182
Pucci, Emilio 135, 136
Pullen, Doris 58–9

Queen of Palm Beach, *see* Sanford, Mary
Quijo-Duggan, Edgar 201, 212

Radziwill, Prince Stanislaw 181
Redé, Baron de, *see* Rosenberg, Alexis von
Reed, Martha 267–8, *269*

Ridley, Group Captain Peter, *see* 'Caroline, Lady'
Riley-Smith, Douglas 231–2
Rivera, Mara 110–11
Roberts, Beverly, 177, 178–9
Roberts, Squadron Leader Alan 178
Roca, Agustina 185–6
Roosevelt, James 84
Rosenberg, Alexis von, Baron de Redé 126, 127–8, 200, 234–5
Rothermere, Lady, *see* Harmsworth, Patricia ('Bubbles')
Rothschild, Éric de 122
Rothschild, Guy de 126
Rothschild, Marie-Hélène 126, 127, 235
Rothschild, Miriam 239
Roussel, Henri Julien Gaston 244
Roussel, Thierry 244, 261, 263–4
Roxburghe, Duchess of (Mary) 153, 156
Rubirosa, Porfirio 67
Rueda, Delfín
Ryan, María Luisa Lobo 152–3

Saavedra, Beto 11–13, 14, 18–19, 20, 207, 212
Sáez Germain, Alejandro 184–6, 187, 188–9
Salvo, Mario 224
Samuel 221–2
Sanford, Laddie 67–8
Sanford, Mary (Queen of Palm Beach) 67–70, 71, 73, 168
Sanok, Ludovico 247–8, 251–2, 261
Santa Marina, Jorge 4
Santos, Juan Manuel 207, 209, 213
Santostefano, Fulco di (Duke of Verdura) 71, 73, 75, 223
Sassoon, Victor 263, 264
Saunders, Didi 247–8

303

Schneider, Paul 273
Sellers, Peter 157–9
Shaffer, Anthony 198
Sherman, Wendy 74
Simpson, Wallis, *see* Windsor, Duchess of
Simunek, Nicholas 166, 167
Sinclair, Mary Stewart 195
Singer, Franklin Forbes 181
Smith, Graham 138
Smith, Shelley *249*
Snowdon, Lord 158, 170, 198
Soldano, Eduardo 4–5
Somerset, David, Duke of Beaufort 247, 248
Somoza, Anastasio 'Tachito' 82, 153
Somoza, Hope Portocarrero 82
Sosa, Héctor (Luis's father) 1–2, 3, 13
Sosa, María Teresa, *see* Etcheverrigaray, Marité Sosa de
Spencer, Lady Diana 216
Spencer, Lady Sarah 207, 208–209
Spencer-Churchill, Lady Sarah 51, *251*
Stark, Ray 158
Stein, David 50
Sutherland, Duchess of (Clare) 153, 154

Taylor, Sergeant Ralph 253, 255
Tennant, Victoria 97
Thyssen, Fiona 145
Tiscornia, Cecilia *109*, *111*
Torri, Pier Luigi 138
Townley, DI Robert 253, 254, 255, 256, 259

Unzué, Clara Leloir (Aunt Clara) 24–6, 45

Vanderbilt, Consuelo 51, 250
Vandières, Baron Armand de 14, 93–4
Vanini, Peppo 97, 104
Veltri, Jacobo 90–1
Vestey, Lord 80, *207*, 236
Vidal-Quadras, Alejo 158

Wales, Prince of, *see* Charles, Prince
Walton, Ike 47, 199
Warhol, Andy 128
Welborn, Tessa (Marie Therese Prendergast) 171–4, *173*, 221
White, Sir Gordon *249*
Wickser, Bob 47, 49, 67, 80, 81, 181
Wildenstein, Guy 177, *203*, 213
Wilson, Charles 153
Windsor, Barbara 217
Windsor, Duchess of (Wallis Simpson) 72
Witheridge, Annette 209
Wyss, Susi 122, 124–5

Yatian, Santiago 166

Zilkha, Cristina 271
Zuccotti, Angelo 168

Printed in Dunstable, United Kingdom